WOMEN AND POPULAR STRUGGLES

Women and Popular Struggles

A History of British Working-class Women, 1560-1984

JAMES D. YOUNG

MAINSTREAM
PUBLISHING·EDINBURGH

First published in 1985 by
MAINSTREAM PUBLISHING COMPANY (EDINBURGH) LTD.
7 Albany Street
Edinburgh EH1 3UG

The publisher gratefully acknowldges the financial assistance of the
Lipman Trust in the publication of this volume.

ISBN 0 906391 59 8

Typeset in 11 point Bembo by Studioscope in conjunction with
Mainstream Publishing.
Printed by Billing & Sons, Worcester.

Contents

Dedicated to the memory of my mother

Jemima Paterson Young
1907-65

Preface

FIVE YEARS have elapsed since I published *The Rousing of the Scottish Working Class*. Although socialist historians are always expected to confront their own world with a tough-minded, optimistic, unbending intransigence, I must confess that this book has been written with a much greater sense of detachment than *The Rousing of the Scottish Working Class*. In a world increasingly descending into barbarism, sceptical dissent is more important than totalitarian decrees or mindless militancy. But in 'the land of cakes and the Kailyard', true socialist feminism seems to me to be the only realistic alternative to a world threatened with nuclear extinction. If there is not very much to be optimistic about in a world of mass unemployment, death by starvation in the Third World and growing militarism in the East and the West, there is no reason why historians should pretend to be above politics.

I could not pretend to be above politics, anyway. I was fortunate to be born into a Christian working-class family. Though my parents were poor, they taught me the importance of commitment and concern. The material poverty experienced by my parents was in inverse proportion to the rich spiritual culture that they communicated to their children. While my father was an individual member of the Labour Party in the Depression years, when working people were expected to keep their mouths shut, my mother never fully trusted any political party or institution. By sympathising with her almost natural, left-wing 'anarchistic' disaffection, and by publishing *Women and Popular Struggles*, I hope to make a small contribution to the social history of British working-class women.

A major theme of *Women and Popular Struggles* is the role of consciousness in the history of the Scottish and English working class. It is, therefore, important to stress that this is a part of a much wider international debate on the role of consciousness in the dynamic of working-class history. In contrast to the dominant schools of labour historiography, whether of the right or the left, the emphasis in *Women*

9

and Popular Struggles is on the hidden history of British working-class women in playing a part in the relative autonomy of cultural change over several centuries. As such, it challenges the economic reductionism of conservative and authoritarian socialist historiography in chronicling the way-of-life of British plebeian and working-class women.

Although authorship is a lonely, sedentary and individualistic occupation, it nevertheless depends on the active encouragement of others. I want to begin by paying tribute to my publishers at Mainstream for their helpfulness and support and to Jackie Hendrie who contributed so much in the editing of the book. In the academic world I have received a great deal of gregarious encouragement and kindness from Royden Harrison, Sam Shepperson, Harry Dickinson, Carl Levy, Arthur Lipow, Richard Price, David Montgomery, Bernard Crick, James Cornford, R F Mackenzie and Dave McKie. A small army of friends in the British and American labour movement have encouraged me to write this book. They have included Saul Landau, Peter and Mia Gilmour, Gray Allan (a prince of librarians), Bob Kennedy, Rowland Sheret, Charles Bowie, Marie Kane, Elspeth King, Corrie McCord, Dick Hook, Andreé Molyneux and Ann and Vincent Flynn.

I also wish to thank the Social Science Research Council, the Carnegie Trust for the Universities of Scotland, the University of Stirling and the Institute for Policy Studies, Washington, DC, for giving me research grants to allow me to work in libraries in Britain, Holland and America. In the course of doing research in these libraries, I have received so much help from so many librarians that it would take a small chapter to name them. The sharing of knowledge without ideological strings is one of the few remaining freedoms we enjoy in a bureaucratised world. In my penultimate acknowledgement, I wish to thank Miss Margaret Hendry for typing the manuscript with her customary efficiency and humour.

But my deepest debts and gratitude are to my immediate family — and, indeed, my friends — Lorna, Alison and David.

1

Calvinism and Scottish
and English Women, 1560-1690

IN MOST COUNTRIES, progressive, socialist and Marxist historians have always portrayed the Reformation as a major revolutionary upheaval and the beginnings of a progressive development, but most Scottish progressive and socialist historians have seen the Reformation as an historical tragedy with absolutely no redeeming features at all.

In the years between the two World Wars Thomas Johnston, Edwin Muir, Willa Muir and others began to develop an ultra-critical, ahistoric and denunciatory analysis of John Knox and the Reformation in Scotland. Throughout their books and essays there is a sort of obsessive, and historically one-sided, hatred of the Calvinism introduced into Scotland in the sixteenth century. Also implicit in their writings is the Reformation's devastating and oppressive influence on plebeian women. Contemporary Scottish cultural life and historical writings are still dominated by this legacy. A Scottish Marxist historiography did not emerge until the early 1970s.

In the writings of historians such as Thomas Johnston, Edwin and Willa Muir, Elspeth King and Eveline Hunter, the Reformation is portrayed as an historical tragedy which was responsible for one of the major witch hunts in Europe, which heightened the level of misogyny, and which ensured the continuity of women's oppression into the twentieth century. Although John Knox and the Reformation have been blamed for actually *creating* misogyny, repressing women and initiating witch hunts, the evidence for these charges is really very slender.

Although the Scottish witch hunt was 'arguably one of the major witch-hunts in Europe',[1] witch-hunting and witch-burning existed in Europe for at least a hundred years before the Reformation. Archibald Robertson, the English Marxist historian, states: 'In 1448 Pope Innocent VIII commissioned the grand inquisitor of Germany, Jakob Sprenger, to

11

regularise the procedure against witches . . . He (Sprenger) is said to have condemned hundreds yearly'.[2] However, witch-burning was a more serious problem in Scotland than in England. This greater incidence of witch-burning in Scotland is often cited as evidence of the advent of a correspondingly higher level of misogyny.

The witch cult, a relic of paganism, was tolerated by the Roman Catholic Church until the thirteenth century, but by the fourteenth century the Church began to fear the coalescence of a revolt by the artisan heretics in the towns and the witch cult in the countryside. In suggesting that the witch cult probably 'contributed more to radical Protestantism than has yet been appreciated', Christopher Hill emphasises the importance of the witch-cult as an 'underground' religion which was 'anti-State and anti-State Church'.[3]

A dominant feature of Scottish progressive and socialist historiography in the years between the First and Second World Wars was that few historians offered any sociological accounts of what motivated the witch hunts and witch-burnings. This is exemplified in the writings of Willa Muir. However, although ideological factors were behind the intensification of the witch hunting, already in 1920 Thomas Johnston vaguely appreciates some of the other material reasons, as he explains: 'For some time after the Reformation the civil magistrates refused to carry out the witchcraft sentences. . . . Further, the magistrates were encouraged to assist the Kirk by being granted the property belonging to executed witches; and when the great Chirurgeon (surgeon) craft found its trade attacked in every parish by one or more female folk herbalists, there was added another economic interest to the anti-witch campaign'.[4] None of these insights have been followed up as yet by Scottish progressive or socialist historians.

Standing on the fringe of Europe, and hardly touched by civilisation except in the Lowlands, medieval Scotland was a very backward country. Both paganism and superstition were powerful currents within its social life, but the 'lower-class' Scots and English enjoyed a rich social and communal way of life before the two countries took divergent paths after 1660. The differences in each country's way of life continued to develop throughout the ascendency of Protestantism.

A characteristic feature of Protestantism in Scotland in the sixteenth and seventeenth centuries was its offensive against paganism and Catholicism as well as witchcraft. In 1579, the practice of making 'pilgrimages to wells from superstitious motives' was prohibited by an Act of Parliament. In Stirling in 1617 a woman who had practised this superstitious rite of taking water from Christ's well was punished by the Kirk.[5] The Protestants waged war on May Day observances and processions to holy wells and shrines because they were 'rallying points' of Roman Catholicism.[6] Throughout Europe the Protestant offensive against paganism and Catholicism was motivated by the same ideology which was responsible for intensifying the witch hunts, as Christopher Hill explains: 'Persecution of witches started before the Reformation, but it became fiercest in Protestant countries just because Protestantism was itself a product of the more radical urban culture, and was hostile to all forms of magic, pagan or Catholic'.[7]

In the sixteenth and seventeenth centuries, witch-hunting and women-hunting were sometimes indistinguishable.[8] In an important essay, *The Scottish Women's Suffrage Movement*, Elspeth King argues that the Reformation was an unmitigated tragedy for women: 'The old Catholic Church, with its Mariological doctrines, female saints, and nunneries, had at least allowed women *a part to play*, however small. The Reformed Church, and the contemporary political events which allowed the establishment of a theocracy in Scotland, brought with it a severely masculine, if not misogynist, theology'.[9] An essay by Eveline Hunter in *A Scottish Woman's Place* also attributes women's oppression in present-day Scotland to 'the anti-female climate' originally created by John Knox.[10] However, these criticisms as well as putting too much blame on Knox and Calvinism for sexual oppression in the nineteenth and twentieth centuries, are also somewhat unfair, abstract and ahistoric. The important historical question is whether the level of misogyny in medieval Scotland was heightened as a result of the Reformation. In *Enemies of God: The Witch-Hunt in Scotland*, Christina Larner argues: 'It is quite possible that witch-hunting had the effect of increasing the level of misogyny rather than the other way about. The status of women can be so high that it threatens patriarchy or so low that women are peripheral property without necessarily provoking a witch-hunt'.[11] The level of misogyny was probably heightened by the Reformation both in Scotland and in Germany. Alongside this heightened level of misogyny, the Reformation in Scotland unleashed simmering social tensions and sharpened existing class antagonisms. In the countryside, the petty lairds and the 'lower orders' waged 'a long and bitter fight against the feudal nobility'. Furthermore, it was only in Scotland that 'a Presbyterian Assembly carved out a powerful position for itself alongside the older Parliament'.[12]

When Thomas Johnston, Edwin and Willa Muir, Elspeth King and Eveline Hunter argue that the Reformation had a devastating impact on the lives of plebeian women, they have an abundance of evidence on their side. What they have ignored, however, was the positive role of the Calvinists in the unorthodox Protestant groups and sects in the seventeenth century in raising the status of women.

While, in the late eighteenth and nineteenth centuries, the 'lower orders' in Scotland and England developed their own distinctive characteristics and culture, the process of national cultural differentation had already begun to evolve in the medieval period. If the Scottish and English working classes, and in particular the women, began to develop distinctive national characteristics after the process of industrialisation got underway, the cultural divergences had already been shaped to some extent by the Reformation itself.

Although England did become a Protestant country, the Reformation was more radical and far-reaching in Scotland, as George Lichtheim argues: 'Historians of the Reformation have yet to agree on the reasons why Calvinism took hold in Scotland but not, on the whole, in England. There is a fairly obvious answer: namely that the English in the end rejected it because it had been taken up by the Scots, whom they detested for political and cultural reasons rooted in a long-standing national enmity'.[13] Kautsky argues: 'With the exception of England, where the Reformation *assumed a peculiar character*, the Reformation countries were economically-backward lands, where absolutism had not developed to the point it had reached in the Romance countries, where peasants and kings still possessed a certain degree of power'. Furthermore, English dependence on the Papacy had begun to disappear in the fourteenth century; and the Popes 'could only extract money from England on condition of sharing the spoils with the Kings'.[14]

Contemporary Marxist as well as liberal historians might be tempted to question Engels' general dictum that: 'There is no great historical evil without a compensating historical progress', but in coming to grips with the history of the Reformation in Scotland — and particularly its later impact on working-class consciousness — Engels' insight is very useful. The manifold evils of the Reformation in Scotland were certainly accompanied by a compensating historical progress. Medieval Scotland was not really enlightened about the role of women in society until the Reformation. The Reformation created the potential for women's liberation.

The compensating historical progress was evident and most significant in relation to the Protestants' perception of the need for education for women. In contrast to Henry VIII's frenzy against education for women, John Knox supported the concept of education for both sexes.[15] Although Knox had been accused of being against education for women,[16] he did champion the cause of education for women.[17] Moreover, the Scottish Calvinists' austere, puritanical anti-pleasure principles were inseparable from their contribution to raising the status of plebeian women.

14

In pre-1917 Marxism it was self-evident that the Reformation had been more successful in some countries than in others. Furthermore, the degree of the radicalisation of the masses in medieval Europe was said to have had an important impact on the subsequent character of capitalism in particular countries. Because Martin Luther's personal cowardice contributed to the belatedness of capitalist development in Germany, Engels was much more critical of Luther than of Calvin. Just as the radical reformers in England were defeated in 1660, so had they already been defeated in Germany in 1525. In commenting on the German Reformation, George Litchtheim argues: 'The real disaster which struck Germany in 1525 was not the failure of the doomed peasants' revolt, but the defeat of what contemporary historians have come to describe as "the radical Reformation"'.[18]

In a brilliant study, *Thomas More and His Utopia*, Karl Kautsky focuses on the duality of the Reformation in medieval Europe. Although only a very few progressive socialist or Marxist historians have glanced at the consequences of the Reformation in Scotland, most of them, at least before 1917, were vaguely aware of Scottish peculiarities. Being aware of the devastating impact of the Reformation in Scotland on the 'lower orders', Kautsky wrote:

> It was not by chance that the *brunt* of the Reformation fell on two of the most backward nations in Europe: Sweden and Scotland.
> This is, of course, not to be understood as a condemnation of the Reformation. We have recorded the above facts because it explains why the most cultivated minds in Germany as in England would have nothing to do with the Reformation, a phenomenon which is unintelligible if we adopt the traditional view that the Reformation was essentially of a spiritual nature, a struggle between Protestant light and Catholic darkness.

But he did not stop there; for he described the Reformation in Europe as a 'struggle of barbarians against civilisation'.[19]

Most pre-1917 Marxist historians were sensitive to the fact that the Reformation was backward except in England. Because the Reformation in Scotland took place within one of the most backward countries in Europe, Kautsky's comments on the inherent antagonisms within European socialism are unusually illuminating:

> The condemnation of communism as a "horrid heresy" by the English communist, Thomas More, seems a strange phenomenon but it is bound up with the essence of socialist beginnings. The antagonism between More and Munzer contains the seed of the great antagonism which runs

15

through the entire history of socialism, and which was only resolved by the *Communist Manifesto*, the antagonism between Utopianism and the labour movement.[20]

But although Scottish — and particularly progressive and socialist — historians have often been denunciatory in their analysis of the role of the Reformation in Scottish history, American and English feminist historians, too, have sometimes portrayed Protestantism in Scotland as a total disaster for women.

In Scotland, the Protestant clergymen punished plebeian women for practising pagan rituals.[21] Scottish plebian women often bore the brunt of the Reformation more than their counterparts in England. In his misogynistic tract on women, John Knox described the female sex as 'weak, frail, impatient, feeble, foolish, inconstant, variable and cruel'.[22] But the early success of Scottish Calvinism meant that until the seventeenth century the Scots produced far fewer female martyrs than the English. However, Matilda J Gage, the American feminist, had no trouble in locating evidence against John Knox and the Scottish Reformation. As Gage puts it: 'Knox himself suffered a woman to be burned at St. Andrews whom one word from him would have saved'. Nevertheless, Calvinism in Scotland was exceedingly complex.

In tracing the 'deep democratic trend' in Scottish life back to the ideology enunciated by John Knox in the *First Book of Discipline*, David Daiches focuses on a major paradox in Scottish history and culture, as he puts it: 'Democracy applied only to the faithful, and could and did go frequently together with the fiercest intolerance of all others'.[23] In the sixteenth and seventeenth centuries, the Protestant commonalty in Scotland were 'utterly incapable of imagining a conscientious dissent' and Calvinist intolerance impinged on 'the popular mind as a tyranny only somewhat less formidable than that which had been put away'.[24] This deep democratic trend identified by David Daiches did not exist in England.

Moreover, the Reformation in Scotland was a vast popular movement. It was profoundly anti-feudal, and it embodied a deep democratic tendency together with an intolerant Protestant fanaticism. What the Rev Robert Burns in 1828 described as 'a levelling Presbyterian democracy'[25] began to develop from the sixteenth century. It clearly made an impact on popular consciousness, and it gradually pushed plebeian women to the forefront of political struggles. Alongside the deep democratic trend and the intolerant Protestant fanaticism towards Catholics and gypsies, the disastrous cultural consequences of the Reformation already began to reveal themselves in 1570 when the Presbyterians suppressed traditional games and 'the

Robin Hood plays of Catholic and unthinking times'.[26]

Before looking at the consequences of witch-hunting in Scotland, I will look at the actual status of plebeian women. Scottish 'lower-class' women enjoyed a comparatively high status before the Reformation, as A D Hope puts it: 'There is no reason to doubt that the female sex in William Dunbar's day, both in the upper and lower classes of society, was less formidable than their sisters of earlier or later times, or that they were less determined to have maistrie (mastery) of the opposite sex. . . . (This) older tradition was "an unconscionable time a-dying" and indeed is, even now, not quite extinct in Scotland'.[27] Although from the sixteenth century onwards plays and the theatre were frowned upon in Scotland, in 1570 a plebeian counter-culture already existed amongst the Protestant 'lower orders'. In discussing the Presbyterians' suppression of games and the Robin Hood plays, Robert Chalmers says: 'Still, while the upper and more serious classes frowned, the common part of people loved the sport too much to resign it without a struggle. It came to be one of the first difficulties of the men who had carried through the Reformation, how to wrestle the people out of their love of the May-games'.[28] Thus Calvinism was anti-traditional and innovative.

But John Knox and the Reformation did not create misogyny or superstition. They already existed throughout Europe before the Reformation. The existence of both 'flyting' women and misogyny was reflected in the poetry of William Dunbar in the fourteenth and fifteenth centuries. Knox and the Reformation began the struggles which led to the centuries-old struggle for women's liberation. The advent of Calvinism in Scotland was quite distinctive from Protestantism in England.

In Scotland and England, however, the Reformation impinged on the consciousness of plebeian women, but because the Reformation in England did not go as far as it did in Scotland, the cultural consequences for the 'lower orders' were identifiable and significant. The process of cultural differentiation between the Scottish and the English working classes, which was evident in the late eighteenth century, was already latent in the sixteenth and seventeenth centuries. Consequently, the year 1660 in English history was of enormous importance to the culture and way of life of plebeian women.

By 1660, patriarchy in England was, as Sheila Rowbotham suggests, 'once more secure and the agitation of "inferiors" suppressed'.[29] However, the significance of the year 1660 in the later history of the English working class was not simply the restoration of patriarchy. In England, the year 1660 signalled the slowing down and 'humanising' of the tempo of the class struggle against deviants in the 'lower classes'. By contrast, towards the end of the seventeenth century, the agitations of 'lower-class' women in Scotland were still being put down.

After 1660, the English puritan sects abandoned politics, and 'many of the old revolutionaries emigrated'. [30] In a vivid description of what 1660 meant for plebeian women, Lawrence Stone observes: 'Far more important in loosening popular conventions about sexual behaviour in England was the reaction after 1660 to the draconian imposition of military rule in the 1650s of the more austere anti-pleasure principles of the puritans. Stage plays, horse-racing, cock-fighting, maypoles, and brothels had all been suppressed; ale-houses had been severely limited in numbers, and adultery made punishable by death. The result was exactly the opposite of what the puritan leaders expected. Instead of producing a regenerate nation of the godly, they created a society bitterly resentful of public interference with their normal recreations'. [31]

Although the Reformation did not altogether represent a struggle of Protestant light against Catholic darkness, it would be a profound mistake to assume that Catholic enlightenment towards plebeian women actually existed in Scotland before the Reformation. Yet, this is precisely what Elspeth King implies in her otherwise useful and perceptive essay *The Scottish Women's Suffrage Movement*, when she argues: 'On account of the repression of women in theocratic Scotland, there was no comparable tradition of prophetesses and women preachers, such as developed in England within religious sects like the Diggers, Levellers and Shakers'. [32] The truth is that the long-term consequences of the Reformation in Scotland for plebeian women were positive as well as negative.

Although plebeian women enjoyed a comparatively high status in medieval Scotland before the advent of the Reformation, the Catholic clergy was most certainly unenlightened towards them. To create an image of plebeian women occupying a more prominent role in 'political' life before the Reformation does nothing to advance our understanding of ordinary day to day life in medieval Scotland.

An important consequence of the Reformation in Europe for the later national history of the working classes was its role in initiating cultural resistance to an evolving capitalism. At the same time as it sought to foster capitalist values, it often, if unwittingly, contributed to the opposite process, too. Though Protestantism played a major role in shaping popular consciousness to fit in with the objective needs of a developing capitalist economy, it was not omnipotent. In late-nineteenth-century Germany, for example, 'the widespread survival of "superstition" in peasant belief' and the 'existence of Protestant pilgrimage and miracle shrines' showed that 'an attempted acculturation of popular culture' was 'in many ways unsuccessful'. [33] In

18

Scotland, too, Protestantism and the dissenting sects played a major role in shaping the consciousness of plebeian women.

In hardening the condemnation of the Reformation developed by the Scottish socialist historian, Thomas Johnston, in 1920, Edwin Muir portrayed John Knox and the Reformation as unmitigated historical evils. Without making much allowance for the cultural sediments of the past, he argues: 'Among these are his tradition of denunciation and his habit of prophecy. The first, I am convinced, is still a feature of Scottish life; and the second was carried on and developed richly by the Covenanters. The Covenanters, their work done, are now, thank God, dead and buried'. Yet, Muir does concede, though grudgingly, that Protestantism probably 'stiffened the independent political spirit of the people, if with the other hand it imposed a spiritual and moral tyranny'.

Protestantism in Europe as a whole, including Scotland, was culture-bound. Nevertheless, the Protestants' innate potential for contributing to the agitation for women's emancipation was incalculable. Edwin Muir's considered judgment on the role of John Knox in Scottish political and religious life is utterly negative. Apparently unaware of the unevenness of the Renaissance throughout Europe, he argues: 'What Knox really did was to rob Scotland of all the benefits of the Renaissance. Scotland never enjoyed these as England did, and no doubt the lack of that immense advantage has had a permanent effect'.[34] Some English historians, however, are much less denunciatory of the effects of the Reformation in Scotland. In identifying some of the common features of plebeian life in Scotland and England, John Langdon-Davies is less judgmental, as he puts it: 'When the sex-horror, which seems almost indissoluble from religious genius, thundered out of the mouths of Luther and Calvin and Knox, fewer people listened, and these listened half-heartedly. For there was a sap in the trees and men, and the spirit of the times desired colour and vivacity. . . . In the circumstances women came into their own. . . . A tangible recognition of this is of course the recognition of the humanity of the priests and the marriage of the clergy'.[35]

Although the anti-pleasure principles of the Protestants in England were overturned in 1660 with profound consequences for the later history of the working class, misogynistic tendencies were already even more prominent in sixteenth-century England than in Scotland. The most cultivated communist minds in England (in contrast to the less cultivated minds in Scotland) were hostile to the agitation for women's rights. In an authoritative study of *The Family, Sex and Marriage in England, 1500-1800*, Lawrence Stone observes: 'Thomas More's Utopia is remarkable in that the subjection of wives to husbands is the one authoritarian feature in an otherwise egalitarian society. Some

Elizabethans revived the Platonic doubts about whether a woman could be considered as a reasoning creature; others questioned whether she had a soul'.[36] In England, too, from the mid sixteenth century onwards 'scolding' women annoyed the authorities; so did Puritanism, as Sheila Rowbotham puts it: 'An anxious proclamation of 1547 forbade the women of London to "meet and talk" and ordered husbands to "keep their wives at home". Enforcement was another problem'.[37]

In Scotland, from the mid sixteenth century onwards, women began to enjoy a comparatively high status. Nevertheless, the Reformation also attempted to impose a severe patriarchal culture upon a recalcitrant commonalty, and the women were the chief sufferers. Consequently, from the late sixteenth century onwards, women were subjected to 'ducking', 'scouring', and 'placarding' when they were found guilty of 'crimes' by ecclesiastical courts.[38] But, in contrast to what Shiela Rowbotham says about the attempt to punish scolding or 'flyting' women in London as early as 1547, similar attempts to punish their Scottish counterparts did not begin on a significant scale until the early seventeenth century.

Despite frequent assertions to the contrary, witch-hunting and witch-burning existed in Scotland long before the Reformation. Many witches, for example, were burnt in Edinburgh in 1479.[39] A sustained campaign against witchcraft however, did not gather momentum until after the Reformation. Although John Knox helped to foster the Parliamentary legislation against witchcraft in 1563, the Presbyterian clergymen initially hesitated to administer the anti-witch legislation.

In the sixteenth century, Catholics and Protestants alike believed in witch-hunting and witch-burning. Archibald Robertson explains: 'A word may be said here on a feature of these times often wrongly regarded as a peculiar feature of the Reformation — the horrible practice of witch-burning. The fact is that on the issue of witchcraft Catholics and Reformers were at one'.[40]

Witch-hunting was intensified from the 1560s onwards, as Thomas Thomson observes in his *History of the Scottish People*: 'In the same year (1569) the Regent Moray in one of his progresses caused certain witches to be burned in St Andrews and some others in Dundee. At the commencement, however, of this new crusade against the works and worshippers of the Prince of Darkness it was not merely to beldames of the lower classes, the old, the ugly, and unbefriended, that this charge was confined: the example of Lady Glammis seems to have animated the accusers to aim at higher game, and females of rank were suspected of practising the black art who, but for their high position, might have suffered at the stake'.[41] Although a few warlocks were burnt at the stake, too, the chief victims were the women of the 'lower orders'.

Even by medieval standards, the brutality inflicted on 'lower-class' women suspected of witchcraft was very, very savage. In a vivid description of incredible brutality, Thomas Thomson says: 'Accordingly, when a woman was apprehended on suspicion or with the witch's mark on her person, she was thrust into the worst dungeon of the prison; and to subdue her obstinacy and force her to confess she was kept from sleep both day and night, for which purpose an iron bridle, called a witch's collar, was sometimes put upon her neck. This instrument had a hoop which, passing from the head, secured an iron four-pronged bridle within her mouth, of which two prongs were pointed against her tongue and palate and two outwards against her cheek, so that not the least movement of the head could be made without an awakening shock of pain; and thus encased in the infernal machine, the poor wretch was kept in a sitting posture by a hook or ring at the back of the headpiece, which was fastened to an iron staple in the wall'.[42] Confessions secured by these means were usually followed by executions.

However, it is conceivable that the Calvinists' role in witch-hunting in Scotland and England in the sixteenth century was exaggerated by partisan historians and chroniclers. In a scholarly and well-documented study of *The Reformation in Scotland*, David H Fleming argues: 'As far as the extant records show, the persecutions for witchcraft in Scotland were much more numerous after the Reformation than before it, but that may be partly due to the paucity of records. Witches were apparently far more abundant in England than in Scotland and infinitely more so on the Continent. The number put to death in some Roman Catholic countries is so appalling as to be almost incredible'.[43] Moreover, in his authoritative study, *Witchcraft in Tudor and Stuart England*, Alan Macfarlane offers similar, though even better documented, conclusions. He sums up: 'There were a number of witchcraft trials in the early 1560s and 1570s, before Puritan teaching could have spread widely. Nor did persecutions end in 1586 after the crushing of the Puritanical Classical movement by Bishop Aylmer; they continued in full force well into the 1590s. Finally, when the Puritans were in power between 1641 and 1660 prosecutions did not continue. After 1660 there were no more executions for witchcraft'.[44]

In Scotland, there were many executions for witchcraft in the late sixteenth century and at various times in the seventeenth century. Witch-hunting was particularly prevalent in the year 1640. Thomas Thomson describes it: 'Of the numerous executions of witches during the whole of the present period we have no wish further to speak; they

21

were merciless hecatombs of old women offered up to the presiding ignorance and superstition of the day. It was also easy to find a victim; for the bare suspicion was often enough to lead to conviction. If a woman, under the effects of stupidity or age, had acquired a habit of mumbling or maundering she might be accused of conversing with her familiar. If of a fiery malignant temper, and prone to utter imprecations, and deal her impatient curses against those she hated, this might bring her under suspicion of being a witch'.[45]

The promiscuous and 'deviant' sexual behaviour of the 'lower orders' was an important feature of the witch cult in Scotland. Just as the English ruling class punished and interfered with the power of the 'wise women' who were 'formidable rivals to the established professions of medicine and the Church',[46] so did the Scots.[47] In the trial of Major Weir, who was nominally a pious Covenanter within a 'lower-class' sect in the 1640s, illicit and 'deviant' sexual behaviour was one of the charges which led to him being 'strangled and burnt at the stake'.[48] Although Weir's sister was also executed, she received much less sympathy from nineteenth-century Presbyterian male historians. With typical patriarchal prejudice, Thomas Thomson wrote: 'She assented to much that her brother had confessed, and was condemned to die as his accomplice. She, too, was skilled in sorcery, and inherited the power from her mother, who was a witch'. This extremely prejudiced comment about Grizel Weir was written in 1892.[49]

The evidence assembled by modern historians would seem to suggest that the English Puritans did not punish 'scolding' women quite as severely as the Scots did, but Protestant attitudes to women in Scotland were not fixed and unchanging. The burning of witches seems to have decreased during the period when the Covenanters were active and also during the Cromwellian period when troops in Scotland would not permit the torture of suspected witches. Yet witch-burning was still practised in the Catholic and Episcopalian areas of Scotland. Moreover, the 'rigid Covenanters' were opposed to witch-burning, and they stamped it out.[50] In describing the reign of Charles II between 1660 and 1673, Robert Chambers says: 'A caustic wit of our age has remarked, "Whatever satisfaction the return of King Charles II might afford to the younger females in his dominions it certainly brought nothing save torture to the unfortunate old women, or witches in Scotland, against whom, immediately on the Restoration, innumerable warrants were issued forth"'.[51]

Although the initial phases of the Reformation in Scotland were probably responsible for intensifying witch-hunting and witch-burning, the Reformation contributed almost immediately to the process of improving the status of women. While divorce in England could not be obtained outside of the ecclesiastical courts until 1857, the Calvinists in Scotland as early as 1560 had already introduced comparatively egalitarian divorce laws in the courts.[52] Moreover, Blackstone, the great medieval authority on English law, had 'declared categorically that "by marriage, a woman's *very being or legal existence is suspended*"'.

These gains in the status of Scottish women, however, were accompanied simultaneously by very regressive developments. At the same time as women gained greater education and legal status, they were also prevented from practising medicine and healing. All over Europe where the Reformation had occurred and in America, too, people were being punished for consulting 'witches' about health matters. As Barbara Ehrenreich and Deirde English argue: 'The charges levelled against the "witches" included every misogynist fantasy harboured by the monks and priests. . . . But again and again the "crimes" included what would now be regarded as legitimate acts — providing contraceptive measures, performing abortions, offering drugs to ease the pain of labour. In fact, in the peculiar legal theology of the witch-hunters, healing on the part of women, was itself a crime'.[53] In Scotland, the long process of witch-hunting ended with women being edged out of their role as healers and replaced by men.

Although the attempt to push women out of their traditional role as healers did not gather momentum until the 1660s, the process began in Scotland in the 1620s. In 1621, for example, a weaver in Falkirk was punished by the Kirk because he had 'consulted a reputed witch in Stirling regarding the state of his health'.[54] Throughout the sixteenth and seventeenth centuries 'the practice of midwifery was still almost soley confined to the female sex'.[55] In Scotland and in England a new sexual division of labour was shaped by an innovative Protestantism within the framework of a nascent capitalism.

The campaign against the Scottish 'witches' — that is, women who were providing the 'lower orders' with medical treatment — was resumed in 1660. Indeed, in the 1660s, 'references were frequent in the records of the Kirk Sessions to the offence of seeking one's health from a woman, implying an invocation of hidden powers to effect a miraculous cure'. In 1664, Barbara Drummond of Dunblane was imprisoned for being suspected of witchcraft, including the administration of medical treatment to women. In *The History of Dunblane*, Alexander Barty says: 'She presented a petition stating that she had been for twelve months imprisoned in Stirling and still remained there in great misery. The Privy Council ordered the persons to whom her trial had been entrusted to meet within fifteen days under pain of being denounced and their property forfeited. Later on she presented further supplication narrating that she had been kept for three years in prison at Dunblane,

Edinburgh and Stirling, stating that her accusers were afraid to appear to try the commission and that she was still in a most miserable condition and starving'.[56] Then Barbara Drummond disappeared from the Kirk's records and history altogether.

Instead of identifying and analysing the communist tendencies within the radical Reformation, Thomas Johnston dismisses them by arguing that 'the revolutionary theological tradition and the evangelistic fervour which has come down to us is distinctly of mercantile and bourgeois origin'. By adopting this dismissive approach, Johnston helps to obscure the prominent role 'lower-class' women occupied in the struggles of the Protestant and other unorthodox sects. Yet, when he discusses witch-hunting in seventeenth-century Scotland, he weakens his own analysis by acknowledging class tensions: 'The juries were composed of the "landowners and other responsible residenters", and that the common people were quite alive to the class nature of the inquisitions is evident in the fact that the executioner or other officials in charge of the witch-burnings were sometimes pelted with stones'.

A major factor in shaping the comparatively high pre-Reformation status of Scottish women was the political activity of the dissenting sects. The Lollards were the most important heretics in Scotland before the Reformation and from the beginning of their movement they enrolled women.

They were particularly sympathetic to the women's cause and between 1407 and 1438, there was a considerable 'growth of Lollardism'. They and other heretics treated the women of the 'lower orders' as equals. Plebeian women were very prominent in the Lollard movement. In 1494, for example, the 'lower-class' women within the Lollard Movement in Kyle, Ayrshire, were called before the King for engaging in heresy.[58]

The Lollards' agitations shook 'the Papacy to its foundations in Scotland' and such agitations opened up the way for the struggles which culminated in the Reformation. Throughout the sixteenth and seventeenth centuries, dissenting Presbyterian sects, including the Covenanters, fostered the process George H Williams characterises as 'the radical Reformation within the Reformation'. Because Scottish women were to play such a prominent role in the struggles of the Calvinistic Presbyterian sects, it is worthwhile quoting James King Hewson: 'Many of the Covenanters were descendants of the Lollards of Kyle. The standpoint of the Covenanters was identical with that of John Knox and his associates. Theirs was to hold the same field and to maintain against Pope, King and Parliament the theological and political dogmas of the Reformed Church'.

The principles born out of the sixteenth-century Scottish Reformation were sustained throughout the seventeenth century, as James Anderson puts it: 'The Covenant in is various forms, signed between 1556 and 1690, was simply an extension of Knox's principles'. From the early seventeenth century 'the Covenant was unhappily converted into a powerful instrument, when, by the fatal mistake of the Stuart kings, whose residence in England had extinguished their Scottish spirit, and who claimed complete jurisdiction, spiritual as well over the body politic, the State became involved in conflict with the Church'. The Kirk's independence was finally secured 'by the Acts of Parliament which were the immediate issue of the Revolution of 1688'.[59]

Although sixteenth-century Scotland produced such female martyrs as Helen Stark, Isabel Scrimger, Elizabeth and Marjory Bowes, Elizabeth Knox and Elizabeth Campbell, Scottish Protestant women were less persecuted than their counterparts elsewhere in Europe. In his massive two-volume history of *The Ladies of the Reformation* in Europe, James Anderson attributes the lack of materials regarding Scottish women to a number of factors including the Catholic élite's neglect of the education of women. He sums up: 'The other cause of the scantiness of our information respecting the ladies attached to the Reformation in Scotland, is the circumstance that Popish persecutors were not permitted in the providence of God, to visit them, in very many instances with the penalties of heresy. The most powerful of the Scottish nobility, and ultimately the Scottish government itself, having early become favourable to the Reformation, the Scottish Popish priesthood was soon deprived of the power of wielding the sword of the State for the extermination of heretics. It was different in most other countries of Europe where the Reformation took footing. In England, for example, though Henry cast off the Papal supremacy, yet still continuing in all other respects a dogmatic Papist, he ceased not to persecute the Reformers. . . . Thus England furnishes a much more numerous list of martyrs, of both sexes, than Scotland, the number of whose martyrs is comparatively small'.[60]

Yet, despite 'the defective state of female education' in mid-sixteenth-century Scotland, the Reformation marked the beginning of a sustained struggle for women's rights. Besides, although 'the ladies attached to the Reformation in Scotland were not called, to any great extent, to suffer persecution and martydom', they did play an important role in the struggle against an oppressive feudalism. Plebeian women agitators were active in the Reformation from the very beginning. Also, in contrast to England, France, Italy and Germany, where the

Protestant women agitators belonged to the 'middle ranks', in Scotland and the Netherlands 'lower-class' women played a crucial role in the struggle against Catholicism.[61] Although Scottish women did not appear on the political scene in a significant way until 1637, Protestantism provided them with education and social and religious rights.

The struggles of the Covenanters between 1637 and 1685 gave the women of Scotland an opportunity to display their intelligence, courage and political and religious principles. The women in the Covenanting, dissident and Protestant and communist sects played a major role in the political struggles of those years; and they were often more radical, outspoken and courageous than their menfolk. In 1637 'a public-spirited interest in the cause of religious and ecclesiastical freedom prevailed among women of all classes in Scotland'. At the same time as Jenny Geddes erupted on to the Edinburgh scene, other women in 'the humbler ranks became famous for their resolute opposition to the reading of the "black service-book" which was to be read for the first time by the Dean of Edinburgh in the Old Church, on Sabbath, July 23, 1637'. But, although Jenny Geddes always gets the credit for throwing a cutty stool at the Dean, Robert Chalmers claims that it was Mrs Mean who 'threw the first stool when the service book was read in the New Kirk'. He also asserts that 'many of the lassies that carried on the fray were preachers in disguise, for they threw stools to a great length'.[62]

Throughout Scotland, the Protestant women intervened independently of their menfolk in the struggle to uphold Presbyterian principles. 'Lower-class' women were particularly prominent in the agitations against Catholicism and Episcopalianism. James Anderson puts it: 'At that period the gentler sex were particularly unceremonious towards the turncoat or time-serving ministers. Baillie gives a very graphic account of the treatment William Annan, the prelatic minister of Ayr, received from the women of Glasgow: "At the outgoing of the Church, about thirty or forty of our honest women, in one voice, before the Bishops and magistrates, did fall in railing, cursing, scolding, with clamours, on William Annan; some two of the meanest were taken to the Tolbooth. All the day over, up and down the street where he went, he got threats of sundry in words and looks; then at night some hundreds of *inraged* women of all qualities are about him, with neaves, and staves and peats . . . he escaped all bloody wounds; yet he was in great danger even of killing"'.[63]

In 1649 'lower-class' women again struggled in defence of Calvinistic Presbyterian 'democratic' principles. An important new development was that the members of the Privy Council, who questioned women about whether they had been put up to the business of opposing the prelatic ministers, had to acknowledge the total independence of the Scottish ministers' wives. In his book, *The Ladies of the Covenant*, James Anderson observes:

> This was true even as to the more ignorant of women in the lower ranks. Many of this class signalised themselves by their opposition to the intrusion of the curates, as in Irongray, where a body of them assailed a party of the King's guard, who came to the parish with the view of promoting the intrusion of the curate into the place of their favourite ejected minister, Mr John Welsh.

The women's political struggles sometimes assumed less dramatic forms, as Thomas Thomson writes: 'On another occasion a minister, annoyed by the scantiness of his congregation, commanded the women of the parish to attend church on the following Sunday, on pain of being informed against and fined. They came, but each brought a baby in her arms; and when the minister, overwhelmed with a chorus of squalling, rebuked mothers for bringing their infants, they excused themselves on the plea that they could not leave their helpless babies at home'.[64] He never again tried to intimidate Calvinistic women.

Although the chiliastic sect, the Anabaptists, who hid 'behind an appearance of humility and detachment', first emerged in early sixteenth-century Germany,[65] the Anabaptist communists were active in Scotland by 1650. Instead of recognising and analysing the role of the Anabaptists and other communist sects in seventeenth-century Scotland, many contemporary historians, of the right and the left, foster an image of women's unrelenting oppression at the hands of the patriarchal Calvinists. Indeed, the dominant, though usually tacit, assumption is that 'the Anabaptist and other orthodox sects flourished far less in seventeenth-century Scotland than in England, because Scotland was economically and socially a far more backward country'.[66] But, although John Knox frequently expressed horrible patriarchal attitudes, he initiated a long historical process which was ultimately beneficial to women's struggles for emancipation.

The general Marxist view that the Reformation was extremely 'progressive', but very mixed and confused like all progress, was particularly applicable to the experience of 'lower-class' women in Scotland. Although the population of Edinburgh and Leith did not exceed 22,000 people, many Anabaptists challenged the values of the dominant ruling-class culture. Indeed, 'sundry hundreds' of 'the women of the lower orders' and women of 'good rank' were challenging the ruling class by being re-baptised.[67] Within the radical Reformation represented by the Anabaptists, the radical Calvinists in Scotland repudiated personal property and the Catholics' anti-democratic attitudes and opposition to the education of women.

The Anabaptists contributed a great deal to the agitation for women's rights throughout Europe. They demanded re-baptism or rather adult baptism, as Ernest Belford Bax puts it, 'to which only an adult capable of thinking for himself should be subjected'. Bax formulates the point in that way, because he was a notorious opponent of the agitation for women's rights. But, because the Anabaptists struggled for 'divorce and re-marriage', too, Anabaptism has been described as an 'Abortive Counter Revolt within the Reformation'. Since the Anabaptist and other Protestant sects developed later in Scotland than in Germany and elsewhere, the Scottish women's seventeenth-century agitations were more important than the absence of peasant revolts.[68]

Because the Scots developed many dissenting and extremist Protestant sects in which the 'woman question' came to the forefront of politics, I will quote Richard Evans' extensive comment on the general relationship between Protestantism and the later history of feminism:

> Equally important in the development and inspiration of feminism as the Enlightenment or the French revolution was the social ideology of liberal Protestantism. The Protestant religion was founded on the belief that the individual, not the priest or the Church, was responsible for his own salvation. Like the rationalist individualism the Protestant faith was, in theory at least, equally applicable to both sexes. In practice, of course, the leading figures of the major Protestant churches in the Reformation era believed firmly in the inferiority of women. . . . Nevertheless, their belief in the priesthood of all believers did explicitly include women. . . . More than this, the Protestant Reformation quickly spawned a whole brood of extremist religious sects whose doctrines went even further than those of Luther and Calvin, attacking conventional marriage and advocating free love and the complete independence of the female sex.[69]

In England, between 1640 and 1660, women gained many new rights. In his brilliant study of this period, *The World Upside Down*, Christopher Hill states: 'In many ways the legal position of (English) women was inferior to that of men. . . . But women's position was improving, most of all in London, naturally enough. There it was actionable to call a woman "whore", and wife-beating was also an offence. Dutch merchants were still horrified by the Englishman's habit of beating his wife, though this was frowned on in Yorkshire'.[70] In England wife-beating, patriarchy and the legal teachings of Blackstone were applied

28

after 1660, as Hill puts it: 'Property triumphed. Bishops returned to a State church, the universities and the tithes survived. Women were put back into their place'. Because the compromise of 1660 was 'directed against the lower classes', the wives of the poor became 'drudges for their absent husbands rather than partners in a family workshop'. From the top of the 'social scale', the idea of 'leisure, white-handed and delicate, spread down into the middle, novel-reading classes'.[71]

The struggles of Scottish women began to reach a peak after the agitations of the English Protestant women had been suppressed. In Ancrum the women 'had a local pattern for being more valiant, in their own 'maiden Lylliard' resting close by, whose epitaph declares:

> Upon the English louns she laid mony thumps, And, when
> her legs were cut off, she fought upon her stumps.[72]

In documenting the independent political activity of plebeian women, James Anderson cites a contemporary witness who relates the Covenanters' experience in Galloway and Nithsdale in 1666: 'Many husbands here who yield to the full length, are punished by fining, cess and quarter, for their wives' non-obedience, and ye know, Sir, that is hard. There are many wives who will not be commanded by their husbands in lesser things than this'.[73] By 1660 patriarchy in England was once again secure. In Scotland it was being challenged directly by the women in the Protestant groups.

The 're-introduction of Episcopacy into Scotland was accompanied by a restoration of all the most severe restrictions upon the liberty of the press and a revival of the absurd and flagitious proceedings against poor, old and friendless creatures, ignorantly or maliciously accused of witchcraft'.[74] Being better educated and more militant in politics, and with the medieval canon law which permitted wife-beating already outlawed in the mid sixteenth century, Scottish women began to play a dominant part in politics in the seventeenth century.

Again and again in the seventeenth century, the representatives of the patriarchal Royalist élite in Scotland expressed what seems to have been a feigned surprise over the Protestant women's obviously independent intervention in political struggles. However, the women within the orthodox Protestant groups were just as hostile to the principles of Royalist Episcopalianism as their sisters in the more extreme Calvinist sects. In 1674, when a number of Edinburgh ministers' wives and other women petitioned for the release of the imprisoned Presbyterian ministers, the Duke of Lauderdale interrogated the women in the old Scots Parliament. Having just escaped the wrath of hundreds of women outside Parliament, he asked them individually if they had acted independently rather than having been prompted by men, as Robert Wodrow states: 'Upon examination they all declared, that no man had any hand in the petition, that they were moved thereto from the sense of their perishing starved condition, under the want of the gospel, having none to preach to them but ignorant and profane men, whom they could not hear. Then they were put together in a room, and the Provost of Edinburgh was sent to dismiss the rest. . . . The Privy Council, when they heard this, were pleased to send the rest out; and so this tumult, about which so much noise was made, ended'. The ringleaders were banished from Edinburgh.[75]

In contrast to the women in the Scottish Catholic and Episcopalian communities, the Scottish Protestant women were provided with education. This was especially true of the female Covenanters. In 1681, two female Covenanters were tried by the Royalist Privy Council in Edinburgh for agitating for their democratic, Republican and socialistic principles. The dialogue in the court was very revealing:

> *Privy Council (PC):* 'Do you own what Donald Cargill has done against the civil magistrates?'
> *Isobel Ailson:* 'I do own it.'
> *PC:* 'Can you read the Bible?'
> *Isabel Ailson:* 'Yes'.
> *PC:* 'Do you own the Sanquhar Declaration?'
> *Isabel Ailson:* 'I do own it'.
> *PC:* 'Do you own the papers taken at the Queensferry on Henry Hall?'
> *Isabel Ailson:* 'You need not question that'.
> *PC:* 'We pity you; for we find reason and a quick wit in you; and would have you take that matter into consideration.'
> *Isabel Ailson:* 'I have been advising on it these seven years and I hope not to change now.'
> *PC:* 'Your ministers do not approve of these things; and you have said more than some of your ministers; for your ministers have brought you on these opinions and left you there'.
> *Isabel Ailson:* 'That's not true'.
> *PC:* 'We pity you'.
> *PC:* 'Do you lecture any? asked they *mockingly*.'
> *Isabel Ailson:* 'Quakeresses use to do so.'
> *PC:* 'Do you own Presbyterian principles?'
> *Isabel Ailson: 'I do.'*

As the unmarried, twenty-seven-year-old Perth woman continued to throw defiance in the face of her accusers, women and men in the numerous Covenanting communities engaged in armed combat with the Royalist troops. The years between 1681 and 1685 became known in Scottish history as 'The Killing Times'.

On the same day as Isabel Ailson's trial, Marion Harvey, a sixteen-year-old servant girl from Bo'ness , was tried for the crime of treason against the Royalist government in Scotland. The Royalist troops had already attacked the Conventicles in which the Covenanters preached their Presbyterian faith. As they were physically attacked, they moved much further to the left in politics. Richard Cameron, one of the leaders of the Conventiclers, rode into Sanquhar on 22 June, 1680 and pinned up the Sanquhar Declaration which effectively declared war on Charles II. The social programme of the Sanquhar Declaration was very radical and wide-ranging. This was the background against which Marion Harvey was questioned in court by the Privy Council:

> PC: 'Where were you born?'
> Marion Harvey: 'In Borrowstounness.'
> PC: 'What was your occupation?'
> Marion Harvey: 'I served.'
> PC: 'Do you appove of the killing of Lord St. Andrews?'
> Marion Harvey: 'In so far as the Lord raised up instruments to execute his judgement upon him, I have nothing to say against it; for he was a perjured wretch, and a betrayer of the Kirk of Scotland.'
> PC: 'Can you write?'
> Marion Harvey: 'Yes.'
> PC: 'Will you subscribe what you have said?'
> Marion Harvey: 'No.'
> PC: 'Do you desire to converse with your ministers?'
> Marion Harvey: 'What ministers?'
> PC: 'Mr Riddell.'
> Marion Harvey: 'I will have none of your ministers.'

The high educational accomplishments of Isabel Ailson and Marion Harvey were notable in these trials. It was also evident that the Covenanters had developed very democratic conceptions about women's role in society.[76]

In 1681, a communist sect in Bo'ness emerged from within the Covenanting community to which Marion Harvey belonged. A sect largely composed of 'lower-class' women, the Sweet-Singers or Gibbites were advocates of 'free love' and the abolition of private property. They published a paper which went far beyond the Republican doctrines expounded in the Covenanters' Sanquhar Declaration. They agitated for the abolition of all ministers, churches, monarchy, for the oppression of landowners and for pure communism. The female Sweet-Singers were imprisoned in Edinburgh and their leader, John Gibb, a sailor, was exiled to America.[77]

Certainly, the Covenanters attached great importance to women's need for education. In discussing the different attitudes of Catholics and Protestants towards the education of women, James Aikman observes: 'All the women in Scotland at this time ought to have been taught to read. From every account, traditionally or otherwise, it appears the daughters of the Covenanters generally were; and some of their published diaries, which have been held up to scorn, are even in point of elegance equal to many English writers who have been praised as the improvers of the English language; but this is a subject which deserves greater attention than I can afford in a note'.[78] In the various court cases in which Protestant women were tried for taking part in 'Church disorders', the judges were often surprised to discover the extraordinarily high level of the women's educational accomplishments and aggressive intellectualism. Helen Campbell, a Highland woman, was one such woman. Although her husband fled when the Royalist government sent its Commissioners into the Highlands, Helen Campbell defended herself in court:

> Under examination, Helen Campbell displayed a dignity of bearing and superior intelligence, which struck her adversaries with conviction, and the judges with admiration, one of whom spoke in her favour in the face of the court. Her uncompromising fortitude also stands favourably contrasted with the timidity of the most of those (men) brought before the Commissioners of that day.[79]

Moreover, the Protestants' comparatively democratic conceptions of women's role in society provoked the Royalist Episcopalians into expressing their patriarchal views. A private letter written by a 'contemporary belonging to the Government party' revealed the extent of their patriarchal conceptions of women: 'There were hanged in Edinburgh two women of ordinary rank, for their uttering treasonable words, and other principles contrary to all our government; the one was Isabel Ailson, a Perth woman, the other Marion Harvey, from Bo'ness; they were of Cameron's faction, bigots and sworn enemies to the Kirk and Bishops; of the stamp with Rathillet, Skene, Stewart and Potter; of whom, *supra, et seq,* where we debate how far men (*for women are scarce to be honoured* with that *martyrdom,* as they think it) are to be punished capitally. Some thought the threatening to drown them privately in the North Loch, without giving them the credit of a public suffering, would have more effectively reclaimed them nor any arguments which were used'.

Clearly the Covenanting women were very strong-minded and

courageous. They were also independent and most of them insisted on retaining their maiden names on marriage.

In the field meetings and Convencticles the women in the Scottish Covenanting communities were provided with education and equal rights. Be that as it may, in 1684 the Covenanters' womenfolk were accused by Government agents of being 'the chief fomenters of the disorders'.[79] In 1685, the women of the 'lower orders' were sometimes more prominent than their menfolk in the Covenanters' struggles.

In Galloway, in 1685, Margaret MacLauchlan, widow of John Mulligan, was persecuted for agitating on behalf of Presbyterian principles: 'She was a plain country woman. Being strictly Presbyterian in her principles, she had regularly absenced herself from hearing the curate of the parish of Kirkinner; she had also attended the sermons of the persecuted ministers, and had afforded shelter and relief to her persecuted non-conforming relations and acquaintances in their wanderings and distresses. . . . Then she was immediately carried to prison, in which she lay for a long time, and was treated with great harshness'. The prisons throughout Scotland were soon overcrowded with Protestant women, as James Hewson puts it: 'Meanwhile the Town Council in Glasgow busied itself with a scheme for emptying the overflowing jails. It was better to banish them to the cake-brakes than to let them die of cold and hunger, as the begger witch Marion Purdy, died. The Glasgow magistrates, "pestered with many silly old women", were ordered to whip, brand and dismiss them'.[80]

Although the Covenanters and the unorthodox sects like the Sweet-Singers were usually portrayed as 'intolerant fanatics', they did play an enormous role in helping to improve the status of Scottish women. James Aikman states: 'It may be imagined, but I hardly think even imagination could conjure up a worse species of punishment than what was practised on well educated females — and such were the wives and daughters of the Covenanters for no fault but their opinions: to be sent off the country as common felons, and sold in the colonies as common slaves; and not only was this villany effected, but worse; their companions who came to visit them and take farewell of their young friends — some of whom had been prematurely, illegally, and cruelly created widows — were frequently subjected to a similar fate, being seized and sent themselves to the plantations'. Some of the ships lying in the Clyde were, as James Aikman adds, 'prelatical slave ships'.[81] But the legacy of the Protestants' enlightened attitudes towards women lived on in Scotland and in England. In Scotland this was seen in the inordinately important role played by 'lower-class' women in the Church and the militia riots in the late eighteenth century.

While the evidence of the role of Presbyterianism is raising the status of women at the same time as its strengthened patriarchal attitudes in Scotland was not perceptible before the early seventeenth century, the process was clearly accelerated by the Covenanters. Although the Covenanters were often 'intolerant' and 'fanatical', they did at least achieve this at a time when an unmitigated patriarchy had already been restored in England. By the 1660s, when patriarchy was again secure in England, the Covenanters were differentiated from the Catholics and Episcopalians by their more liberal and enlightened attitudes towards women.

Underneath the small communist sects and even where the 'lower orders' seemed to be 'humble' and 'detached', resistance to the evolving capitalist culture was widespread. The cultural attitudes retained by plebeian women and men in Scotland were incompatible with the objective needs of capitalism, resulting in increasing class tensions. Although the power of the Kirk to enforce its discipline and maintain conformity was 'formidable', the resistance of the 'lower orders' in the sixteenth and seventeenth centuries was stubborn and sustained. In his massive study, *The Domestic Annals of Scotland*, Robert Chambers describes the resistance of the commonalty in Aberdeen:

> Notwithstanding all efforts at repression, cases of excessive conviviality and of questionable frolics are not infrequent in these moral registers. It seems to have been a favourite prank to interchange the dresses of the sexes, and make a parade through the town at night, singing merry songs. . . . A month later in the same place, a group of women, "tryit presently as dancers in men's claithes, under silence of night, in house and throught the town", are assured that if found hereafter in the same fault, they shall be "debarrit fra all benefit of the Kirk, and openly proclaimed in the pulpit".[82]

The Presbyterian ministers and the civil magistrates frowned upon, discouraged and punished those plebeian women who participated in the 'penny weddings'. These are explained by Thomas Thomson: 'It was still the fashion among the poorer classes to make a contribution among themselves for giving the young couple a fair start in life; and in this custom originated these weddings, which were all the more profitable the more numerously they chanced to be attended'. Yet the extensive punishments did not result in the penny weddings being eradicated. In fact, they survived among the commonalty into the nineteenth century. Thomson sums up: 'The decrees against the penny weddings are both numerous and strict; and from their number and constant iteration we can conclude that their strictness caused them to be of little or no avail'.[83]

In contrast to England, where the Puritans' anti-pleasure principles were reversed after 1660, the Presbyterian clergy and magistrates sustained an unrelenting campaign against the rumbustious sexual behaviour and culture of the 'lower orders' long after the advent of the Reformation. A typical example of the Presbyterians' obsession with illicit sexual behaviour in the early sixteenth century was evident when 'a ship of war anchored for some short time at Aberdeen'. Although this was 'no extraordinary circumstance', the Kirk 'resolved that if any living proof should appear of an improper intercourse between the sailors of the ship and the women of the city, the offending females should be imprisoned eight days in the Church vault upon bread and water, and afterwards publicly ducked at the quay-head'.[84] Similar attempts at social and sexual repression were commonplace throughout the late sixteenth and seventeenth centuries.

Perhaps the most important single difference between the historical development of Scotland and England was simply that capitalism had taken root earlier in England. In both countries urbanisation broke down traditional Church controls over 'lower-class' women. In England the Reformation had been — at least in terms of the Puritans' anti-pleasure principles — reversed by 1660, whereas in Scotland the opposite had happened. Nevertheless, the dissenting Protestant sects in Scotland, until the 'crushing' of the Covenanters in the late seventeenth century, increasingly developed a form of democratic thinking about women's inalienable social and religious rights. This important historical development was somewhat ignored by progressive and socialist historians writing in Scotland in the years between the First and Second World Wars. The positive features of Protestantism in Scottish working-class history still need to be properly documented from a Marxist perspective.

Although Hamish Henderson's comment about Calvinism's 'numbing effect on the Scottish psyche' not being marked until the nineteenth century is valid,[85] the roots of Presbyterian sexual repression were planted in the sixteenth and seventeenth centuries. The cultural divergences in the history of the Scottish and English working classes were not solely the consequence of economic factors. As a result of the English experience of 1660, there was much less sexual repression and more social freedom in England than in Scotland during the Industrial Revolution. While Antonio Gramsci's observation about any industrial society's inherent need for moral restraint and discipline is undeniable, the anti-pleasure principles of Calvinism probably did have more lasting impact on the 'lower classes' in Scotland than they had elsewhere in the United Kingdom.

The Kirk had been attacking plebeian sexual behaviour with very little effect for centuries before the advent of industrialisation, though it was armed with judicial powers. If in the sixteenth and seventeenth centuries the brunt of the Reformation fell on Scotland rather than on England, Engels' comment that 'There is no great historical evil without a compensating historical progress' is particularly applicable to the sufferings of 'lower class' women in Scotland. What the Reformation did was reinforce some aspects of plebeian culture. If this plebeian culture existed within the framework of a nascent capitalist patriarchy, 'lower-class' women were already tough, independent and with political opinions of their own.

If the Reformation in Scotland had a dual significance in terms of its innate progressiveness *vis-a-vis* the rise of capitalism, it also had a dual character in relation to plebeian and later on working-class women. In spite of their 'intolerance' and 'fanaticism' in the face of an obscurantist Catholicism, the Protestants — and particularly the communist and Covenanting groups — did contribute enormously to the growth of democratic thinking about women's equality in the sight of God. Because this process was not halted in 1660 as was the case in England, the Presbyterian Establishment's reinforcement of patriarchy and imposition of the new social values appropriate to the needs of capitalism were not quite as successful as traditional progressive and socialist historiography have assumed and asserted.

2

Popular Culture and Women's Struggles, 1770-1850

IN THE LATE eighteenth century, Scotland was to the left of England. In explaining why this was so, A L Morton, the English Marxist historian, writes: 'In Scotland, whose people were on the whole more educated and who had national grievances of their own, the movement grew more rapidly than in England'. There was, in fact, much greater militancy and popular agitation in Scotland than in England during the last three decades of the eighteenth century, as the American historian, Robert Palmer, argues:

> In Scotland the disaffection was more broadly based. . . . A lingering feeling against England, a sense of exclusion from public life (there were only about 1,300 actual freehold voters in a population of one million), a Presbyterian habit of participation in popular affairs, the repeated splits and disputes among the Presbyterians since the Union, the connection between church and state, the existence of severe poverty along with a widespread literacy, the sermons of itinerant and unauthorised preachers, who were frowned upon by the Presbyterians, and much inclined to anti-aristocratic outbursts, combined to spread discontent in Scotland, especially as the American and French revolutions, over the period of a generation, began to arouse a new political consciousness.[1]

Clearly the force of cultural tradition played an enormous role in shaping the national differences in the development of the Scottish and English labour and women's movements.

In England, the radical Reformation had been defeated in 1660. Consequently, the coalescence after 1660 of a combination of factors reinforced patriarchal authority.[2] It was otherwise in Calvinist Scotland. Although patriarchal authority was strengthened in Scotland after the Reformation, the new capitalist values encountered greater resistance than in England. Although resistance was to be found in

England, the English were already less sympathetic to the idea of greater freedom for women than the Scots.

In Scotland, the success of the Reformation meant that the Calvinists' austere anti-pleasure principles were to play a major role in the social, cultural and intellectual formation of the Scottish working class. Moreover, in an illuminating comment which sheds new light on the seventeenth-century background to the formation of the English working class, Lawrence Stone describes the reversal of the Puritans' anti-pleasure principles: 'The most obvious sign of this major shift of values was a progressive separation of sin from law, which resulted in a marked decline in attempts to enforce the laws concerning sexual behaviour'.[3]

English sexual attitudes do not seem to have penetrated Scotland until the eighteenth century. But, although eighteenth-century Scottish literary men sided with 'the English middle class and its repressive sexual ethic', English Putitanism was not as punitive as Scottish Calvinism. By 1740 'shame punishments' for fornication or pre-nuptial conception had 'virtually disappeared altogether'. Even so, some penalties were imposed on the plebeian mothers of illegitimate children. They were sometimes sent to the Houses of Correction or 'eventually driven into prostitution'. In *The Domestic Annals of Scotland*, Robert Chambers cites what happened in Edinburgh in August, 1743: 'Notwithstanding the late execution of Margaret Stewart for child-murder, yet we were told that two new-born children have since been found dead, with marks of violence on them'.[4]

In the 1770s, prostitutes in Scotland were still being subjected to shame punishments. The *Glasgow Mercury* reported one such case in 1778: 'On Monday Barbara Barber was tried before the Magistrates of this city for keeping a bawdy house. She was sentenced to remain in prison till Wednesday 12 August next, and then to stand on the Tolbooth stairhead with a label on her breast, having these words: "For keeping a notorious bawdy house; and afterwards to be banished from the city and liberties for seven years"'.[5] But by the 1790s mothers of illegitimate children were simply being banished from Scotland for periods ranging from seven years to life. The serious problem of child murder was a consequence of the shame punishments imposed upon women by the Kirk-Sessions.

An important aspect of the shame punishments on the mothers of illegitimate children and prostitutes was the double-standard of the hypocritical Presbyterian clergy*men*. Although Robert Wallace, moderator of the General Assembly of the Church of Scotland, was already aware of the poverty which forced some plebeian women into prostitution, before his death in 1771, A C Chitnis observes: 'It must be recalled that Wallace was a moderator of the Church of Scotland during the meetings of which, according to a well-known Edinburgh working-class tradition, the prostitutes of Rose Street, Edinburgh, never had so much custom. More sound support for the tradition comes from the following passage in a letter of a whisky agent, who was a magistrate, to his manufacturer, dated 20 May 1814: "I have the Police Court at present, and I will be needed very much to keep the whores and ministers in order during the sitting of the Assembly'".[6] While the élitist comment by Dr Chitnis was written before women's liberation began to influence professional historians in the Scottish universities, he certainly exposes the hypocrisy of the so-called Moderate clergymen in sexual matters.

Although the Scottish ruling class had long been hypocritical in sexual matters, they were not totally unenlightened, however in relation to women. By the eighteenth century they were beginning to raise new questions about the role of women in society. In contrast to the English before the French Revolution the Scots did not produce a Mary Wollstonecraft or an Anna Wheeler, but this does not mean that the Scots were more patriarchal or less liberal than the English. Quite the opposite was true in fact. In spite of the constant assertion and re-assertion of the austere anti-pleasure principles of the Calvinist clergymen, Scottish 'lower-class' women were more militant than their English counterparts and this was probably assisted by the cultural residues of the earlier political activities of the Covenanting women. Contrary to the argument of Edward Shorter, the Industrial Revolution in England did not 'emancipate' 'lower-class' women,[7] as Lawrence Stone argues: 'With this reassertion of patriarchal authority in the early nineteenth century, the status of English women inevitably declined, despite the hollow blast on the trumpet of female liberation issued by Mary Wollstonecraft in 1792. The standard advice of the moralists was now that "in everything the women attempt, they show their consciousness of dependence"'.[8]

The English ruling class was much less sympathetic to the political claims of women than were their Scottish counterparts. While Horace Walpole was describing Mary Wollstonecraft as 'a hyena in petticoats', the Scottish male intelligentsia was analysing the historical reasons for women's enslavement. In opening up the space for a critical discussion about women's role in previous societies, the Scottish Enlightenment was making a very important contribution to human progress.

In the sphere of marriage English women had, in Janet Dunbar's phrase, 'no legal status of any kind'. In England, 'The savage criminal law was more cruel to women than men. This no doubt arose partly from the fact that the life of the family was felt to depend more on women than men, and that women's misconduct was therefore regarded as specially dangerous to the community. But it seems to have been largely due to the belief that women were subjects whose offences against their masters were in the nature of a revolt and must be put down with the severity usual in punishing the rebellion of slaves'.[9] This shrewd judgment by the English feminist historian, I B O'Malley, is reinforced by the careful historical research of Erna Reiss. Reiss argues: 'According to English law a woman owed complete obedience to her husband; he had the right to her absolute fidelity, to her society and to her services — in legal language, to her consortium' including the right to beat her.[10] Janet Dunbar sums up: 'The worst legal disability for a woman was the fact that she could not be released from a bad husband, no matter how cruelly he treated her; for a woman could not easily obtain a divorce before 1857'.[11]

Although, in the seventeenth and eighteenth centuries, Scottish women experienced a similar legal status to their English counterparts, the position began to change from the early nineteenth century onwards. The original divergence in the legal status of Scottish and English women was a result of the Reformation, as Alfred Waddilove puts it: 'It would seem that, previous to the Reformation, marriage was held to be indissoluble in Scotland as well as in England and Ireland. But the Presbyterian tenets which prevailed, which repudiated everything of a Roman Catholic tendency, discarded the sacramental character of marriage; and the Scottish nation, grounding its views on the precept of our Redeemer, resolved at the instance of *either* husband or wife, on the proof of the other's adultery'.[12] Although the great legal authorities in seventeenth-century Scotland also argued that the husband was 'the ruler and governor of his wife' at a time when the Covenanting women were displaying their Republican defiance of the established social order, from 1804 onwards a divergence in the legal status of Scottish and English women increasingly opened up.

Between 1770 and 1850, English men had a legal right under common law to beat their wives, provided that the stick they used was no thicker than a man's thumb. In a series of Scottish legal cases between 1804 and 1850 the Scots were no longer allowed to beat their wives or to 'use personal chastisement to compel obedience or conjugal obligations'. Unlike in England, a woman in Scotland could *not* be imprisoned in her husband's home. Moreover, as early as 1847 (a decade before the introduction of legal divorce in England), a Scottish court pronounced 'a decree of separation at the instance of a wife of a tenant farmer on account of beating her, holding her down forcibly on a bed', etc.[13] In England 'The right of husbands to imprison wives in their own homes did not end till 1891'. Besides, divorce was impossible outside of the ecclesiastical courts and wife-beating was permitted. Commenting on the absence of divorce in England down to the middle of the nineteenth century, C G Hartley writes: 'Wherever divorce is difficult, there women's lot is hard and her position low. It is part of the patriarchal custom which regards women as property'.[14]

In the eighteenth and early nineteenth century, Scottish women 'spoke and did exactly as they chose'. They were, as Henry Cockburn puts it, 'strong headed' and 'high spirited'.[15] Unlike English women who 'took their husbands opinions in politics and religion',[16] Scots women frequently intervened in politics independently of what their husbands said or did. When Scottish plebeian women married, they retained their own maiden names. As R De Bruce Trotter explains: 'Fok disna lose their name there whun they'r mairry't, and tak shelter in their man's yin'. They *insist on equal rights* there, and the wife's as gude as the man onyday, an' whiles a gey deal better'.[17] Writing in 1935, Marie Stopes, the English feminist, commented on the continuity of Scottish women's independent identity from medieval times onwards: 'In this country (England) married couples are generally called Mr and Mrs X Y. Many people wrongly imagine that there is a "law" that a woman should be called by her husband's name directly she marries. If they are educated and know anything of history, they may remember that many prominent women in the (medieval) past kept their own names. . . . In Scotland one has only to look at the tombstones around the country Kirks to realise that the custom of a married woman retaining her own name after marriage was the usual one'.[18] Unlike English women, marriage for the Scots did not entail the surrender of 'the few and inefficient rights they had enjoyed before marriage and thrown back into the class of children and idiots'.[19]

Although in the early nineteenth century there were often heated discussions in Scottish working-class homes about the role of wives and whether their mastery over men was desirable or not, Sarah Troop, a weaver's wife in Paisley, was quite representative of some Scottish women in her insistence that 'in every weel regulated hoose the wife is the maister'.[20] In reporting on an extraordinary occurrence in Glasgow in the 1830s, William Cameron, better known as Hawkie, says that the wives of working-class men 'were for once fairly out-talked'.[21] In their social lives as well as in their politics, the differences in the status and behaviour of Scottish and English 'lower-class' women were clearly visible and tangible.

Although the comparatively higher status of Scottish over English plebeian women was most obvious in the sphere of political activity,

41

Scottish plebeian women frequently did most of the manual work. In seventeenth-and early eighteenth-century Scotland the cottars' wives were, as Thomas Johnston puts it, 'the pack horses of the period, carrying everything — grain, hay, and manure — in creels on their backs'.[22] While Lawrence Stone disputes Engels' assertion that 'work brought equality between the sexes', the Scottish historical experience probably lends some support to Engels' argument.[23] The uniqueness of Scotland in this respect deserves careful analysis.

In early nineteenth-century Scotland, women still played an important role in the economy. Perhaps the actual backwardness of capitalism in Scotland contributed to the comparatively higher status enjoyed by Scottish plebeian women. In this connection, the characterisation of early industrial society as gynocentric is illuminating, as Barbara Ehrenreich and Deirdre English explain: 'And yet, to a degree that is almost unimaginable from our vantage point within industrial society, the Old Order is gynocentric; the skills and work of women are indispensable to survival. Woman is always subordinate, but she is far from being a helpless dependent'.[24] Although capitalism in Scotland was still steadily imposing patriarchal authority on working-class women, the force of their cultural legacy remained enormously powerful in unleashing the militancy of women in a whole range of industrial and political disputes. However, a major aspect of the militancy of Scottish working-class women was their comparatively greater importance in the economy. This was made clear in the abstract of the occupations of British working-class women and men in 1844, at least in coal-mining, factory work and agriculture:

England		Scotland	
Coal Miners		**Coal Miners**	
Male	Females	Male	Females
86,192	1,321	16,152	767
Factory Workers		Factory Workers	
Male	Female	Male	Female
7,396	8,787	1,860	4,373
Agricultural Workers		Agricultural Workers	
Male	Female	Male	Female
854,660	35,262	148,215	18,883

Therefore the percentage of female workers in the total labour force in England engaged in coal-mining, factory work and agriculture respectively was 1.50, 54.29 and 3.96. In Scotland the corresponding percentage of female workers in coal-mining, factory work and agriculture respectively was 4.53, 70.15 and 11.30.[25]

Irish immigrants and Highlanders soon became integrated into the Scottish working class and each ethnic group contributed its own unique features to the making of a Scottish working-class culture. Nevertheless, these ethnic groups retained their own values and distinctive behaviour. Illegitimacy rates for example, were higher among the Lowland Scots and the Highlanders than amongst the Irish. Prostitution, which was already a serious social problem amongst the Lowland Scots, scarcely existed amongst the Irish immigrants.[26] As David Vincent puts it: 'The Irish working class population observed a much stricter code of sexual morality than their Scottish counterparts'.[27] But, in spite of the cultural and other diversities within the Scottish working class, the puritanical principles of the Calvinist past merged with and shaped the distinctiveness of capitalism in Scotland.

Although they sometimes operated on the margins of some aspects of Scottish life, the Calvinist clergymen always denounced the licentiousness of the theatre, bawdy songs, illicit sexual behaviour and the strikes and political activities of plebeian women. The continuity of the clergy's denunciation of plebeian social life and sexual behaviour existed from the Reformation onwards, but what Scottish historiography has not yet taken sufficient account of was the tenacity with which for centuries afterwards the commonalty of women continued to cling to their pre-Reformation culture. There was a continuity of resistance to the social values dictated by the objective needs of a rising patriarchal capitalism. It was not, therefore, accidental that sympathy for 'free love' doctrines in the early nineteenth century created a climate of opinion in which Utopian socialism could develop amongst a minority of Scots, as Abram Combe, the Scottish Owenite, puts it: 'The new system has had its origins in Scotland; and the great exertions which the Presbyterian clergymen are making, to retard the adoption of the only means by which the questions can ever be set at rest, will tend greatly to accelerate its progress'.[28] Moreover, the birth of Utopian socialism owed a great deal to the Scottish Enlightenment. In explaining the connection between the Scottish Enlightenment and Owenite socialism, J F C Harrison says: 'What is significant is the relationship between Owenism and the "Scottish inquiry" of the eighteenth century'.[29] By 1849, Utopian socialism and the doctrine of phrenology were 'still exercising considerable influence over the press and people of Edinburgh'.[30] Utopian socialism in Scotland came out of and blended in with the residues of the Scottish Enlightenment and the older communal culture.

Although Calvinism played a detrimental role in Scottish social life up until the middle of the nineteenth century, it was never as powerful or as 'totalitarian' as it is still repeatedly portrayed in Scottish historiography. But, because a centuries-old Calvinism has been portrayed as unchanging, classless and utterly and unyieldingly 'totalitarian', Scottish historians have largely ignored plebeian women's formidable resistance to the juggernaut of industrial capitalism. Moreover, the cultural baggage of the past — penny weddings, bawdy songs, rumbustious behaviour and plebeian women's tough-minded independence and militancy — was carried into the new communities created by industrialisation.

The genesis of Calvinism as an oppressive force in later Scottish working-class life began to take shape in the eighteenth century. In *The Picture of Scotland* and *Traditions of Edinburgh*, Robert Chambers portrayed the lives of 'lower-class' women in eighteenth-century Scotland as austere, joyless and dour. Certainly, that was what the ruling class had aimed at for centuries beforehand. Although the 'evidence' mustered by Chambers has had a strong influence on modern historians, Henry G Graham documents the defiance of the women of the 'lower orders' in dancing 'promisky' in spite of the Calvinist clergy's admonitions. Nevertheless, the Calvinist Reformation had already had some influence on the austerity of social life in Scotland. In a colourful description of the differences between the lives of the 'lower orders' in Scotland and England in the early nineteenth century, Elizabeth Spence writes: 'The fair here (in Glasgow) does not exhibit, as in England, such gay booths, stalls, etc., covered with toy trinkets, ribbons, gingerbread, etc. The chief amusement seems to be walking through the streets until the evening, when the public houses are filled with holiday people, who dance till day-light to the sound of the bagpipe. In Scotland all the lower orders of young persons go to the dancing school. There are no variety of sports, and very few exhibitions'.[31] So alongside the very obvious austerity fashioned out of extreme poverty and the positive traditions of the Reformation, plebeian women were still enjoying themselves by dancing and drinking in public houses.

In the eighteenth century, an anonymous Italian traveller was impressed by a 'vivacity far superior to the English' of plebeian women in Paisley and indeed Scotland as a whole. Though theatres did not exist in Paisley, plebeian women enjoyed themselves by dancing and drinking in public houses with their menfolk.[32] By 1828 Robert Chambers was describing plebeian women in Paisley as 'a race of slatterns'.[33] But contrary to Chambers' portrait of the lives of plebeian women and exaggerated account of the success of Calvinism's unyielding repressiveness, the Calvinist clergymen did not eradicate dancing and drinking. It is clear from the *Old Statistical Account* that dancing and drinking were popular in urban as well as in rural communities. This was still the case in the early nineteenth century. Robert Dale Owen describes the popularity of dancing at New Lanark: 'The villagers were almost all Presbyterians; but in those days at least dancing, a favourite national amusement from the earliest times, was not forbidden by the Kirk'.[34]

The Italian's observation on working-class women in Paisley is of particular interest. When there was a debate in the British labour movement in 1919 about the reasons for the much greater militancy and socialist radicalism in Glasgow than in any other British city during the First World War, Augustin Hamon, a French socialist writer, argued that the Scots were 'more supple-minded' and displayed 'more intellectual vivacity than the English workers'.[35] Victor Kiernan also depicts 'the Scottish intellectual (including the theological) tradition more widely shared than any systematic thinking in England' as a major factor in the advent of the Red Clyde.[36] Although the cultural consequences of a past rooted in the Calvinists' struggles of the sixteenth and seventeenth centuries contributed to Scottish plebeian and proletarian women's greater intellectual vivacity and militancy, the negative side of the 'dialectic' in the formation of the Scottish working class was seen in their very austere way of life. As industrialisation gathered momentum, so did the austerity of social life.

The exclusion of Scottish working-class women from public houses was a slow process. Although women were still frequenting pubs in Glasgow and the west of Scotland in the 1810s, the practice had already ended in Edinburgh by the end of 1790s, as David Craig puts it: 'Although so much of the social life centred in pubs, their "equivocal" character made it unwise for women of "delicacy and propriety" to go into them. Scotland still suffers from the lack of a natural, integrated social life (in comparison with, for example, France and England) because there are so few pubs where women are welcomed on equal terms with men'.[37] The Calvinist clergy's patriarchal ideology had begun to influence workers' behaviour. By the 1830s and 1840s the process of excluding women from Scottish public houses was complete.

The Calvinist clergymen, however, did not dominate Scotland in a 'totalitarian' way. They contributed significantly to an ethos in which their austere anti-pleasure principles became part of working-class consciousness. Though English working-class women were also victims of a patriarchal capitalism, they continued to enjoy a much richer social life than the Scots. In the north of England in the mid nineteenth century, for example, working-class women 'went on outings' and drank in pubs.[38]

The Scottish ruling class did not exercise a 'totalitarian' control over the 'lower orders'. If the peculiarities of Scottish social life and culture were coloured by the Calvinist ethos of an industrialising nation, the plebeian counter-culture was nevertheless unruly and rumbustious.

45

What Antonio Gramsci says about Italian folksong is equally true of Scottish chapbooks and folk songs. It was an independent view of life developed by those who live outside of 'official' society and culture. When he discussed Dugald Graham's superb eighteenth-century chapbooks in 1883, George MacGregor wrote: 'The coarse language here used is in no way an exaggerated account of what may have actually occurred at the period with which the author is dealing. Great laxity of morals and speech prevailed; but vice it must also be stated, came more to the surface than now. The people were uncultivated, and did not seek to *cast a veil of prudery* over their failings, however much these were to be reprobated'.[39] In discussing the same chapbooks, another historian argued that Dugald Graham 'painted with cynical truth how peasants spoke, how they drank, how they courted, how they wed, and how they forgot to wed . . . how little they respected the menaces of the Kirk-Session'.[40]

By insisting on the Presbyterian clergymen's total control over working-class social life, the discontinuity in Scottish social life between the pre-industrial, the industrial and the post-industrial period is inevitably glossed over. In presenting the dominant historiography of the Scottish left, Thomas Johnston writes: 'The Kirk of the seventeenth century is ever with us, in our language, our habits, our traditions, our lives; it penetrates everywhere, prescribing for us the decorum in which we must perforce spend one-seventh of our days, enveloping us at baptism, at marriage, at death, and playing no mean or unimportant part in the education of our children and the making of our laws'.[41]

Contrary to the dominant school of Scottish progressive and socialist historiography, the Calvinist Kirk did not totally dominate working-class Scotland. In criticising this particular historiography, it is quite reasonable to ask the following questions: 'Did the Kirk really dominate Thomas Chalmers' Glasgow? How and when could this have happened when Glasgow became half-Catholic?' In analysing these questions, Scottish capitalism will be found to have possessed much less strong 'totalitarian' attitudes than Thomas Johnston and Edwin and Willa Muir allowed it in their portrayal of Scottish history.

In both Scotland and England ruling-class 'dominance' was the outcome of cultural leadership rather than totalitarian control. As E P Thompson explains in his essay on English 'Patrician Society and Plebeian Culture' in the eighteenth century:

> Nevertheless, the analysis allows us to see that ruling-class control in the eighteenth century was located primarily in a cultural hegemony, and only secondarily in an experience of economic or physical (military) power. To say that it was "cultural" is not to say that it was immaterial, too fragile for

analysis, insubstantial. To define control in terms of cultural hegemony is not to give up attempts at analysis, but to prepare for analysis at the points at which it should be made: into images of power and authority, the popular mentalities of subordination.

By the nineteenth century, the English Tories resisted 'Methodistical fanaticism' in relation to plebeian cultural traditions. Hence the growth of 'the politics of beer and Britannia' in later Victorian England.[42]

Moreover, the Calvinist Kirk did not require to exercise any control over the sexual behaviour of the Irish immigrants. The Irish who came into Scotland practised a much stricter code of sexual morality than the working-class Scots. It is nonsense to insist that because the sexual behaviour of many plebeian women was unruly and defiant, the Calvinist clergy exercised 'totalitarian' control over the Scottish working class. Nevertheless, the Kirk-Sessions possessed considerable power and authority through their control of the magistrates in the courts and the machinery for administering poor relief. Since the unemployed, the sick and the old had to 'truckle and cringe to a fellow called a minister', the Scottish radicals always focused their propaganda on the absence of Poor Laws.[43] In that specific way the ruling class was able to exert some control over the Lowland Scots, the Highlanders and the Irish immigrants.

This process began to develop in the late eighteenth century. A prominent feature of plebeian life in eighteenth-century Britain as a whole was its anti-capitalist culture. In paying homage to the counter-culture of the English 'lower class' in the eighteenth century, E P Thompson says: 'Nor should we underestimate the creative culture forming process from below. Not only the obvious things — folk songs, trades clubs and corn dollies — were made from below, but also interpretations of life, satisfactions and ceremonials. The wife sale, in its crude and perhaps exotic way, performed a function of ritual divorce both more available and more civilised than anything the polite culture could offer'.[44] Although the Calvinists' puritanical principles had cast a long oppressive shadow over Scottish life since the Reformation, plebeian resistance had existed alongside it.

Many features of the pre-industrial culture of Scottish and English working people have always been separated. But in Scotland there was a strong, distinctive and hidden 'matriarchal' dimension to plebeian culture, which did not exist in England. In addressing the question of why it was the women, rather than the men, who offered such resistance as there was to the Highland Clearances in the nineteenth century, Hamish Henderson argues that: 'It is when we examine the role of the women in resisting the evictors that the folklorist begins to feel that he might be able to offer the historian some revealing evidence. One of the most noticeable and most easily documentable characteristics of Celtic society, from the early Irish saga onwards, is the place in it of tough, strong-minded women'. Frederick Engels was also very sensitive to the existence of this hidden 'matriarchal' women's world in nineteenth-century Scotland and Ireland.[45] In explaining why it was the women who resisted the evictors in the Highlands, Henderson provides the empirical evidence to support Engels' theorising about the Scottish experience.

In the late eigtheenth century capitalism had begun to create a new sexual division of labour. By then, the Scottish ruling class was attempting to impose sexual repression, reticence and prudery on the rebellious 'lower orders'. In 1873, in analysing the eighteenth-century chapbooks, John Fraser wrote: 'The coarseness of the conversation between persons of the opposite sex surpasses belief, and the dialogue in *Jockie and Maggie's Courtship* and the *Coalman's Courtship*, is only a literal, short-hand report of what might be heard any day in almost any clachan in the land.'.[46] In the eighteenth century, Patrick Walker, the pious Presbyterian chapman pedlar, was upset by the growth of illicit sexual behaviour, as he put it: 'It is said by some intelligent publick Persons, That adultery exceeds fornication in Scotland; that they find more married people in Bawdy-houses than lads and lassies: This vile Abomination is known to abound in England'.[47]

With the dramatic growth of brothels in Edinburgh and Glasgow plebeian (as distinct from upper-class) women were being punished by the magistrates for "muffling" their faces in plaids in case they were or would be mistaken for prostitutes. These punishments were intended to eradicate prostitution. This was also consistent with the wider process of attempting to *idealise* women by portraying them as asexual. Thus, in Edinburgh and Glasgow, plebeian women were again being punished by the magistrates for 'muffling' their faces in plaids. An important consequence of the new idealisation of women was that 'The better ranks of women appear(ed) little in the streets'.[48] Street-walking became an exclusively 'lower-class' pastime.

Because the Scots pre-industrial plebeian culture had a strong 'matriarchal' dimension, the ruling class sought to strengthen patriarchal authority by defining new roles for women. In discussing this development in England, Gail Malmgreen writes: 'The threat of female independence was exorcised to some extent, by the popularisation of the new domestic ideal of womanhood, paralleling a similar development among the middle class by the 1830s'. Although this new bourgeois ideal of women's role in society was clearly influential in English working-class communities, it met with greater resistance among the Scots. Within the fishing communities on the east coast of Scotland 'the women did the work of men and had the manners of men'.[49] If the 'matriarchal' aspect of this culture has not been recognised by historians, contemporaries had no doubt about its existence and persuasiveness.

Between 1770 and 1850, the development of the new capitalist mode of production gave a new lease of life to the influence of the Calvinist clergy. Because capitalism needed a new sexual division of labour, the Calvinist clergy and the civil magistrates sought to impose sexual repression, prudery and censorship on Scottish society. Although many of the older 'matriarchal' mental attitudes and elements of the pre-industrial culture survived and interacted with the wider forces of the nineteenth century to create a new working-class culture, some working-class Scots already became austere, reserved and prudish. In spite of the 'matriarchal' dimension of traditional culture, a number of Scottish working-class women, in *some* communities, became reticent, taciturn and prosaic — except when they were engaged in political struggles.

In England and Scotland, the new domestic ideal of womanhood defined man as the 'breadwinner'. By the 1830s, working-class women in England were increasingly accepting this new role for themselves,[50] but in Scotland women 'factory hands' as well as women in the fishing villages refused to accept the new ideas of domesticity. In Inveresk, Musselburgh and Buckhaven eighteenth- and early ninteenth-century fisherwomen were notorious for their 'independence'. Robert Chambers described them in 1828: 'A woman of Fisher-row would have but little cause of boasting, if she could not by this species of industry gain money sufficient to maintain a domestic establishment, independent of the exertions, whatever they might be, of her husband. On hearing of any such effeminate person about to be married, it is customary for the fishwives to exclaim, in a tone of sovereign contempt, "Her! what would she do with a man, that canna win a man's bread?"' The wives of the salters in Prestonpans were also very tough-minded and independent. They earned their own money by carrying salt to Edinburgh.[51]

This 'matriarchal' dimension to Scottish plebeian culture did not exist in eighteenth-century coal-mining communities. In one of Dugald Graham's chapbooks the women in the fishing communities articulate their contempt for their sisters in the coal-mining communities:

> A muckle lazy useless jade . . . she canna tak a creel on her back, and apply to merchandising as I do to win a man's bread.

They also criticised the women in the coal-mining communities for doing housework or 'husband-work'. Although the women in the fishing villages remained hostile to the notion that housework was exclusively women's work, they were *eventually* drawn into practising the *mores* induced by the new sexual division of labour. The process was very uneven, however, and in some fishing communities the older 'matriarchal' attitudes survived into the twentieth century. In other fishing communities, they seem to have been *disappearing* by 1850.[52]

The Scottish colliers and their womanfolk were serfs until 1799. But although women were not removed from underground work in Scottish and English pits until protective legislation was passed in 1842, the Scottish coal-owners had been responsible for inducing the development of patriarchal attitudes long before the Industrial Revolution. As industrialisation got underway in other countries, the coal miners became notorious for their extreme patriarchal attitudes towards women.

In 1842, Janet Selkirk, a Scottish coal-bearer, told a Parliamentary committee that 'Men only marry us early because we are of advantage to them'. An old collier in the Lothians, who had been born in 1768, told the same committee that he had been 'obliged to get a woman early' to avoid paying away all the money he earned as a hewer. By the 1830s, the aggressive, independent, tough-mindedness of the women in the fishing communities stood out in sharp contrast to the subordination of the colliers' womenfolk in their day to day social lives. By then 'the patriarchs of the tribe whose duty it was to legislate for the commonwealth of collierdom were excluding women from trade union meetings, as A Millar sums up: 'Women or boys were dismissed into the interior of the workings, while the adult male portion, in their picturesque garb, held the council meeting'.[53]

By the 1840s, some of the features of the older communal culture had already been transformed by an urban industrial environment, but some aspects of the old culture, in particular some of the women's traditional mental attitudes, survived. In a fascinating account of life in a weaving factory in the north-east of Scotland, William Thom, the poet-weaver, describes the impact of industrialisation on the lives of working people: 'Between three and four hundred male and female workers were promiscuously distributed over the work; the distinctive character of all sank away. Man became less manly. Woman unlovely and rude. . . . Vacancies daily made, were daily filled — often by queer people, and from all parts, none too coarse for using'. In an anonymous book entitled *Chapters in the Life of a Dundee Factory Boy*, a middle-class journalist complains about the so-called corrupting role played by factory women and girls, as he puts it: 'I have known them myself living one week in a brothel, working the next in a mill, and so on for a number of months. Such abandoned females mixing with the young, undermine any good principles which they have inherited from the parents or imbibed at school, and prepare them to recruit to the ranks of drunkenness and prostitution'. On the other hand, a Calvinist minister in Glasgow in the 1790s was already appalled because some young women and girls seemed to prefer prostitution to working in 'the numerous manufactures established among us'.[54]

By the 1830s, the conflict between 'lower-class' women and the Presbyterian clergymen was just as fierce as ever before. In Lanarkshire the women coal miners were criticised for their obscene songs and immoral jests. The anonymous author of *Chapters in the Life of a Dundee Factory Boy* also criticised the factory and mill women for singing obscene songs and ballads. He singles out a popular ballad called *Sally Kelly* as the butt of his wrath and moral indignation: 'This horrible compound of doggerel and obscenity is still popular among mill boys and girls which convinces me that, as a class, they have made little moral progress in the last twenty years'. In spite of the centuries' old fulmination against bawdy songs, the ruling class had not eradicated them. What these authors were really objecting to was the employment of women in factories, mills and pits as well as the surviving elements of the older communal culture,[55] yet they had less success than their English counterparts.

In Scotland the 1830s and 1840s were a transitional period. The older communal culture merged with the wider forces of the nineteenth century to create a new working-class culture. On the one hand, it was a politically radical culture. On the other hand, it was already a sexually — and indeed socially — repressive culture. But, although sections of the female working class were militant and politically aggressive, others were sometimes timid.

In other ways, too, the merging of a repressive Calivinism with rapid industrialisation between 1770 and 1850 contributed to the social and cultural peculiarities of the Scottish working class. In contrast to their English counterparts, the Scots — except those in the 'lowest ranks' were becoming prudish, reticent and ultra-respectable. If wife-sales were defensible as a form of ritualised divorce á la E P Thompson, the Scots were reluctant to acknowledge their existence. A wife-sale in Dumfries in 1847 caused more consternation than a riot would have done, as the editor of the *Glasgow Examiner* put it: 'Not infrequently a statement like the following, which we extract from a letter written by a friend in Dumfries is to be met with in the English newspapers; but we are glad to know, the illegal, as well as shameless and unnatural practice which it records, but seldom, if ever, disgraces our country. From this circumstance, the case before us becomes more noteworthy'. Because the English ruling class was more tolerant of the residues of their older — and different — communal culture than the Scots were of theirs, English newspapers and magazines reported wife-sales without any inhibition or reticence. In 1832, when offering his wife for sale, a small tenant farmer near Carlisle said at the public auction: 'Gentlemen, I speak from my heart, when I say, may God deliver us from troublesome wives and frolicsome widows. Avoid them as you would a mad dog, a roaring lion, a loaded pistol, cholera morbus, or other pestilental phenomena in nature'.[56]

The 'dominant' Calvinism in Scotland did not eradicate resistance to the new values being imposed by patriarchal capitalism. What it did was to make some working-class women less open and more prudish than the English about their own day to day social and sexual behaviour. Because wife-sales, though very rare, were conducted in private and without the articulate auctioneering which accompanied those in England, the Scots became more cautious about some aspects of their social behaviour. Thus the *Glasgow Free Press* had written in 1834: 'The English sell their wives by public auction; the Scots a more cautious race, arrange the matter by a private bargain'.[57]

Although English society was more liberal and tolerant in the latitude it allowed working women's drinking and other social activities, it probably punished women more for non-sexual crimes than the Scots did. In an English town as late as 1838, for example, a working-class woman was punished for 'scolding' by having a scold's bridle put on her tongue.[58] This had long since ceased to happen in Scotland. While the Scots and the English imposed a patriarchal ideology on working-class women, Scottish society was in some tangible ways less consciously patriarchal.

Nevertheless, economics played an important role in shaping the hidden history of Scottish women. If Victor Kiernan's argument that 'a feudal-collective frame of mind' lingered longer in Scotland than in England has validity, then this unique factor played a crucial role in the making of the Scottish working class. In Scotland, everything old had a longer life than in England because of the weaker current of economic change, but the Scottish bourgeoisie's sustained assault on the older communal culture was fierce and ferocious. Women were now idealised in order to achieve working-class males' acceptance of the bourgeois conception of women's new role in society.

In the late eighteenth century, a particular target of the new culture of patriarchal capitalism was the hitherto uninhibited sexual behaviour of plebeian women whose social attitudes and mentalities were portrayed in the chapbooks of Dugald Graham and Patrick Walker. By the 1820s, literary censorship in conformity with the new bourgeois culture was widespread. Because the short stories and poetry of James Hogg, the Ettrick Shepherd, reflected the values and attitudes of the older communal culture, he became a victim of censorship. In 1828, for example, Thomas Pringle, the editor of *Friendship Offering*, wrote to insist on the need to censor Hogg's poem, *The Shepherd's Callendar*: 'I think it ought to be a rule to admit not a single expression which would call up a blush in the Cheek of the most delicate female if reading aloud to a mixt company'.[59] When William Cameron's autobiography was published in 1888, the editor said he had exorcised 'some spicy bits here and there . . . applying to the standards of the time'.

By the 1830s and 1840s, a process, originating in the eighteenth century, was reaching a peak. Although eighteenth-century Scottish literary men identified with what George Legman, the authority on international folk-literature, characterises as 'the repressive sexual ethic' of the English middle class, working-class women in urban (as distinct from rural) Scotland before the 1830s do not seem to have been very influenced by the new sexual morality. In the 1830s, Hawkie, a perceptive itinerant pedlar and observer of Scottish life, noted the new sexual attitudes of working-class women in Glasgow. He met with great hostility when he tried to sell them printed sheets of bawdy ballads. In summing up this point, he said: 'I have had the cheek, when *I was drunk* to sing such songs; but at my worst, I would not take £5 and sing one of them in the presence of a female; and yet the morality of England, even by dress and looks among families from whom "refinity" might be looked for, I found in the circle of the profane'.[60]

When J D Burn's *The Autobiography of a Beggar Boy* was subsequently republished, the passing references to 'sex and bodily functions', which appeared in the original 1855 edition, were deleted. Although sexual attitudes did not become really rigid until Victorian times, the process had begun in the 1770s. By the 1840s, the middle-class repressive sexual ethic had gained wide acceptance throughout Britain. This was reflected in nineteenth-century working-class autobiographies, as David Vincent argues: 'Those published in working-class journals for a working-class readership were no more explicit than those appearing under the imprint of a major London publishing house'.[61] The middle-class attitude to sexuality seems to have wrought more havoc in Scottish than in English working-class communities, hence William Thom's double standards and somewhat sanctimonious comments about Scottish factory and mill women.

A friend of the editor of the English Chartist newspaper, the *Northern Star*, Thom was also a Chartist. If his comments on Scottish factory and mill women were often unsympathetic, he was not insincere. A radical in politics, he was quite conservative in other matters. What David Vincent has to say about Thom's personal life throws much light on the extent to which the new culture of patriarchal capitalism persuaded even working-class radicals to become prudish and reticent:

> This was particularly the case with the Scottish weaver and poet William Thom, whose first wife left him after three years of marriage in 1831, and as a divorce was out of the question, he then formed a successful common law marriage with Jean Whitecross until her death in 1840, and then with Jean Stephens until his death in 1848. Despite the eminent respectability of both relationships, he felt it necessary to conceal the existence of his first wife and implied that he was legally married to the mothers of his seven children.

Although members of 'the lowest section of society' in Scotland and England described 'sexual or travelling partners' as their 'wives', by the early eighteenth century, the Calvinist clergy had already had considerable success in stamping out wife-sales. In spite of a few scattered references to wife-sales in the nineteenth century, the Calvinist ethos was hostile to them. Wife-sales (as distinct from mutually agreed trial marriages for a year and a day) were rare in the eighteenth and nineteenth centuries.[62] However, in the sphere of political activity, the legacy of the Scottish cultural past proved stronger; the women retained their militancy and independent identity.

The most dramatic turning-point in the agitation for women's rights came in the late eighteenth century. The Scottish Enlightenment played a crucial role in the agitation for women's rights, for, in contrast to most eighteenth-century English intellectuals, John Miller, Dr John Gregory, David Hume, Lord Kames and other Scots began to discuss women's role in history and contemporary society.

Although none of these enlightened Scottish liberal intellectuals championed the cause of complete sexual equality for women, they went much further than their English counterparts. By discussing the 'woman question' in history and contemporary society, they were reflecting the importance of the Scottish Protestant heritage in the struggle for women's rights. In common with other Enlightenment thinkers elsewhere in Europe, the Scots believed in what Engels described as 'the absurd notion that in the beginning of society women was the slave of man'.[63] Nevertheless, the Scots were not unsympathetic to the claims of women.

In an uncompleted essay which he wrote in the 1790s, Dugald Stewart presented 'a formal argument in defence of the exclusion of women from political privileges'.[64] When James Mill published an article in the *Encyclopaedia Britannica* in 1824, he dismissed in 'a sentence all claim of women to political privileges'.[65] By focusing too exclusively on this sort of evidence of the Scottish Enlightenment's hostility to the agitation for the female franchise, it is only too easy to overlook the Scottish intellectuals' very real contribution to women's struggles for emancipation. If the Scottish middle classes' agitation for women's rights had not been halted by the Tory witch-hunt which developed after the French Revolution of 1789, Stewart and Mill would probably have gone beyond their initial opposition to the agitation for the extension of votes to women in Parliamentary elections.

In *The Origins of the Distinction of Ranks*, John Millar argues that what he identified as an evolutionary improvement in the status of women in eighteenth-century Europe was a consequence of 'real improvements arising from wealth and opulence'.[66] Although Millar does not comment on the agitation for women's rights, Michael Ignatieff's remarks on Millar's significance should be emphasised: 'Given the immense effort it has cost us to reach this understanding, it may come as some surprise to return to Scottish political economy and to discover in, for example, John Millar's *Origins of Ranks* an economic history which tried to investigate the intertwining of sexual and accumulated desire and the corruption of sexual need by acquisitive individualism in commercial society'.[67] By raising such questions as early as 1771, Millar was contributing to a climate of opinion in which the 'woman question' could be discussed intelligently and rationally.

Scottish bourgeois intellectuals were usually more liberal than their English counterparts. Dugald Stewart, David Hume, Lord Kaimes, Dr John Gregory and John Millar did not feel threatened by intellectual women. In contrast to their English counterparts, who were, in Lawrence Stone's phrase, 'erecting a whole battery of philosophical and biological arguments to protect themselves' against the threat of intellectual women, the Scots were more questioning and inquiring. By focusing on the role of the Scottish Enlightenment in the development of Owenite socialism, J F C Harrison throws some light on the Scottish intellectuals' importance in the agitation for women's rights in Britain and America:

> The number of Scots among the early Owenites has already been remarked upon. When it is also remembered that a man's formative intellectual influences are those received in early manhood (so that a mature person's position may be explicable by the ideas current twenty-five years earlier) the

importance of a Scottish upbringing for several prominent
Owenites is further enhanced. Thus Frances Wright (1795-
1852), founder of the Nashoba community and collaborator
with Robert Dale Owen as a Free Enquirer and popular
educator in America, was raised in a liberal Scottish
environment. After her father's early death she was
befriended by Robina Millar, the widowed daughter-in-law
of John Millar who had published *The Origin of the Distinction
of Ranks* (1771), and by James Mylne, professor of moral
philosophy and a friend of Owen's. Fanny Wright attained
notoriety as the alleged champion of two of the most
unpopular tenets associated with Owenism, Free Love and
Free Inquiry, both which (in their true form of female
emancipation and deism) were aspects of a basic liberalism
stemming from Enlightment ideals.[68]

In the 1770s middle-class women were admitted into the literary and
philosophical debating societies in Dundee, Glasgow and Edinburgh.
This was seen as evidence of 'the levelling tendencies' of the age. As
aristocrats, intellectuals and scholars 'separated themselves and
gathered together in societies which were no longer open to those in the
middle ranks of society' around 1770, the 'middle ranks' were thrown
on to their own resources. The most important consequence of this
division was 'a growing democratisation of the Scots middle class'. Out
of this process 'the inclusion of women in traditionally masculine
pursuits such as public debating societies became a marked feature of
Scottish intellectual life. Although this particular development came to
an abrupt end after the outbreak of the French Revolution, it was a
long-term consequence of the radical Reformation. Moreover, John
Millar and other Scottish intellectuals believed that the Scottish
Enlightenment itself was a direct consequence of the Reformation'.

John Millar always argued that 'the Roman Catholic religion may be
regarded as a deeply laid system of superstition which took a firmer
hold on the human mind than any other that has ever appeared in the
world'.[69] In Millar's view the greatest significance of the Reformation
in Scotland was its development of the democratic assumptions
underlying the *First Book of Discipline* written by John Knox.[70]

Although this development in Scottish life stood out in sharp contrast
to Lawrence Stone's brilliant portrayal of women's total exclusion
from social and intellectual life in England, it met at first with some
opposition from Scottish males who believed in patriarchal domination.
However, the latter lost this particular battle. Davis McElroy describes
it: 'The first society in my records to admit women to its proceedings
was the Speculative Society of Dundee. The debate in the press was

started almost immediately. The provocation was a letter from Dundee dated 22 January 1774 published in the *Weekly Magazine, or Edinburgh Amusement*, which claimed "pre-eminence amongst the several entertainments of Dundee for the Speculative Society". According to the letter, the Society "hath the resort of great numbers who feast on knowledge and ingenuity of the speakers. Tribes of females, deserting the card table, flock thither and acknowledge the superiority of philosophy'".[71]

In spite of the Scottish intellectuals' antipathy towards the agitation for women's votes, they were among the first thinkers anywhere to analyse women's role in history and contemporary society in a serious sociological way. Although Lord Kaimes was 'complacent about the subordinate role of women', he argued that they should nevertheless attain a position of 'importance in society'.[72] Moreover, he devoted, as Ramsay of Ochtertyre put it 'unwearied attention to form the minds of young people of both sexes'.[73] Dugald Stewart also took 'the view that, though women as a group appeared to be inferior intellectually to men, the differences were due to education'.[74] Dr John Gregory argued that women were 'the companions and equals of men'.[75] In contrast to his English counterparts, Gregory warned his daughters of the dangers of venereal disease, as well as offering other 'sparks of enlightenment'.[76]

Many of the intellectuals in eighteenth-century society were very liberal. Consequently, Scots law was, as Nan Wilson puts it, 'powerfully influenced by theories of social realism'. Towards the end of the century, Dugald Stewart, John Millar and other intellectuals influenced the Scottish judiciary's decision to repudiate the concept of Negro or other slavery before the English did so. Millar argued that the slavery of the salters, colliers and female coal-bearers was an anachronism. Because Millar was quicker off the mark in identifying the economic inefficiency of slavery in Scotland in conditions of developing *laissez-faire* capitalism, he advocated its abolition.[77] The Scots legal attitude towards women was also more liberal than the attitude of the English. In spite of the otherwise repressive social climate of opinion in Scotland, the intellectual climate was comparatively liberal. Although this liberal intellectual stance was driven underground in the 1790s, it was not altogether eradicated.

Nevertheless, the liberal bourgeois intellectuals in the Scottish universities were, in the 1790s, the victims of a Tory witch hunt. Born out of the fears engendered by the French Revolution, the Tory witch-hunters played a detrimental role in the lives of men like Dugald Stewart. But, in spite of the dictatorship of Henry Dundas and other Scottish Tories, progressive thought survived in the universities.

By the 1840s, Scottish university teachers were no longer

encouraging such left-wing intellectuals as Fanny Wright. Progressive middle-class (as distinct from working-class) women found it increasingly difficult to play a role in Scottish politics at all. This process began in 1798 when a Mrs Fletcher, a progresssive English woman, attempted to set up an innoccuous Female Benefit Society for maid-servants. The authorities prevented her from doing so, as Elizabeth Haldane explains: 'The "innovation" was looked on with deep suspicion, in as much as the ladies were suspected of democratic principles, and the Deputy Sheriff and Magistrates (who had to be consulted) actually opposed the scheme when asked to sanction the rules. For many years after this, it was considered wrong for women to take part in any public scheme, whether for educational or philanthropic objects, and very wrong to speak in meetings even among their own sex'. In an article he published in the *Edinburgh Review* in 1833, Francis Jeffrey, a Whig intellectual and lawyer, argued that 'the proper sphere of female talent' was in the home'.[78] Consequently, middle-class women in Scotland were discouraged thereafter from playing any role in politics or public life. This complexity — that is, the survival of the progressive intellectual legacy of the Scottish Enlightenment in relation to women's struggles for emancipation alongside political repression — explains why Fanny Wright could develop as a champion of women and yet be denied the opportunity of functioning politically in Scotland.

The daughter of a wealthy merchant, Frances Wright was born in Dundee in 1795. A passionate supporter of the French Revolution and publisher of a cheap edition of Tom Paine's book *The Rights of Man*, Wright's father died soon after her birth. James Mylne, a radical professor at the University of Glasgow, said she was 'the child of her father and must have inherited her views and principles in the blood'.

In 1818, at the age of twenty-three, Frances Wright went to America. In 1821, she published her first book *Views of Society and Manners in America*, before she took up permanent residence in America and became the first female lecturer in the history of that country. But, although Wright's 'contempt for the English travellers in America was great', she published her first book under the pseudonym 'By an Englishwoman'. In addition to pioneering Utopian socialism and birth control in America, she subsequently contributed articles to the English Chartist newspaper, the *Northern Star*.[79]

The *Northern Star* also provided an outlet for some of the writings of Helen Macfarlane. Moving in the same circles as Karl Marx, Frederick Engels and Julian Harney, very little is known about Macfarlane's biography except that she had had a Scottish upbringing and that by the late 1840s, she was on friendly terms with the wives of Marx and

Harney.

Mary Cameron, who married Julian Harney in 1840, was the daughter of an Ayrshire weaver 'with a long record of radicalism'. However, Mary did not become a Chartist speaker until she moved to London in 1841. By then she was very close to Helen Macfarlane, who wrote under the pseudonym of 'H.M.' Macfarlane's contribution to British working-class radicalism is summed up by Harney's American biographer, A R Schoyen:

> The possessor of an intimate knowledge of the *Communist Manifesto* with the initials "H.M.": who could be but Helen Macfarlane, the admired acquaintance of Marx and Engels and translator of the first printed English translation of the *Manifesto*, which appeared in the four November issues of the *Red Republican*? Of Macfarlane almost no contemporary reference is to be found, though from her signed articles in the *Democratic Review* it is possible to gather that she was a remarkable person — an ardent feminist, thoroughly emancipated and advanced in her expression; well-read in philosophy and an admirer of Hegel; and evidently a travelled woman as well, having witnessed the Vienna revolution in 1848. If her identity as "Howard Morton" is accepted, it is evident that one of the most vigorous minds in the last period of Chartism was a feminine one.[80]

Frances Wright's role in the struggle for women's liberation was, and is, far better known in America than in Scotland. Writing in 1912, at a time when Wright's name was certainly unknown in Scotland, Earl Barnes wrote: 'The initial impulse to secure suffrage for American women came from Europe. After the Revolution, Frances Wright, a young Scotswoman, came to America to lecture and write, claiming equal political rights with men'.[81] But, by the early 1830s, all memory of the earlier agitations for women's suffrage in England had been almost eradicated. When the agitation for women's rights was reborn in the 1840s, it came 'chiefly from America and created only a faint echo' in England.[82]

Although 'echoes of the American movement' did not reach England until 1850, the American Women's Movement was stimulated by the male chauvinism of the English. The American movement was born in 1840 at an international Anti-Slavery Convention in London. In her book, *The Evolution of Woman*, G W Johnson, the English feminist historian, describes the origins of the American Women's Movement:

> To this Convention delegates were invited from all countries, but the conveners forgot to say that in their view the word "delegates" was of the masculine gender. There

were a number of women among the delegates sent from
America, who, after travelling three thousand miles to
attend a world's convention, were surprised to discover that
"women formed no part of the constituent elements of the
moral world". The conveners explained at the opening of
the Convention that it never occurred to them that they
were inviting ladies, and that it was quite contrary to the
English sentiment for "ladies" to appear in any public
capacity; and after a long debate, the rejection of the women
delegates was carried by an overwhelming majority.

As Johnson sums up: 'Their eyes being thus opened to the contemptible
and contemptuous attitude of the dominant male sex, these women on
their return to America at once took steps to establish Women's Rights
Associations'.[83]

In the future, international feminists would again and again argue
that the degree of partriarchal oppression was much worse in England
than in any other country in Western Europe or America. The
significant thing was that Frances Wright's concept of women's
emancipation from patriarchal capitalism was gestated within her
comparatively liberal Scottish *milieu*. It was then taken into America
and came to England in 1850.

The exclusion of Scottish middle-class women from politics was to
have profound consequences. There was no longer much scope for
bourgeois feminism, therefore women like Fanny Wright and Helen
Macfarlane were compelled to find an outlet for their talents and
radicalism outside of Scotland altogether. Not surprisingly, many
Scottish middle-class women became reticent and inhibited in public
for a long, long time afterwards, but many working-class women defied
the patriarchal notion that ' a woman's place was in the home'. In
popular disturbances, riots and strikes, Scottish 'lower-class' women
often displayed articulacy and volubility.

Though Scotland did not provide Frances Wright and Helen
Macfarlane with enough scope for their talents, it had at least given
them sufficient support, stimulus and confidence to push them on to the
stage of international politics. But although they were clearly a product
of the legacy of the Scottish Enlightenment, they also owed a great debt
to the long tradition of Scottish women's militancy and prominence in
popular struggles. This tradition of militancy was sustained throughout
the period of the Industrial Revolution.

The first recorded strike of women workers in the world seems to
have occurred in 1768 in the Scottish town of Paisley. In attempting to

explain why the first women's strike took place in 'backward' Scotland, it seems to me that George Lichtheim's concept of the role of the cultural legacy of the past in shaping a nation's history is more useful than any mechanistic 'Marxist' one.[84]

Throughout the years between 1770 and 1850, Scottish women workers were more prominent than their English sisters in such significant occupations as coal mining, factory work and agriculture. In contrast to the situation in England, there was often a serious shortage of labour in Scotland. The Scottish peasantry developed 'a great aversion to the novel system of working in factories' and they refused to enter the new cotton mills and factories.[85]

Unlike English male workers, the Scots *did not* demonstrate against the employment of women during the Industrial Revolution. In her important book, *Women and a Changing Civilisation*, Winifred Holtby describes what happened in England:

> Therefore, from their entry into industry, women were compulsory blacklegs, and the men of 1834 liked being displaced no more than the men of 1934. In more than one town there were riots against female labour. One working man suggested complaining to the Prince Consort. A gentleman called W. R. Grey wrote a serious essay called *Why are Women Redundant?* In 1841 a deputation of working men petitioned Mr Gladstone for "the gradual withdrawal of all females from factories", maintaining that "the home, its cares and its employments, is the woman's true sphere".[86]

This outspoken opposition to the employment of women in industry and agriculture did not create an echo in Scotland. Although patriarchal attitudes existed in Scotland, after the French Revolution they were much stronger amongst the ruling classes than the working class. Consequently, although, after comparative calm in the 1820s, strikes of woman workers broke out in Scotland and in England in the 1830s and 1840s, the Scottish strikes were the most extensive. In contrast to the strikes of women workers in England, those in Scotland were usually supported by male trade unionists. In the mass strikes of the female operatives in Aberdeen in 1834, for example, the women workers were actively supported by the male workers in the tailors', shoemakers' and weavers' trade unions.

When Mary Brodie addressed a meeting of 4,000 workers of both sexes in Aberdeen in 1834, she stated:

> Mr Kay then said, that he would send for an officer and caused me to be conveyed to the Bridewell for disobeying his commands. I told him that he might do as he pleased; but I

61

was determined not to go to the reels. He then gave me my
leave; and called two men to be witnessed that he did so. He
then pushed me away from him, and abused me very much. Is
such conduct to be tolerated? (No! no! never!). No, it shall
not. We will unite together to the utmost of our ability to
resist such cruel barbarity.

The Aberdeen Female Operatives' Union was born out of this conflict,
though it did not survive for very long. Similar women's trade unions
were formed throughout Scotland. However, at this period, most
women's trade unions in Britain were still very fragile, unstable and
impermanent.

In Scotland, no-one seems to have made denunciatory comments just
because women came out on strike, but, in England, the strikes of
working-class women were seen as being actually subversive, as Sheila
Rowbotham puts it: 'Unions were regarded by the middle class with
horror, but when women organised, it was seen not only as a threat to
class power but to the basis of authority in society'.[88] A strike of 1,500
card-setters in the West Riding in 1835 led Jack Wade to comment:
'Alarmists may view these indications of female independence as more
menacing to established institutions than "the education of the lower
orders"'.[89] On the other hand, the Scottish ruling class was very
confident about the efficacy of offering popular education to 'lower-
class' women.[90]

Strikes are often a crucial index to the class consciousness of
working-class women. Because it is assumed by the dominant bourgeois
and élitist 'socialist' historiography that working people did not have
any consciousness of their own, the 'lower orders', including women,
are portrayed as 'docile'. If 'it take a very jaundiced eye to read a
people's history as a record of undiluted compliance and docility', both
T C Smout, a bourgeois liberal historian and John Foster, a self-
proclaimed Stalinist historian, have portrayed the Scottish working
class as compliant and docile.[91] In a review of Smout's book, A History of
the Scottish People, 1560-1830, Foster accepts Smout's account of the
docility of Scottish working people down to 1830. Then he adds the
comment that 'the real (sic!) Scottish people' had yet to emerge after
1830.[92]

Because it is often argued that Scottish plebeian women did not have
any consciousness, it is not considered necessary to look at the struggles
they waged against their employers. This explains why the strikes of
Scottish women have been so badly neglected by historians. A report in
the bourgeois press of the women's strike in Paisley in 1768 tells a
different story to the one articulated by Smout and Foster. The Glasgow
Journal reported that 'a female combination . . . has been entered into by

the young women of this place, employed in the clipping of lawns, who refuse to work, unless on higher wages. They, in number betwixt two and three hundred, mostly clothed in white, drew up this day in Maxwelltoun, and marched in procession, four in rank to this place, and paraded through the streets. This white regiment was escorted by great crowds of journeymen weavers and others'.[93] It is inconceivable that they were not conscious of the class antagonism they were so defiantly articulating.

There was a continuity of women's strikes in Scotland during the transition to a fully industrialised society. In 1819, the English working-class women at Peterloo had been drawn into the conflict through sympathy with the plight of their menfolk rather than through consciousness of 'their own wrongs'.[94] The Scots inherited different traditions. Consequently, the strikes of Scottish women caused no surprise or consternation. In a path-breaking essay on Highland history, Hamish Henderson explains the women's resistance in terms of the survival from the Middle Ages of the 'matriarchal' character of Scottish plebeian culture.[95] This factor has always played an important role in shaping the class consciousness of Scottish women.

In attempting to explain why Scottish women became more militant than English women, a close examination of the interplay between this cultural legacy and the influence of the new capitalist mode of production has far greater relevance than any interpretation based solely on economic considerations. It must be acknowledged, however, that material differences also played a part in shaping the history of the British working class.

Although factory labour did not attract most women workers in Britain, it did attract a proportionally greater number in Scotland than in England. Yet, that important material fact should not conceal the distinctive character of Scottish women's participation in the class struggle. Moreover, if Irish women probably contributed to the Scottish proletariat's narrower sexual code, the Irish women in Scotland were no less militant than the natural born Scots. In the early nineteenth century, Irish women workers in the west of Scotland began their own long tradition of militancy by resisting the poor wages offered to them by Scottish farmers. On one occasion, a Scottish farmer was 'pelted from the Glasgow Cross by indignant Irish female reapers who felt themselves insulted by the wages he offered'.[96]

In differentiating the sociological character of the popular disturbances of plebeian women in Scotland in the late eighteenth and early nineteenth centuries, Ken Logue argues: '(Scottish) women formed 46.4% of all those charged with mobbing and rioting in cases where the motivation was in opposition to the exercise of church patronage by lay patrons against the popular wishes of the congregation. Far from being a "bread and butter" issue, the question of who should decide on the appointment of a minister to a church was a sophisticated politico-religious one, of concern to the whole congregation'. Besides, there were plenty of active, outspoken women in working-class communities throughout Scotland. This was particularly noticeable in the Highlands, as Logue puts it: 'In this way they were at the beginning of a long tradition in the Highland area of popular resistance to landlordism, in the first instance at least, by the women'.[97]

Plebeian women in Scotland were also very active in the widespread militia riots. In attempting to account for the continuity of opposition in Scotland to compulsory military service between the late eighteenth and the late nineteenth century, George MacGregor focuses on the anti-militarist sentiments expressed in Dugald Graham's chapbooks: 'Although the Scots have always been more or less a military nation, the common people have generally had a sort of pitying contempt for mercenary soldiery, as opposed to the old feudal system of raising an army. It would be difficult to account for this feeling, but it is still the fact that even now service in the army is regarded as the last resource of a respectable tradesman or countryman'. Such attitudes were shared by the womenfolk, as Christopher Campbell, who was transported for five years for his own role in the militia riot at Markinch in 1797, explained: 'He heard it said in the mob that a woman with a yellow ribbon in the Milntown of Balgownie spoke a great deal'.

Although there were no political riots in Linlithgow in the 1790s, plebeian women were subsequently hostile to war with revolutionary France. Scottish women not only participated in strikes, riots and demonstrations, they led and spoke at them, too, and they did so in the Lowlands as well as in the Highlands. Dorothy Thompson argues that, by contrast with the Scots, English plebeian women in 1819, were, 'new to politics'. Unlike the women in the Luddite Movement elsewhere in Europe who did not participate in 'the actual strikes', the Scottish women did. In a Luddite strike in Dunfermline in 1823, Alexander Stewart depicts the role of the women: 'On arriving at the doomed mills the work of destruction went furiously on, and the women sometimes vied with the men in their efforts to destroy dwellings and looms'.[98] These national differences were not accidental.

The distinctive feature of Scottish women's militancy was already visible in the late eighteenth century and it was sustained in the nineteenth century. In discussing Scottish women's role in popular struggles, Ken Logue says: 'Women took part in most disturbances for much the same reasons and generally in the same way as men did. They were concerned to resist the imposition of unpopular ministers by lay patrons as their male counterparts were. Their opposition to compulsory military service was frequently demonstrated. . . . While we have sought to highlight the role which women played in popular disturbances in this period, that role should not be seen as being in any sense separate from the role of the men. Women sometimes used different tactics from men — using the "privilege of their sex" on a few occasions only — but their reasons for taking part were the same. If there was a woman's view of popular direct action, there is no evidence of it'.

Quite apart from the somewhat chauvinistic formulation about 'the privilege of their sex', Ken Logue does not seem to appreciate that, in contrast to their English counterparts, Scottish 'lower-class' women intervened in popular politics independently of what their menfolk thought about political questions. At a time when English women participated only in food riots, Scottish women were often in the forefront of political struggles.

In England in the late eighteenth and early nineteenth century 'lower-class' women were not allowed to play a part in the labour movement. This was not the case in Scotland. During the struggle against the Militia Act in the Scottish town of Tranent in 1797 'the women were particularly clamorous, and for some time seemed to take the lead; for the men, either ashamed of the business, or wishing to conceal their strength, at first kept out of sight'. At approximately the same time, 'a rabble of women' at Bathgate Muir, who were also protesting against the Militia Act, said: 'There they go with their pensions and houses and lands; if it were not for those things it would not be so ill with us today'.[99]

During the years between 1770 and 1850, there was a very sharp contrast between the role of Scottish and English women in popular struggles. In Scotland 'lower-class' women constantly and consistently played an independent, autonomous and prominent role in working-class politics, irrespective of the opinions of their menfolk. In England, working-class women were not allowed to participate in popular politics until 1816, as I B O'Malley puts it: 'In the past their share in working-class agitation had been almost entirely confined to food-riots: in these they had, on more than one occasion, taken a leading part, roused to do so by the patent, practical facts that their families were perishing for the lack of the necessaries of life and that the farmers and the shopkeepers who possessed a good supply of these accessories were withholding them. It took such facts as these to goad the female poor to violence, and they were *not interested in philosophy*'.

In 1816, English working women began to accompany 'their

husbands and sweethearts to the reform meetings which were being held up and down the countryside. The meetings were not without danger, for the ruling class were even more frightened by this widespread constitutional popular movement than they had been by earlier manifestation of what they called indiscriminately "Jacobinism"; the magistrates were hostile and ready to call for help by the soldiery, a peaceful gathering might end in bloodshed. The women naturally wished to share these perils or at least to see what happened to their menfolk; a new sense of comradeship awoke in their hearts; and, as they listened to the speakers, in green fields under the evening sky, they were conscious of a new hope'.[100]

According to I B O'Malley, patriarchal authority in English working-class communities began to be undermined in 1816 when William Cobbett, the great populist and radical journalist, *invited* 'lower-class' women to play a part in the Labour Movement. If this was true, it was ironical, since Cobbett was an opponent of the agitation to give women the right to vote. It was only in 1818 that working-class women were allowed to vote at Labour Movement meetings, as Samuel Bamford puts it: 'This was a new idea; and the women who attended numerously on that bleak ridge, were mightily pleased with it. The men being nothing dissentient, when the resolution was put the women held up their hands amid much laughter; and ever from that time females voted with the men at radical meetings.[101]

This new decision by men to allow working-class women to vote at English Labour Movement or radical meetings was not a universal one. Indeed, the *Gorgon*, a London radical and trade union newspaper, and other such newspapers continued to oppose the agitation to allow women to vote in Parliamentary elections: 'First, it might be urged, that females are under the control of their husbands, that they are too much occupied with domestic affairs, that were they to vote at variance with their husbands it might cause dissension'.[102]

By 1819, female reform associations were springing up in many towns and cities in the north of England. In 1819 the *Annual Register* recorded:

> An entirely novel and truly portentous circumstance was the formation of a Female Reform Society at Blackburn, near Manchester, from which circular letters were issued inviting the wives and daughters of workmen in different branches of manufacture to form sister societies for the purpose of co-operating with the men, and of instilling into the minds of their children a deep rooted hatred of our tyrannical rulers. A deputation from this society attended the Blackburn Reform Meetings and, mounting the scaffold, presented a

cap of liberty and an address to the assembly. The example of
these females was successfully recommended to imitation by
orators at other meetings.[103]

This was the background against which English working-class women
became involved in the bloody and infamous Peterloo meeting for
Parliamentary reform. Millicent Fawcett stated: 'The picture
represents women in every part of the fray, and certainly taking their
share in its horrors. In the many descriptions of the event, no word of
reprobation has come to my notice of the women who were taking part
in the meeting; they were neither "hyenas" nor "witches", but
patriotic women helping their husbands and brothers to obtain political
liberty; in a word, they were *working for men and not for themselves*, and this
made an immense difference in the judgment meted out to them'.[104]
Nevertheless, the women's role in the Peterloo episode has been
unfairly neglected by modern male historians.

But, although some contemporaries in the radical movement at least
recognised the important role of the women in the Peterloo struggle,
Lord Castlereagh denounced English working-class women for
beginning to play a part in popular politics. When he introduced the
Seditious Meetings Prevention Bill in November 1819, he denounced
the women with particular venom:

> There was one point on which he should propose no law; it
> was the part which women had played in the late
> transaction, for he trusted that it would be sufficient to
> restrain them from such conduct in the future, to let them
> know, that when the French Republicans were carrying on
> their bloody orgies, they could find no female to join them
> except by ransacking the bagnious or public brothels. He
> was happy that no female had attended any public meeting in
> the metropolis. Such a drama, would, he trusted, be put an
> end to by the innate decorum and the innate sense and
> modesty which the women of this country possessed and
> which would purge the country of this disgrace.[105]

According to I B O'Malley, the female reformers in the English
working-class communities, were silenced for a long time after the
setback suffered by the radicals in 1819.

The decade of the 1820s was one of comparative calm and quiescence
in Scotland and in England. Around 1830, when working-class politics
began to revive, there would be significant differences once again in the
pattern of Scottish and English working-class women's involvement in
popular politics.

Although patriarchal authority was strengthened in Scotland and in England, Scottish 'lower-class' women resisted it much more than their English sisters. The process of cultural change is always an interaction between past and present. The cultural legacy of the past was of particular importance in explaining the history of Scottish women — that is, their greater militancy, and the relative difference in the degree of sexual oppression in Scotland and England. Consequently, Scottish women were bold and outspoken, This was seen in the women's strikes in the 1830s. In arguing that 'The attempt by the Glasgow Spinners' Association to negotiate equal rates of pay was quite exceptional', Sheila Rowbotham unwittingly reinforces the hidden history of Scottish women. What her interesting comment obscures is the role played by factory women in the struggle for equality. In giving evidence, in 1833, before a Parliamentary Select Committee on Manufacturers a Glasgow employer said: 'We had an intimation that they had meetings, and I saw a letter signed by a woman, calling upon one house to raise wages equal to the men's'.[106] The voluminous literature on British (but not Scottish) working-class woman offers no hint that the English women were as self-assertive in the struggle for equality.

In contrast to the portrait of English working-class women depicted by such historians as Sheila Rowbotham, Ivy Pinchbeck and Sheila Lewenhak, the Scots were more outspoken about the need for equal rights. Despite the absence of a radical bourgeois culture in Scotland, working-class radicals championed the cause of women's rights without being encumbered by the inhibitions which led English radicals into ambiguous attitudes towards the 'woman question'. In a poignant description of women in the English Labour Movement, Edward Royle and James Walvin argue:

> Women were certainly active with their menfolk in radical agitations, and enjoyed a certain amount of autonomy in areas where the cotton textile industry had given them a measure of economic independence, but overall their role can be compared to that of the womenfolk at a village cricket match. Their place was in the pavillion making the teas, and washing the whites afterwards. Seldom were they permitted to field a team of their own.[107]

Scottish trade union and Chartist newspapers such as *The Herald to Trades Advocate* and the *Chartist Circular* agitated for equal educational opportunity for women.[108]

Scottish plebeian women were prominent in political life in the 1830s and 1840s. When the Owenite socialists criticised 'legal prostitution' and agitated for 'free love', they attracted considerable working-class support. From 1839, when Robert Owen founded Halls of Science in the major Scottish towns and 'proclaimed the orphanhood of mankind', working-class women raised fundamental questions in the Owenite halls and dissenting Calvinist churches. A Mrs Hamilton, an Owenite lecturer, gained entry into the Voluntary Churches by criticising the Established Church at a time when the latter was very unpopular with working-class women. She complained of 'the tyranny with which males lorded it over females and advised women to be ruled no longer'. Agnes Walker, a lecturer in theology at the Glasgow Mechanics Institute, also lectured to audiences of women on the need for 'if not supremacy, at least the perfect equality of her sex to that of the male'. She also vindicated 'her sex from the bondage in which they had been held for the last 1,800 years'.[109]

Although ordinary rank and file women were very active in political struggles in the late eighteenth and early nineteenth centuries, the agitation for women's rights rose to a crescendo in the 1830s and 1840s. At question time during a Parliamentary election in Paisley in 1834 a woman weaver asked the Liberal candidate if he 'would, if elected, support a petition for female emancipation and the betterment of her sex'. Scottish women frequently fielded their own team in working-class struggles without asking their menfolk for permission to do so.

In a letter published in the *Northern Star* in 1838 a working-class woman who signed herself 'A Real Democrat' wrote:

> I address you as a plain working woman — a weaver of Glasgow. You cannot expect me to be grammatical in my expression, as I did not get an education, like others of my fellow women that I ought to have got, and which is the right of every human being. . . . It is the right of every woman to have a vote in the legislature of her country, and doubly more so now that we have got a woman at the head of the government.

In quoting this letter in her important essay on English working-class women, Dorothy Thompson says it was one of 'the rare cases in these years in which the demand for the vote is put specifically by a working woman'. But this sort of demand by working-class women in Scotland was actually far from rare, as we can see from a report of the proceedings of the Gorbals Female Suffrage Association by the *Glasgow Constitutional*: 'We read in Monday's *Chronicle* of the Gorbals Female Association where a brazen-faced jade of the name Miss Agnes McLarty Lennox, having been called to the chair by acclamation, Mr Wattie Currie, the secretary, read the minutes of former assemblages

— and the meeting proceeded to the election of office-bearers, when Miss S J Buchanan was elected secretary for the females; and an assistant secretary for the males'. In concluding this report the editor of the *Glasgow Constitutional* said: 'We observe she (Miss Lennox) sat down amidst much cheering. In concluding her harrange, she sung out for, "*Equal rights and equal laws*", which we were we her mother — would respond to with the taws'.[110]

In contrast to many English Chartists, there is no evidence of any Scottish Chartists actually opposing the agitation for female suffrage. If the English Chartist movement was, as Dorothy Thompson argues, 'always ambiguous' on 'the central question of the admission of women to the suffrage', many English Chartists repeatedly opposed this agitation in unqualified patriarchal language. This opposition was indeed present at the birth of the Chartist movement in London, as Ray Strachey explains: 'There is no need to discuss its underlying causes, nor to account for its rise and fall; the only point we must notice is that in the first draft of the Charter of Rights and Liberties itself, women's suffrage was specifically mentioned'. The English Chartists, however, thought that such a demand would 'retard the suffrage of the men' and it was 'rapidly struck out again'. The Chartists in London also ridiculed the agitation to set up a National Women's Chartist Association.[111]

The Scottish Chartists were unquestionably more sympathetic to the agitation for women's suffrage than the English. When he opposed the plan to create a National Women's Chartist Association, a Mr Cohen and other Chartists objected to 'the interposition of women in political affairs'. In launching a successful campaign against this 'ridiculous notion', Cohen 'put it to the mothers present, whether they did not find themselves more happy in the peacefulness and usefulness of the domestic hearth, than in coming forth in public, and aspiring after political rights'. Harriet Taylor, the wife of John Stuart Mill, also criticised the English Chartists for their patriarchal and élitist mentality. In summing up in an article in the *Westminster Review* tracing the agitation for women's rights to the American women who had come to London in 1840, she said: 'The Chartist, who denies the suffrage to women, is a Chartist only because he is not a Lord; he is one of those levellers who would level only down to themselves'.[112]

The Scottish Chartists, though austere and puritanical, were more sympathetic to the agitation for women's rights than English radicals and reformers. This development during an important transitional period in British history had a strong bearing on the future struggles of Scottish and English working-class women.

3

Women and the Class Struggle in Mid-Victorian Britain

A MIDDLE-CLASS Women's Movement (as distinct from a few scattered individuals) simply did not exist in mid-Victorian Scotland. This was not an inevitable development. It was a consequence of a number of factors including the Tories' witch-hunting of the radical intelligentsia in the 1790s. As a result of the virtual absence of a Women's Movement, the strikes of Scottish women who were by far more militant than their English sisters were largely ignored. The extensive militancy of women in the mills, workshops and factories was not recorded except in brief newspaper reports. Also, there was no tradition of bourgeois radicalism in Scotland. This is why mid-Victorian Scotland did not produce an Emma Paterson, a Harriet Martineau, a Frances Power Cobb or a Harriet Taylor. In the 1870s, however, a small number of middle-class women did gain membership of the School Boards and entry into the medical school in Edinburgh.

To understand why Scottish working-class women were so militant and yet so ignored by the intellectuals in the universities, we must focus on the 'peculiarities' of capitalism in Scotland. One of the 'peculiarities' of Scottish society was its failure to produce a strong middle-class feminist movement. Although a unique conjunction of circumstances gave an enormous impetus to the struggles of the women in the mills, factories and agricultural communities, the extreme polarisation between the contending classes weakened the Feminist Movement's possibility of attracting mass support from working-class women.

Glancing back to the activities of Scottish women in the mid-Victorian period, Ethel Snowden states: 'Miss Flora Stevenson was the woman chairman of the Edinburgh School Board, and her name is affectionately remembered by her fellow citizens for the work she accomplished'. In her interesting and well-researched book, *The Scotland of our Fathers: A Study of Scottish Life in the Nineteenth Century*, Elizabeth Haldane records the struggles of the Scottish feminists:

It was the Education Act of 1872 that gave women the power

to serve on Public Boards, and in the early seventies one or two managed to acquire degrees which would entitle them to practise medicine.

In acknowledging the lesser *degree* of patriarchal dominance in Scotland, Haldane argues: 'We must never forget that there was a noble body of Scottish iconoclasts such as Flora and Louisa Stevenson, Ann Dundas and Clementia Guthrie Wright, who broke open the closely barred male defences and made their way into universities, Hospital-Governorships, School Boards and so on, and in doing so helped in the breaking down of the old tradition of female servitude where it existed. It had never existed everywhere'.[1]

Although the middle-class Feminist Movement in mid-Victorian Scotland was weaker than that in England, it probably gained greater social reforms for women. In addition to the activities of middle-class women such as Flora Stevenson on the School Boards, women like Agnes McLaren fought for women's suffrage. Daughter of the prominent Liberal member of Parliament, Duncan McLaren, Agnes was the secretary of the Edinburgh branch of the National Society for Women's Suffrage.

Edinburgh was the stronghold of the Scottish Feminist Movement, as Elizabeth Stanton and Matilda Gage explain: 'The work in Scotland was chiefly carried on in the way of lectures by Miss Jane Taylor, who during these early years of the movement was an untiring and spirited pioneer, Miss Agnes Mclaren often accompanying her and helping her to organise the meetings'. But there were other feminists who struggled for women's emancipation, as Stanton and Gage sum up: 'We must not omit to mention Mary Burton (sister of John Hill Burton, the historiographer of Scotland), who was also one of the most energetic workers of the Edinburgh committee, especially in the north of Scotland; and Mrs Dick Lauder who had the courage to free herself from the opinions in which she had been educated, and with much sacrifice devoted herself to the work'.[2]

Despite the numerical weakness of the Scottish Women's Movement, Flora and Louisa Stevenson, Ann Dundas and Sophia Jex Blake won concessions from the male-dominated Establishment. In discussing Sophia Jex Blake's important struggle to gain entry into the University of Edinburgh, Eunice Murray says:

> When Sophia Jex Blake in 1869 asked to be allowed to study medicine, she was informed that to study anatomy was impossible for a woman; even to discuss the matter was indelicate. Vulgar-minded people declared that her wish to enter the University was only a cloak to allow her to carry

on her intrigues and flirtations with the students, and ultimately enable her to get a husband.

Miss Jex Blake stood her ground unflinchingly and fought her battle, and won the victory for her sex and profession practically alone.[3]

But, although Flora Stevenson was elected to the new Edinburgh School Board in 1873, she did not achieve her major victories for women's emancipation until the late nineteenth century.

In England, women were often made out to be figures of fun. In 1867 some English women were deprived of the voting rights that they had inherited;[4] and women were widely regarded as 'scolds'. The discovery of ether as an anaesthetic in dentistry prompted *Punch* to publish a cartoon displaying 'the wonderful effect of ether in the case of a scolding wife'.[5]

While the patriarchal working-class family existed in Scotland as well as in England — 'a euphemism', as Robert Briffault put it, 'for the individualistic male with his subordinate dependents' — there were significant social differences in the two countries. Socially, economically and culturally, the status of English working-class women was at zero. English women, for example, were sometimes used instead of horses for hauling canal boats, because, as Karl Marx put it, 'the labour required to produce horses and machines is an accurately known quantity, while that required to maintain the women of the surplus population is below all calculation'.[6] In contrast to their Scottish counterparts, most English trade unions were very hostile to the employment of women in mills, factories and at pit-heads. In the 1850s for example, there was a strike of English whipmakers because women were 'introduced into a branch of the work for which men had been hitherto employed'.[7]

In contrast to what happened in Scotland, where frequent and aggressive women's strikes were often supported by the Labour Movement, strikes of working women in England were a very rare occurrence. Commenting on what was a very unusual strike of workers in an English country town in 1866, Bessie Rayner Parks described the amazement that it caused: 'There were letters and speeches to and fro; placards on the walls, and a liberal expenditure of forcible Anglo-Saxon language. Now, who were these hands "out on strike", these speeches, gathered together in angry knots at the corners of the street — women'.[8] Any attempt to organise English women was ridiculed, and strikes of women were just not taken seriously. This was summed up by John Milne who wrote in 1857: 'The strikes of workmen are feared; those of *workwomen are laughed at*. Yet a strike is almost the only means of asserting a social right that is at present open to work-people'.[9]

The total social context of Scottish society gave working-class women greater scope to engage in militant strikes in the factories and mills. As strikes for better wages and working conditions escalated into bitter class conflict, Scottish rank and file women workers frequently rose above the values being imposed on them by patriarchal capitalism to demand greater social freedom and even the vote in Parliamentary elections. At a time when the Presbyterian Churches were engaged in the task of attempting to make women totally subordinate to males, the Establishment responded to the women's challenge by attacking the notion of female equality. In a book on *A Woman's Thoughts on Women's Rights*, an anonymous Scottish spokeswoman for patriarchal capitalist values saw the implicit threat posed by the women's strikes when she wrote: 'Then, if wives come to consider themselves on a perfect footing of equality with their husbands — if they find that they can be perfectly independent of them — will not there be an end of all wifely submission and obedience? Disobedient wives have disobedient children. Disobedient children grow up unruly men and women'.[10]

The militancy of women workers in the mills and factories was a distinctive and major feature of the class struggle in mid-Victorian Scotland. In attempting to answer the question of *why* the Scots were much more militant than their English sisters, I will not engage in a vulgar 'Marxist' explanation of the immediate importance of the new mode of production. While readily acknowledging the enormous importance of the capitalist mode of production, I will nevertheless try to sketch in the *cultural* determinants of class. The juggernaut of industrial capitalism was still in the process of imposing itself upon an economically under-developed society with older social and cultural traditions and modes of thought which were antithetical to the new social order.[11]

Founded in 1874, the British Women's Protective and Provident League faced much more riducule and opposition from English than from Scottish working-class men. It was founded by Emma Paterson, wife of a London printer, immediately after she returned from her honeymoon in New York. Ray Strachey explains: 'She went to America in 1874, and there she saw women's unions in existence, so that she became fired with the hope of founding similar bodies in England'.

Although there were branches of the Women's Protective and Provident League in Glasgow and Edinburgh, it was essentially an English organisation. In sketching the history of the League between 1874 and 1879, Barbara Drake states: 'The League established in England between thirty and forty women's societies, of which eight were composed of dressmakers and milliners, and there was a general labour union at Oxford. Not many societies, however, counted more than a few hundred members or survived longer than a few years. The early promise failed fulfilment and success was mostly short-lived. Members grew discouraged and left the union'.[12]

Although Emma Paterson envisaged finally emancipating the Women's Protective and Provident League from 'middle-class rule' before her death in 1887, she always insisted that administration by women of 'wealth and leisure' was essential in the early years. Unfortunately, the wealthy English women who supported the League were often hostile to the potential militancy of working-class women, as the English feminist historian, B L Hutchins, explains: 'The founder, although a woman of unusual energy and initiative, whose efforts for the uplifting of women workers should not be forgotten, was in some degree hampered by the narrow individualism characteristic of what may be designated as the Right Wing of the Women's Rights Movement. She was an opponent of factory legislation for grown women, and did not lead the unions under her control to attempt any concerted measure for improving the conditions of their work'.[13]

A major reason for Emma Paterson's prejudice against legal restrictions upon labour was the persistent efforts of English working men to drive their own womenfolk out of industry altogether. In the 1860s in Manchester, for example, 'a union of warpers refused to allow the wives and sisters of their members to warp', for 'if women were introduced into *their* market, the wages of the men would be reduced'. The unholy alliance of English working-class male chauvinism and Emma Paterson's ultra-individualistic liberal economic doctrines combined to stifle the potential militancy of working-class women.

The often riotous militancy of Scottish working-class women in the nineteenth and twentieth centuries can be seen as a continuation of the self-assertion, independent identity and long tradition of women's 'riots' in the seventeenth and eighteenth centuries.[14] In an important book, *Women and Trade Unions*, Sheila Lewenhak identifies, but does not explain what she describes as 'the long tradition of women's militancy' in the Scottish (as distinct from the English) mills and factories.[15] Also, the aggressive women's strikes in the mills and factories were influenced by the same cultural traditions and values that encouraged working people to resist the repressive sexual morality of what William Power depicts as 'the Gradgrind Calvinism' of mid-Victorian Scotland.[16] In a vivid description of the effects of the traditions of the past on the psychology of Scottish women, Lewis Grassic Gibbon (James Leslie Mitchell) argues that:

Catholicism was more mellow and colourful and poetic: it

> was also darker and older and more oppressed by even more
> ancient shames. It produced an attitude of mind more soft
> than the Presbyterian: and also infinitely more servile. Sex
> had always been a shameful thing to the Catholic mind, a
> thing to be transmuted.[17]

An obvious objection to the analytical explanation that I have offered
for the much greater militancy and more frequent strikes of Scottish
than English working-class women is the presence of Irish immigrant
women in the Scottish mills and factories. Certainly, the Irish
immigrants came into industrial Scotland with their own culture,
values, sexual attitudes, traditions of struggle and historical baggage,
but, within Scotland, the Irish immigrant women were subjected to the
same rules of patriarchal capitalism as were the Scottish women and
some of the Roman Catholic priests often tried to be more repressive
than the Presbyterians. This is summed up by Joseph L Melling, who
argues: 'The position of women in the community was the concern not
only of moralists in Dundee, concerned with the amoral mill girls, but
also in Glasgow. The Turkey Red Dyeing Company of Alexandria,
imported hundreds of girls from the west of Ireland for their dye mills at
Alexandria, using a Donegal priest as supplier and building a Roman
Catholic Church for the immigrants. Strict morals were enforced with
regard to women, particularly when administrating the social services
such as the Poor Law'.[18]

The Irish, however, had come into a society in which there was a long
tradition of bitter hostility towards Roman Catholicism. A report in the
North British Daily Mail made it quite clear that the 'bourgeoisie' were
already exploiting existing ethnic divisions within the Scottish working
class. It read:

> The sexes employed in these dye works are nearly equal, but
> the great majority of both are young. The young women
> earn from seven to ten shillings a week. Their work is very
> much heavier than that of their sisters in the calico
> printworks, and the latter, who are mostly natives of the
> place, enjoy a much higher social position, than the former, a
> great proportion of whom are immigrants from Ireland.[19]

Within Scottish working-class communities the Irish immigrants were
segregated and kept apart from the indigenous working class. By the
1850s, the chastity of the women (but not the men) amongst the Irish
immigrants in Scotland was already known. In ascribing the chastity of
the Irish women to the role played by the Irish priests at home, T C
Smout says: 'In the post-famine situation, with late marriage for the
males and few holdings to go round, the teaching of the priests was

reinforced by a quite separate economic sanction. For immigrant industrial workers in Scotland the economic situation was obviously of another kind, but the cultural and moral habit formed in Ireland would not immediately collapse'.[20] While the historical baggage that the Irish — and indeed the Highlanders — brought into Lowland Scotland added a unique dimension to the making of the sexual and social attitudes of the Scottish working class, it did not vitiate the radicalism of the women workers in the mills and factories. Indeed, between 1871 and 1875 Scottish working-class women frequently initiated the 'labour unrest'. In a comprehensive account of women and trade unions in Britain as a whole, Sheila Lewenhak depicts only one solitary strike of women workers in England in those years. This was a strike of weavers who, in 1875, resisted a wage cut in the mills in the Dewsbury district.[21]

In the late nineteenth century, Scottish working women mounted a whole series of spontaneous strikes. In the Wallace factory, Perth, in 1871, the women workers struck for a ten per cent increase in their wages. They only called off their strike after they had forced their employers to offer them at least half of what they originally asked for.[22] A strike of powerloom weavers in Nithsdale, in 1873, provoked their employers to use the partisan machinery of the law against the six hundred workers who struck work for higher wages. Eleven of their leaders were charged in the Sheriff Court with breach of contract (the workers in this factory required to give eleven days' notice before they could leave their employment). Sheriff Hope told them that he would not 'exact penalties', if they persuaded the other women to go back to work. However, in spite of the appeals of the leaders the women had thrown up in the course of their struggle, only sixty of the three hundred were intimidated by the Sheriff's threats. Some months later, the women's demands were met.[23]

In Aberdeen, an unprecedented wave of 'labour unrest' was unleashed by the spontaneous strikes of women workers. This was described in a report from Aberdeen in the *North British Daily Mail*: 'The strike epidemic seems to have at last fairly reached "the northern city cold". Last week the females employed in the powerloom department of Broadford works struck work, and conducted themselves in an uproarious manner within the works. They, however, have now returned to work, an advance being conceded. A large number of females employed in the Banner mills struck on Friday for an advance of wages, evidently being incited to this step by the example of the females at Broadford'.[24] The women mill workers in Aberdeen were given almost immediately an increase of twenty per cent in their wages. It is, however, significant that they do not appear to have formed themselves into trade unions,[25] yet they were accurately blamed for initiating the 'labour unrest' in 1871. Elsewhere in Scotland, women workers frequently triggered off a wave of strikes for higher wages and better working conditions.

The widespread militancy of Scottish women was encouraged by the decision of hundreds of female domestic servants to form themselves into a trade union. The Dundee Female Servants' Union, however, did not complain about their wages. With support from the Trades Council, they campaigned against 'the system of surveillance', the heavy work they had to do and the 'unjust suspicions' of their employers. In a speech characterised by class-conscious resentment against the employers' treatment of female domestic servants, the secretary of the Dundee Trades Council told the domestic servants that 'some time must elapse before they could be strong enough to make a direct stand'.[26] It was the class-consciousness of the Dundee women which provoked an editorial rebuke in the pages of the *Dunfermline Journal*. The Scots were also more politically conscious than their English sisters. During a strike in 1873 of female weavers employed at the Lancefield works in the east end of Glasgow, for example, a rank-and-file striker told a mass meeting of women weavers: 'If it had been on the eve of an election, and if the female workers possessed votes, there would have been a very different story to tell'.[27] Strikes of Scottish women, moreover, were not regarded as being any more subversive than those of the male workers and so they did not receive as much attention as the strike of the women weavers in the Dewsbury district of England.

The cultural traditions of the Scottish past played a distinctive role in fashioning the militancy of women workers in the mills and factories. Yet, if tough, strong-minded women had always occupied a prominent place in Scottish society, the new capitalist mode of production also played a role in shaping the collective experience of women workers. In the coal-mining communities, male chauvinism had existed long before female labour in the mines was abolished under the 1842 Act. The women who were employed as coal-bearers alongside their husbands were also expected to do the housework when they returned home from the pits. With the abolition of female labour in the pits, the miners' womenfolk were increasingly subjected to various forms of subordination by their husbands, fathers and sons. The subservience of the womenfolk in mining communities in Stirlingshire developed very rapidly after the passing of the 1842 Act which eradicated women's labour except at the pit-heads. Writing in 1878, Robert Gillespie commented: 'And girls even now seem to be held somewhat at a discount by the mining community. When a daughter, for example, comes home to the family, she is practically spoken of as a "hutch of dross"; whereas when a little stranger appears in the sex of a son, he has the higher valuation of a "hutch of coals"'.[28]

After 1842, an ugly male chauvinism was intensified in both Scottish and English mining communities. However, in contrast to the miners' womenfolk in England, the Scots women were often more militant than their men. In 1868, for example, a meeting of colliers' wives in Kilmarnock, called by 'the bellman was held in the neighbourhood', and a resolution unanimously carried to the effect that 'the infamous' blacklegs should be assailed by the women when they came home from the pit. A similar situation developed in 1879 in the same area. Once again, the colliers' wives and daughters defeated the attempts of the employers and the blacklegs to weaken the men's trade union.[29]

However, the high value that many working men — the Scottish miners were an exception — placed on women's labour almost certainly reinforced the comparatively high status that Scottish women enjoyed within the wider society. In 1855, the Immigration Officer at Port Adelaide in Australia wrote to the Colonial Secretary in London: 'Anyone accustomed to visit the rural districts of Scotland or Ireland must know well that females there are employed in outdoor farm work in a way not customary in England'.[30] Also, when the women, who were evicted from the Highlands, came into industrial Scotland, they brought their historical baggage of militancy and aggressive self-assertion with them.

One consequence of the strikes of Scottish women workers was that many employers felt a need to defend their entrepreneurial behaviour in the face of working-class criticism. The Woollen Mill Company at Kinross, for example, issued a public statement saying that they had refused their female employees a wage increase because of their heavy investment in the construction of new mills for the purpose of providing more work for females in the district.[31] Far from such arguments having any influence in mitigating the spontaneous strikes of Scottish women, the Labour Movement gave increasing support to women who struck work to get a wide variety of grievances rectified.

In January 1875, a thousand women employed at the Baltic Jute works in Glasgow went on strike for higher wages. They were supported by the Trades Council.[32] A few weeks later, 'nearly a hundred girls employed at the Kinning Park weaving factory struck work because they are only allowed half an hour to meals instead of the full hour'.[33] By August 1875, organised labour in Scotland was fighting defensive battles against wage cuts and a major victory against the employers' determination to impose a second wage reduction on the Dundee mill girls was won as a result of the intervention of the whole of the Labour Movement in Scotland. This strike was particularly significant because while the women and girls resisted a second wage cut they suffered conditions of terrible poverty. Supported by the Scottish Labour Movement as a whole, the remarkable sum of £5,000 was collected by trade union branches to provide the women with bread and soup. In a brief report in a local newspaper, the tough militancy of the women of Dundee was conveyed in a single sentence: 'A woman (Jenny Brown) addressed the meeting in favour of no surrender, and urged all to follow the action of their forefathers, by whose self-sacrifices great battles had been won, notwithstanding extreme privation'.[38]

If Scottish women were sometimes more prominent than male workers in fighting the rearguard action against wage cuts in 1875, there had been very few attempts made before then to organise women into trade unions. One of the first women's trade unions in Britain — the Edinburgh Upholsterers' Sewing Society — had been formed in 1872,[34] but militant women workers in Scotland did not generally form themselves into trade unions at all. The National Union of Working Women had been formed in 1874 under the leadership of Mrs Fawcett and Miss Coleman and by late 1875 it had recruited 2,000 members in England.[35] During the early 1870s, most of the strikes of Scottish women workers, such as the one at Nairn's linoleum factory, had been fought without any formal trade union structure at all.[36]

In 1875 the National Union of Women Workers decided to extend themselves into Scotland. The Edinburgh Trades Council agreed to offer them assistance to organise working women in the Edinburgh district, but they were not very successful.[37]

In the mid-Victorian years both the major Presbyterian Churches — the Established and the Free — competed with each other to confront and suppress the older, often half-pagan popular culture, inherited by proletarian women and men, with its hedonistic sexual attitudes, its fairs, its drink and its dancing. The objective sociological function of the Presbyterian clergymen was to act as a carrier of the new work discipline required by a still-evolving industrial capitalist society. The Presbyterians' onslaught on this older, popular culture was even more vicious and systematic than anything witnessed in England. What E P Thompson identifies as 'the extraordinary correspondence between the virtues which Methodism inculcated in the working class and the desiderata of middle-class utilitarianism' in England[39] did not have an exact replica in Scotland.

There were two main reasons for the difference in the Scottish and English situations. In the first place, if the Methodists waged war until

1832 on the older, popular culture of 'Merry England', they did not receive the unanimous support of the English intelligentsia. Secondly, the advent of capitalist industrialisation in Scotland was a very abrupt development which was still proceeding in the mid-Victorian years.[40]

The social and sexual peculiarities of the modern Scottish working class began to crystallise in the 1850s and 1860s. A distinctive national feature of the social attitudes of Scottish working men and women resided in their sexual reticence and prudery. The cultural roots of some of these attitudes can be traced back to the Reformation, when the Presbyterian clergymen punished men for swimming and women for working in taverns.[41] This latter tradition survived until the First World War.[42] Far from being swept away by the new capitalist mode of production, some of these post-Reformation attitudes towards women and sex played a major role in shaping the consciousness of the Scottish working class, but a major reason for the excessive repression of the Presbyterian clergymen in attempting to impose new social values and a new work discipline on pre-industrial working people was the survival and strength of the older sexual attitudes. There is, as A D Hope puts it, 'some evidence that formal occasions for a sexual free-for-all did exist from the earliest times and survived in some cases to the present in Scotland'.[43]

The bawdy culture of pre-Reformation Scotland probably did not survive in all the new industrial communities in the Lowlands, but the activity of the Presbyterian clergymen in Glasgow in denouncing the pedlars who sold bawdy ballads tells the story of their survival in some industrial areas. This was the time when Kailyard images of Scottish women as un-persons were fostered by such antiquarian 'historians' as De Bruce Trotter. In looking back at the 1830s, Trotter contributes to Kailyard images of Scottish working-class women by creating stereotypes of passive, asexual, comic-like women. This was happening at a time when wife-beating was increasing as a result of the decline of such pre-industrial sanctions against wife-beaters as the riding-of-the-stang. By forcing the culprit to ride on a pole and be beaten by women and men, the wife-beater was punished by the whole community. In Trotter's account, working-class women in Galloway were not beaten by their husbands, except for the few who were married to Englishmen.[44]

In the 1830s, the distinctive Scottish and English patterns of — and class differences in — touching or tactility began to be visible. By the 1850s and 1860s, Scottish working women — and men — were already very reluctant to display affection for each other in public. Being affectionate or demonstrative in public was, in Scottish working-class consciousness, to engage in the pretentious, insincere affections of the

English.[45] In a paper presented to a Workers' Educational Association conference in Edinburgh in 1978 on cultural oppression in Scotland, Janet Hassen said that modern Scotland was for her 'the bleak, authoritarian and sexually repressive society depicted in Henry Grey Graham's study of Scottish social life in the eighteenth century'.[46] This well-established, liberal-left tendency in present-day Scottish social criticism is so blind to the 'dialectic' in our history that it ignores the centuries' old resistance to the sexual *mores* that Presbyterian clergymen began to impose on the commonalty from the sixteenth century onwards. There is also some evidence that should persuade historians to question the extent to which Presbyterian clergymen were successful in imposing the sexual *mores* demanded by capitalism. For 'if the Reformation made little difference to the sexual morals of the ordinary population',[47] T C Smout's comment on sexual behaviour in nineteenth-century Scotland is very relevant: 'Thus in the town the sexual *mores* of working-class groups were probably very various, and it would be impossible to talk of one code of proletarian morality for the urban population as a whole'.[48]

However, the sexual *mores* propagated by the Presbyterian clergymen in eighteenth-century Scotland had to confront the older popular culture of the commonalty, as Henry Grey Graham puts it in an implicit acknowledgement of the struggle between the older sexual attitudes and the newer sexual values represented by patriarchal capitalism:

> All the great domestic events were accompanied by roystering and drinking — at a christening there was much, at a funeral there was more, at a wedding there was most . . . However the Kirk might threaten and punish the people danced defiantly; for to dance "promisky" (i.e. men and women together) as they called it, was their great delight and lairds and farmers sent money and food and drink to supply the festival. That these scenes were often wild and indecorous was certainly the case.[49]

Although in mid-Victorian Scotland the lairds and farmers were no longer supplying either the drink or the food at the great hiring fairs, the wild and unlicensed scenes were said to be an important source of the notoriously high Scottish levels of illegitimacy in some of the rural areas.[50]

To recognise the persistence of the older sexual morals that had existed since before the Reformation is to depict another cultural dimension of the Scots' resistance to the newer values of a patriarchal capitalism. In the middle decades of nineteenth-century Scotland, 'free' love without contraception meant many illegitimate births, and it was the women who were the chief sufferers. Also, there were no longer Utopian socialists to offer a critique of the dominant sexual attitudes, but at least some of the 'lower orders' opted for sexual pleasure in conditions of general sexual repressiveness. Though 'regular institutionalised mass outbursts of free sex' were historically compatible with 'keeping the poor in their place', there have never been 'great social revolutions' without 'cultural dissidence'.[51]

Illegitimacy was a much greater problem in Scotland than in England, as Alfred Leffingwell put it: 'The subject of illegitimacy in Scotland deserves a special study, occurring as it does in a country distinguished above every other in Europe by its zeal for orthodox belief'. In analysing the complex causes of the high levels of illegitimacy in Scotland, T C Smout ignores the question of rape. Although it is now impossible to quantify the importance of rape in contributing to illegitimacy statistics, contemporaries acknowledged that agricultural and factory women were frequently raped. Presbyterian trade unionists in fact wanted 'moral policemen' to supervise the feeing markets where 'a large proportion of illegitimacy (was) the fruit of rape rather than of seduction, and girls were assailed and overcome by force, aided beforehand by being offered intoxicating drink'.[54]

In a collection of essays on *Social Class in Scotland*, Allan MacLaren and T C Smout contribute important arguments about aspects of sexual behaviour in nineteenth-century Scotland. Smout's important essay documents the Presbyterian clergymen's analysis of the economic causes of prostitution in the mid-Victorian period. The clergy's semi-sociological analysis of the causes of prostitution in Scotland was developed in a series of books and essays. Meanwhile, when this development was occurring in Scotland, the bourgeois élite in England was attempting to discourage any public discussion of the problem of prostitution.[52]

Child-murders had ceased to be a major social problem by the end of the eighteenth century. However, a few illegitimate children were occasionally murdered in mid-Victorian Scotland. In 1854, for example, the illegitimate daughter of a domestic servant in the Craigs, Stirling, was murdered within minutes of her birth. Indeed, 'no sooner had the child begun to cry than the grandmother said "she would soon stop its squalling"'. Then she 'burnt the child to death'.[53]

T C Smout's major shortcoming is that he sees social and sexual relations in the one-sided, non-dialectical way of the liberal historian. When he argues, for instance, that 'bastardy itself was not regarded as any kind of sin' and 'the crimes of abortion and infanticide (were) unknown in the countryside', he tells only one part of the story of

Scottish working-class women. The mothers of illegitimate children were often in fact punished by the Boards of Supervision through the simple expedient of depriving them of financial help.

In Smout's nineteenth-century world, where class antagonisms seemingly did not exist, the sexual assaults on domestic servants and factory women received no mention. Allan MacLaren fills the gap with the remark: 'The increasing class polarisation and associated residential segregation created problems for middle-class males customarily denied access to girls of their own class outside of marriage'. The consequence was that 'they turned to working-class girls as temporary partners (sic!), and the two occupations providing such contacts were those of domestic servant and prostitute', but neither he nor Smout hint at the ideological war that raged around the questions of illegitimacy and illicit sexual relations.

Although remnants of the older, pre-industrial plebeian culture survived in many working-class communities, in other communities the new sexual and social *mores* of patriarchal capitalism influenced the consciousness of the 'respectable' and upwardly mobile workers. In the new circumstances of the mid-Victorian period, Scottish working-class women were increasingly expected to do the housework and be generally subservient to men. When James D Burn, a former radical who had been active in the Glasgow Trades Council in the 1830s and 1840s, went to America in the 1860s, he was horrified to discover the comparative 'freedom' experienced by American working-class women. In articulating the patriarchal prejudices which were probably typical of the Scottish 'labour aristocracy', he said: 'In America, female notions of independence have to a great extent reversed the old order of things in the relation of the sexes to each other. Among the class of married people who keep house it is a common thing for the man to do a considerable part of the slip-slop work'.[55]

Nevertheless, the older social and sexual *mores* survived in agricultural and rural communities. Whether abortion existed in the countryside or not, Scottish male trade unionists were horrified by the idea of abortion. In contrasting the widespread abortion he found amongst American working-class women with its allegedly minimal existence in Britain, Burn warned his British countrymen to 'mete out to this class of offenders (i.e. so-called "physicians") such punishments as will reform this growing evil'.[56]

In so far as the authorities could do anything about them, abortion (or, in the language of the period, 'race suicide') and birth control were suppressed. In 1853, an Edinburgh bookseller was sent to jail for twelve months for selling *Every Woman's Book* — a book which contained 'most important instructions for the prudent regulation of Love and the

Number of a Family'.[57] By the early 1870s, however, Annie Besant and other English radicals, who were sympathetic to feminism, had formed the Malthusian League; in Scotland such an organisation simply did not exist. The Malthusian League took birth control information into many English working-class communities. In 1878 a Bristol bookseller republished Charles Knowlton's pamphlet on birth control, *The Fruits of Philosophy*, originally published in America in 1830. *The Fruits of Philosophy* recommended a chemical formula and other methods for preventing conception. Between 1878 and 1881, it sold 185,000 copies. After a sensational trial in a London court, Annie Besant and Charles Bradlaugh were admonished. In glancing back at this famous trial over two decades later, Margaret Elderton attributed the beginning of 'the fall in the English birth rate' to the propaganda of the Malthusian League.[58]

However, cultural dissidence existed alongside Scottish working-class conformity to the sexual morals of the Presbyterian clergymen. Indeed, contradictory attitudes to the values of patriarchal capitalism existed in the same heads of working-class women. Far from the Presbyterians not having any influence on women and men,[59] they sometimes had so much influence that miners, domestic servants, artisans, female weavers, etc, *volunteered* the information to the Kirk Sessions of their 'antenuptial fornication'. In the Kirkintilloch Free church in 1868 and 1869, a weaver, a miner and a farm labourer said that they were 'willing to submit to the discipline of the Church',[60] and in 1876 in Kirkcaldy, a miner and a domestic servant volunteered the information that they had committed 'the sin of antenuptial fornication'.[61]

When the Synod of the Free Church in Fife discussed the sexual behaviour of working women and men, they restricted themselves to examining what was happening in the mining and farming communities, as Kenneth M Boyd puts it: 'The sexual morals of other sections of the Fife population were hardly discussed by the Synod. It was highly reticent about the middle classes, vague about the urban population, and admitted to ignorance of the lives of the sailors'.[62] This was true of the Churches elsewhere in Scotland, too. In Fife, the Free Church clergymen also disapproved of the miners' enjoyment of a weekly dance on the evening of pay-day',[63] and they depicted the miners' drunkenness as yet another cause of illegitimacy. The miners in places as far apart as Langholm, Grangemouth and Hawick were described by the clergymen in the Free Church as 'low, coarse and sensual'.[64]

It was the farm labourers and their womenfolk who were, however, the chief target of the moralistic Presbyterian clergymen. As well as disapproving of dancing, drinking, the ballads and the *expensiveness* of illegitimacy to the privileged elements in Scottish society, the clergy and the elders were horrified by the 'discovery' of the problem of illegitimacy in the farming communities. David Kerr Cameron describes it in his fine book, *The Ballad and the Plough*: 'It was only when the first official statistics about such things began to be published in Scotland in the mid-1880s that the true extent of the problem became known. Then, indeed, were genteel eyebrows raised, for the figure for the ballad counties in particular, from the Mearns north to the land of Moray, was about twice the national average. It was a staggering blow to the forces of morality and to the men of the Free Kirk, so closely associated with the farmtouns, in particular. Their wrath was terrible; Free Kirk ministers took to seeing abomination behind every haystack when all that was happening was the playful struggle of country lovers coming to the right and true end of love'.[65] Yet, in farming communities all over Scotland, the bawdy ballads and the sexual attitudes of an unruly and rumbustious proletariat, who had inherited a culture stretching back to before the Reformation, survived in the farm labourers' underground organisation known as The Horseman's Word.[66] It is, therefore, pertinent to quote what Cameron says about the counter-culture of the folk in the farming communities: 'It might be thought that the ballads though blatant enough about the midnight courtships of the farmtouns would be less outspoken about their inevitable result, but no, that was but further grist for the ballad-writer. Never though is it the slightest tinge of outrage that shines through, just the simple broad humour of folk who live close to nature and, for all the Kirk's preaching, find in bastardy little cause for surprise'.[67]

In the towns as well as in the countryside, the collective experience of working-class women was varied and contradictory. What happened to Scottish working-class women must be seen dialectically within the struggle between the values being imposed by patriarchal capitalism and the influence of a past in which women occupied a dominating position in Scottish society. The older cultural traditions manifested themselves in oblique, rudimentary and diverse ways. In some Scottish working-class communities, for example, many working people 'called themselves man and wife and returned their children to the registrar as legitimate, although they were not married'.[68] It is also possible that the geographical factor was important in so far as the greater equality and value of women's labour in some Highland districts endowed them with a much higher status than in the mining communities, where male chauvinism had gained an enormous grip on the consciousness of working-class males. But, independently of such speculation, there is evidence that in some working-class communities brutality against women was considered intolerable. Thus, in Keith, Banffshire, in 1876, employers who had ill-treated a servant girl provoked a serious 'riot' among working men and women.[69]

In Michael Hechter's imagery, Scottish women — the victims of a harsh and sometimes brutal existence within a peripheral economy — experienced 'a lower standard of living and a higher level of frustration' as 'measured by such indicators as alcoholism'.[70] Yet, within these very unfavourable circumstances, Scottish women's inheritance of some militant folk-memories and attitudes enabled them to engage in a struggle against their employers that had no parallel in England.

Armed with judicial power, the Kirk in Scotland had been attacking plebeian sexual behaviour for centuries after the Reformation. Though it had succeeded to a large extent in this task, it often met with the stubborn resistance of the older popular culture. But, far from urbanisation totally breaking down the traditional sexual discipline of the Kirk, the Presbyterian clergymen were frequently able to impose their sexual morals on both rural and urban communities through their continued ideological dominance of the institutions of Scottish civil society. From 1845, the Central Board of Supervision had been responsible for the administration of poor relief in Scotland, and the members of the Parochial Boards at village, town and city levels accepted and shared the Presbyterian clergymen's criticism of the financial burden of illegitimacy on the upper and middle classes. Certainly, the possessing classes and the members of the local Parochial Boards made it clear that they agreed with the Presbyterian clergymen that those who engaged in illicit sexual behaviour should be punished. The expensiveness of illegitimacy was the *material* reason for the Presbyterians' attack on the older sexual morals of those members of the commonalty who rejected the values of patriarchal capitalism. The *expensiveness* of illegitimacy was also a decisive factor in motivating the members of the Parochial Boards to assist the Presbyterian clergymen's desire to punish those responsible for bringing illegitimate children into the world, as Kenneth M Boyd put it: 'Not least startling was the expense of illegitimacy. Pauperism, already nearly twice as bad as in England, would certainly increase, "as every bastard is apt to be a beggar", and so, according to Begg's speech in elaboration of this report, would crime, which had already risen by 10% between 1857 and 1859'.[71] In 1878, Andrew Wallace, the Poor Law inspector in Govan, Glasgow, told the Glasgow Philosophical Society: 'Women with illegitimate children should not be taken upon the pauper roll if it can be avoided. As they have *transgressed the moral law*, it would be a pity to relieve them of the temporal consequences, and throw the burden upon others. . .'. He also insisted on the necessity of testing deserted wives since 'often too the wife is as much to blame as the husband for the desertion'.[72] The Parochial Boards frequently refused to support single women with children outside of the poorhouses. This ruthless inhumanity — and even downright murder — is described by Thomas Ferguson in his book, *Scottish Social Welfare*:

> In 1876, when pressure to refuse outdoor relief to those mothers of illegitimate children was at its height, an Aberdeen doctor annoyed the Board of Supervision by insisting that the refusal of outdoor relief in these cases often led to the death of the children.[73]

In the absence of a socialist *critique* of bourgeois sexual morality, the Scottish Labour Movement accepted the Presbyterians' criticisms of working-class sexual behaviour without protest or challenge. Since the Labour Movement in Scotland was largely confined to the ranks of Presbyterian artisans and skilled or semi-skilled workers (the miners' unions were not affiliated to the Trades Council), it is not surprising that they acquiesced in the bourgeois sexual morality of the Presbyterian Churches. The Scottish miners' newspaper, *The Glasgow Sentinel*, however, did not accept the Presbyterians' analysis of the causes of illegitimacy. In contrast to T C Smout, a historian who accepts uncritically the Presbyterian clergymen's analysis of the causes of illegitimacy, the editor of *The Glasgow Sentinel* made a number of important comments in three separate articles published between 1870 and 1872.

In the first place, the editor of *The Glasgow Sentinel* observed that illegitimate children in Scotland were 'almost entirely confined' to the labouring and working classes. Secondly, the mothers of such children 'consisted chiefly of those employed about farms or agricultural labour, of factory girls, of domestic servants, and those engaged in needlework and in shops'. Thirdly, he denied that the proportion of illegitimate children was any higher than it 'was a century ago'. With very little knowledge of urban, industrial working-class communities, the Presbyterian Churches had claimed that most illegitimacy was confined to the farm labourers and the miners.

The editor also denied the frequently told story that the high levels of illegitimacy amongst the farm labourers was just a consequence of the bothy system and 'nocturnal courtships'.[74] In a vivid description of *general* working-class courtship practices, the editor of *The Glasgow Sentinel* said: 'But, wherever the place, the meeting is by stealth, in the middle of the night, in darkness, lasts for two or three hours, and is repeated weekly. This is the uniform mode of "courting" amongst the working classes in Scotland. It is not confined to engaged lovers, but even acquaintances, who may or may not become lovers, go a-courting. A girl prides herself on the number of such lovers she may have, and young men do not think it wrong to visit different girls after this fashion. It must be remembered that no-one in the working class, not even the most particular of parents, thinks that anything is wrong in this manner of courtship'.[75] At the same time, however, as he ridiculed the Presbyterians' analysis of working women's sexual behaviour, he nevertheless reflected the general authoritarianism of Scottish society when he called for the insertion of a new clause into the Poor Law Amendment Act, making the desertion of illegitimate children a criminal offence, instead of focusing on the inhuman ways in which the Poor Law was used to punish the mothers of illegitimate children.[76]

The Presbyterian possessing classes exercised extraordinary power over Scottish society. From the perspective of the Presbyterian 'bourgeoisie', the social problems of illicit sexual behaviour, illegitimacy, poverty and wife-beating arose from the 'moral transgressions' of ordinary working women and men. The tensions and frustrations — and indeed the working-class culture — engendered by a brutal and exploitative capitalism were, from their standpoint, unworthy of attention, except when they might be expected to upset social stability or become financially *expensive*.

What characterised mid-Victorian society was not 'the untimely survival of Scottish theocracy'. To formulate the problem in this way is to assume that Calvinism had not changed since the sixteenth century. 'Scottish theocracy' was not a classless phenomenon, as Scottish nationalists like Stephen Maxwell infer. Rather it represented the coalescence of 'bourgeois' Presbyterianism with international capitalism within a specific national setting. In a reference to the outlook of the European middle class in *The Age of Capital*, Eric J Hobsbawm says: 'Moreover, economics apart, in the countries of the Old World the middle class believed that workers should be poor, not only because they had always been, but also because economic inferiority was a proper index of class inferiority'.[77] The men who ruled mid-Victorian Scotland therefore were not men who *necessarily* believed in their 'divine authority'. Rather, they were men whose untrammelled political power within civil society was informed by an almost ancient and superbly confident Calvinist world-outlook.[78]

Nevertheless, 'bourgeois' Presbyterians exercised a pernicious ideological influence over social life. In contrast to what was happening in England, social life in Scotland was overshadowed by the monolithic

Calvinist world-outlook, which was hostile to the agitation for women's rights in any shape or form. 'In 1850,' as Kenneth M Boyd argues, 'few would have denied that the Presbyterian Church still exercised considerable social influence in Scotland.'[79] The Presbyterians' temporal power was vividly symbolised in the person of Robert Wallace who began his career as the minister of Greyfriars Church, Edinburgh, and became, in turn, editor of *The Scotsman* and a Liberal member of Parliament. Unsympathetic to trade unions, strikes and militancy in the factories and mills, Wallace articulated the patriarchal attitudes of the Presbyterian Churches. If in 1876 he only somewhat grudgingly acknowledged the problem of wife-beating in Scottish working-class communities, he wrote about the problem in a more serious tone two years later. While he did not believe that fines or imprisonment would eradicate 'the inexcusable behaviour' of working men, he believed 'some responsibility lay with working-class wives to humour rather than antagonise their drunken husbands'.[80]

The mid-Victorian élite in Scotland did not know very much about the lives of the Jenny Browns or the other female militants. We now know a great deal about the lives of the Scottish miners and the agricultural labourers. But until we know more fully something of the world of the urban workers both women and men we will not properly understand the history of the women who worked in the mills, workshops and factories. Unfortunately, there are not any Scottish equivalents of such important English studies as Thomas Wright, *Some Habits and Customs of the Working Classes* (London, 1868), A Daughter of the People, *The Working Classes* (London, 1869), and A Working Man, *Working Men and Women* (London, 1879). Yet, some insight into the lives of Scottish working-class women can be gleaned from the fragmentary observations on urban community life in James D Burn, *The Autobiography of a Beggar Boy* (London, 1855) and Tom Bell, *Pioneering Days* (London, 1940). The evidence cited by Burn and Bell, together with the considerable support given to women strikers within working-class communities, is sufficient for us to infer that a distinctive working-class culture had already crystallised. Without such a supportive working-class culture, the numerous strikes of Scottish working-class women would not have occurred so frequently. To sum up this point, it is pertinent to quote the comments from the American Marxist historian, Herbert G Gutman: 'Working-class cultures — even those which reject acquisitive individualism — do not necessarily directly challenge inequality and the structures and belief systems that sustain it, but the existence of these cultures themselves is a form of resistance. Under changing historical circumstances they become the source of oppositional social and political movements'.[81]

The Scots did have their own working-class culture, and they were not — contrary to what Kenneth M Boyd argues — 'rootless'. Nor is it true that 'the brutal and brutalising' conditions in industry depersonalised most working men and deprived 'them of any sense of significance'. If that had happened, then wife-beating would undoubtedly have been a much greater problem than it was. In a perceptive comment in *Mrs Grundy in Scotland*, Willa Muir argues that Scottish working-class women 'developed a strength of character and a vitality on which their contentious and cocksure men depended utterly'.[82] Since the Scots did not produce such a strong critical sociological or imaginative literature as the English, I will sketch in the significant differences between wife-beating in Scotland and England.

Instead of using the sort of descriptions of wife-beating in English working-class communities contained in Mary Merryweather's, *Experiences of Factory Life* (London, 1862) or in George Eliot's *Scenes from Clerical Life* (London, 1858), the historian of Scottish working-class life has to depend to a large extent on newspaper reports. In the essay on *Outrages on Women*, the author had no Scottish sources of information except Margaret M Brewster's slender didactic documentary novelette, *Sunbeams in the Cottage or What Women May Do*.[83] Furthermore, most of the 'debates' on wife-beating in Scotland were forced upon the 'bourgeoisie' as a result of the ongoing discussions in England and in the House of Commons.

The first signs of serious wife-beating in Scotland occurred in the early 1850s. In Leith, a seaman, who was in the habit of beating his wife, finally murdered her. This incident was 'witnessed, if not without sympathy, certainly without interference on the part of the neighbours'.[84] The problem was already much more serious in England. In 1872, in the English town of Charterhouse, a miner murdered his wife in the presence of neighbours who ignored her cries for protection. A special feature of this case 'was the cowardice and apathy displayed by the neighbours, some of whom stood looking out of their windows watching Lease murder his wife'.[85]

What Hamish Henderson describes as 'the hidden matriarchal women's world', together with the more liberal divorce laws, probably played some role in determining the different pattern of wife-beating in Scotland. But, Presbyterianism, though constantly undergoing temporal transmutations in response to changing economic and political conditions, also played an oblique and unwitting part in raising the status of working-class women by comparison with what had happened (and was still happening) in England. Just as Calvinism had already eradicated wife-sales by the mid seventeenth century,[86] so did the Presbyterian legacy contribute to the climate of opinion in which

Scottish working-class women were able to come out on strike without provoking either amusement or ridicule. For, if the Scots' strikes in mills, workshops and factories were made possible by the overall working-class culture, it was this same culture which mitigated the problem of wife-beating. In the 'dialectic' of social life, Presbyterianism played a dual, contradictory role.

Conversely, the almost unbridled, patriarchal working-class culture which smothered English women's strikes found another outlet in wife-beating. The problem became a major one in mid-Victorian England. In *Romany Rye*, George Borrow attributes the brutality inflicted on English working-class wives to the new legislation against pugilism.[87] In London, wife-beating was restricted to a 'severe thrashing with the fist'. In the north of England, it took the form of 'kickings, tramplings and "purring" with hob-nailed boots'. In an essay explaining the social causes of *Wife Torture in England*, Frances Power Cobbe, the great English feminist, said: 'They are lives out of which almost every softening and ennobling element has been withdrawn and into which enter brutalising influences almost unknown elsewhere'.[88]

In 1853, a special Act of Parliament was put on the statute book to punish those Englishmen who beat their wives, but, though the punishment envisaged was very mild, this particular Act was soon repealed.[89] Many English lawyers supported the working men's right to beat their wives, provided that the stick they used was 'no thicker than a man's thumb'.[90] In an authoritative book on English law published in 1862, Serjeant Woolrych approved of 'the parent who chastises his child with moderation, the gaoler who coerces his prisoner or even as some say the husband the wife'.[91]

In England the Woman's Movement persistently campaigned against wife-beating. Out of the immense literature that they developed around the ill-treatment of working-class women, perhaps the most perceptive remarks were made by Frances Power Cobbe:

> Every brutal-minded man, and many a man in other relations of life who is not brutal, entertains more or less vaguely the notion that his wife is his thing, and is ready to ask with indignation (as we read again and again in police reports) of any one who interferes with his treatment of her, "May I not do what I like with my own?" It is even sometimes pleaded on behalf of poor men, that they possess nothing else but their wives, and that, consequently, it seems doubly hard to meddle with the exercise of their power in that narrow sphere.[92]

By focusing most of their agitation on the problem of wife-beating in English working-class communities, the Women's Movement was able to gain major legislative 'amelioration' in the form of the Matrimonial Causes Act of 1878. This Act was the brainchild of Frances Power Cobbe. However, Cobbe's ruling-class friends smuggled this legislation through an almost empty House of Commons without any discussion.[93] The lack of any discussion of the cases of wife-beating allowed the Scottish possessing classes to ignore what was happening in England.

As a result of Frances Power Cobbe's efforts in persuading sympathetic members of Parliament to make divorce possible in the civil courts, the concept of the 'aggravated assault' was introduced, as Cobbe explains: 'An "aggravated assault" means a great deal more than a simple blow. It means knocking out an eye, "clogging" with hobnailed boots (i.e. kicking or standing on a woman, setting her hair on fire, breaking her ribs, throwing a paraffin lamp at her), etc.'. In the same year, Annie Besant reported on a wife-beating case in a police court in London: 'A man who dragged his wife out of bed, and, pulling off her nightdress, roasted her before the fire, was punished (?) by being bound over to keep the peace for a short period'.[94]

The English feminists regarded the Matrimonial Causes Act as one of their most important achievements in the mid-Victorian period, as Beatrice Wallace Chapman put it: 'By this Act if a husband is convicted of assaulting his wife, a magistrate may make a separation order, and may command the husband to pay a weekly sum for his wife's maintenance'. In discussing her own considerable achievement in getting this Act on the statute book, Frances Power Cobbe says: 'I hope that at least a hundred poor souls each year thus obtain release from their tormentors, and probably the deterrent effect of witnessing such manumission of ill-treated slaves may have still more largely served to protect women from the violence of brutal husbands'.[95]

Long before the English legislation of 1878, the Scottish courts gave the victims of brutal husbands 'legal separations with aliment'. Moreover, 'wife-beaters, when proven guilty, received a sentence of imprisonment without the option of a fine'. In the evidence presented on the Law in Relation to Brutal Assaults, the Scottish law officers repeatedly asserted that 'assaults of brutal violence on women are of rare occurrence'. It was accepted, therefore, that Scotland did not need special legislation for dealing with wife-beaters. Neither did the Scots produce such a legal category as the 'aggravated assault'. Given the different Scottish and English legal definitions of assault and wife-beating, it is not possible to compare Scottish and English statistics on wife-beating and violence against women.

In the 1870s, while arguing that wife-beating was much worse in England than in Scotland, the editor of the *Dunfermline Journal* wanted to solve the problem by using the lash on wife-beaters.[96] So did the Scottish law officers.[97] In developing a different analysis, the Edinburgh Trades Council sent the following Memorial to the Lord Advocate of Scotland:

> That your memorialists representing the working classes of this city, desire through you, to memorialise Her Majesty's Government, on the subject of the application of the lash as a mode of punishing wife-beaters.
>
> That your memorialists are of the opinion that were such a mode of punishing wife-beaters introduced it would not in any measure tend to render the crime less frequent: the authorities would seldom be called upon to exercise it, as in the majority of cases the unfortunate wife would rather choose to suffer in silence than advance evidence which would lead to the lashing of her husband.
>
> That your memorialists believe that the practice of lashing wife-beaters, would increse the number of cases of wife desertion; if a man is lashed for beating his wife, and this on evidence given by his wife, domestic harmony is all but impossible ever afterward between them.
>
> That the effect of lashing the wife-beater would not be to produce any beneficial influence on the delinquent. It would only further brutalise him. He is thereby reduced to the same treatment as is inflicted on the brute creation, and would seldom, if ever, recover his manhhood.
>
> That your memorialists are strongly of the opinion that to lash wife-beaters would only be to adopt a barbarous practice, whereby the cause of humanity would not in any wise be benefited.[98]

It is, however, interesting to learn from the *Minutes of the Edinburgh Trades Council* that a minority of the delegates moved an amendment for 'the insertion of a few lines advocating the restriction of the intoxicating liquor traffic as being a cause of wife-beating'.[99]

Socialist ideas were almost extinct in mid-Victorian Britain, and the Labour Movement's critique of bourgeois society did not challenge the system of inequality and patriarchal oppression. There were, however, important differences in the response of the Scots and the English to the decrees of capitalist society. What shaped the whole development of the Labour Movement in Scotland from the late eighteenth century onwards was the fate of the Scottish Enlightenment.

Scottish women participated in the literary and philosophical clubs in the major cities before the French Revolution, [100] but, from 1789 onwards, the women of the propertied classes would not again play any significant role in Scottish politics. It was quite otherwise with the women of the 'lower orders' who maintained their almost 'matriarchal' culture.

In mid-Victorian Scotland, the middle-class Women's Movement was very weak. Certainly, a branch of the National Society for Women's Suffrage existed in Edinburgh from 1867. It was, however, dominated by Agnes McLaren, the daughter of the right-wing Liberal Member of Parliament for Edinburgh. Lacking even the support of middle-class women, in 1870 Agnes McLaren turned to the Edinburgh Trades Council for general working-class support.[101]

In contrast to the Labour Movement in England, the Scots were sympathetic to the agitation for votes for women. Since these differences cannot be explained without recalling the influence of the cultural sediments of the Scottish past, we should note the different attitudes of English working men towards this particular agitation. The hostility of English working men towards the agitation for the enfranchisement of women was described in 1867 by Charles Anthony: 'The subject of the enfranchisement of women (in England) usually excites laughter and ridicule'.[102] Then, in 1868, a few progressive intellectuals in the English women's movement invited 'all the delegates to the Trades Union Congress — few in number — to a tea, and they put before them after tea the arguments in favour of women's suffrage'. They had to confront the open hostility of most of the delegates. A miner from Wigan ended the discussion, when he said: 'I agree that the arguments for women are the same as the arguments for men. The only difference is that in the case of working men these arguments apply, and in the case of women they do not apply'.[103]

By contrast, the Trades Councils in Scotland were sympathetic to the agitation for women's suffrage, but the gulf between the Labour Movement and capitalist society was much greater in Scotland than in England. Also, the Scots were always suspicious of the representatives of official society even when the radical working-class critique of existing institutions and civil society was not very searching or challenging. When the Edinburgh branch of the London-based Society for Women's Suffrage appealed to the Trades Council for support, the majority of the delegates 'expressed their opinion as opposed to the Society on the ground that it would create great facilities for faggot voting and would almost disenfranchise the working classes by putting it within the power of the monied class of obtaining votes for the female members of their families'.[104]

It was also paradoxical that the widespread militancy of Scottish working-class women did not culminate in the organisation of women's trade unions. The two or three Scottish branches of Emma Paterson's London-based Women's Protective and Provident League were incredibly transitory, and they made absolutely no impact on the Labour Movement in Scotland. The actual weakness of the Women's Protective and Provident League in Scotland was not particularly important in the mid-Victorian years, however, for Emma Paterson was an advocate of extreme right-wing Liberalism within the English Labour Movement.[105] She was opposed to legislation to protect factory women,[106] and she told the delegates to the British Trades Union Congress in 1877 that 'it was a degrading thing for a woman to be hunted by a factory inspector'.[107]

Scottish working-class women, therefore, experienced a higher status than did their English counterparts and this important cultural factor quite obviously influenced their militancy in the mills, workshops and factories. In contrast to the situation in England, where formal labour organisation existed alongside the comparatively visible quiescence of women workers, the Labour Movement in Scotland was fragile, narrowly based and unstable. But, in the new conditions of the late nineteenth and early twentieth centuries, the slenderness of formal labour organisation would actually assist the Scottish women who struggled to create a better world.

4

Scottish and English Women and Protest, 1880-1914

> At the risk of puzzling those earnest souls who imagine that
> ideas (or "ideologies") grow out of the "social structure" in
> accordance with textbook rules that can be learnt by heart,
> it has to be stated that history operates quite otherwise.
> What happens to people in a given milieu is in part at least
> determined by cultural sediments left behind by earlier
> experiences (or their absence).
>
> *George Lichtheim*

THE STRUGGLE FOR women's liberation gathered momentum
during the years between 1880 and 1914, but, although British women's
agitations were beginning to be increasingly successful, there were still
very significant and visible differences in the experience of Scottish and
English women.

Within the international Women's Movement, England was
regarded as being a more patriarchal country than Scotland. In
discussing the divorce laws in Britain, for example, Eugene Hecker, the
American advocate of women's rights, asserts that 'Scotland in this as in
other respects has been *more liberal* than England'. In making a similar point,
Ethel Snowden, the English socialist feminist, says: 'In many respects
British women are more fortunate than German women; but within
these islands there are differences, Irish and Scottish women being, in
some matters, in a *much better position* than English women'.

In the light of Scotland's present-day reputation for being a much
more male chauvinist country than England, it is very interesting to
note that the opposite was true before the First World War.[1] Indeed,
while focusing on the higher status of Scottish women, feminists in the
international women's movement always emphasised the contrast
between the extreme positions of the most oppressed and the most
'emancipated' women within the advanced industrial nations — the
English and the Americans. In Ethel Snowden's view 'The American
woman has long held the title of queen amongst women'.

Although the common law of England, with 'its relatively low position for women, was carried over to the new world', Ethel Snowden attributed 'the privileges' of modern women in the United States, Australia and New Zealand to 'the atmosphere created by the colonial scarcity of women'. In discussing the tangible differences in the collective experience of Scottish, English and American women, feminists such as Ethel Snowden, Eugene Hecker and W E Carson always concentrated on the divorce laws, wife-beating and political rights. In England, wife-beating was, in Snowden's phrase, 'a crime which generally meets with very lenient treatment'.[2]

In contrast to American and Scottish police magistrates, the English ones actually defended men's right to beat their wives. Indeed, one English police magistrate said that working men should not be deprived of this particular right, since they had few other rights. In commenting on a case in London in 1914 in which a police magistrate advised a working man that he had the right to beat his wife with a stick, W E Carson said: 'If such advice as this had been given in open court by an American police magistrate it is easy to imagine what an outburst of indignation it would have excited from one end of the country to the other'.[3] In a comment typifying the attitudes of many police magistrates in England, Alfred Plowden said: 'It is wonderful how many black eyes they will put up with, before they make up their minds to complain; and when at last they are driven to seek the protection of the law, there is, generally speaking, much more than a spark of pity left for their husbands. They extenuate all that they can'.[4]

In the sphere of political rights, Scottish middle-class women were better off than their English counterparts. Commenting on this important difference, Ethel Snowden said: 'By the qualifications of the Women's Act of 1907, the right to stand for all those public bodies for which they may vote was extended to Scottish women. Previous of this Act they could only sit on the Parish Councils and School Boards. Marriage is no disqualification for the woman candidate in Scotland'. Such political developments were the outcome of the struggles and protests of such Scottish feminists as Flora and Louisa Stevenson.

Between 1880 and 1914 the Stevenson sisters and other Scottish feminists also successfully struggled for greater educational opportunities for women. Under the Act of 1889, the Scottish universities were empowered to 'admit women to graduation in one or more Faculties and to provide for their instruction'. Although women were not admitted into Edinburgh and Glasgow until 1894, Louisa Stevenson's role in winning this struggle against patriarchal prejudice was subsequently described by an anonymous chronicler: 'She was one of the band of pioneers who finally accomplished the opening of the

Scottish universities to women in 1894, after years of struggle to promote University teaching for them outside its walls, and the classes, held first at 117 George Street, and later at 15 Shandwick Place, will always be associated with her, by all who attended them'.

Similar struggles were waged in England. However, the universities of Oxford and Cambridge were much less progressive in relation to the claims of women, as S J Curtis and M E Boultwood explained: 'Women were admitted to full membership of the university at Oxford in 1920, but Cambridge was more conservative and did not admit them until the Michaelmas term, 1948'.[5]

However, at all levels of social class, women's oppression was just as real and tangible in Scottish as in English communities, but, although the difference in the collective experience of Scottish and English women was only one of degree, it was reflected in the distinctive social behaviour of Scottish and English working-class men towards their womenfolk. In a perceptive comment on English working men, Peter Sterns, the American historian, says: 'The working man's world was a man's world. The image of virility crops up constantly, to the point that one wonders if some were not protesting too much. A group of strikers agrees not to return to work until blackleg labourers are fired, "for this could be contrary to our manhood"'.

Although Peter Sterns' important essay is entitled *Working-Class Women in Britain, 1890-1914* and although he does seem to understand the historical and cultural differences between Scotland and England, most of his evidence is drawn from the experience of the English working class. If we substitute the words 'England' and 'the English' for 'Britain' and 'the British', it will become clear that he has captured the essence of the history of the English working class when he says:

> Continental trade unions admitted women much faster than those in Britain, as many British organisers noted. Though strikes against women workers were not unknown (particularly among French printers), they were far less common than in Britain. British workingmen did not think that women should work. As more and more did so, if only before marriage, men's attitudes stiffened.[6]

Although in 1888 and in 1909 the Scottish Tailors' and Clay Pipe trade unions organised two solitary strikes to oust female workers, they were unsuccessful.[7] The stronger patriarchal attitudes identified in Stern's essay on the English working class can be seen in the statistical evidence. In contrast to what happened in England between 1881 and 1911, the female percentage of the total labour force in agriculture and coal mining in Scotland actually increased.[8]

In *Women, Church and State*, Matilda Gage, the American feminist, describes the social behaviour of *English* trade unionists in the 1880s: 'Among the male painters of pottery a combination was formed to prevent the use by women of the arm-rests required in the work. Tramway trains carry London workmen at reduced rates, but a combination was entered into by male labourers to prevent women workers from using the low-priced trains'.[9] Though Scottish trade unionists (like their Continental counterparts) often expressed patriarchal prejudices, they never went to such extremes as the English trade unionists.

In contrast to the significant increase in the percentage of women workers employed in Scottish agriculture up until the outbreak of the First World War, English women were increasingly pushed out of employment in agriculture. In discussing the acceleration of this trend in the late nineteenth century, O Jocelyn Dunlop says:

> In 1881 the number of women engaged in agriculture had been 40,346; by 1891 it had fallen to 24,150. This reduction is explained partly by the Gangs and Education Acts which by rendering children unavailable for the gangs, led to their decline. Where the gang disappeared women's employment tended to disappear . . . Further, the whole influence of the unions had been directed against women's labour, and even where as in Norfolk, their employment was still common, there was said to be an increased objection to it on the part of fathers and husbands.[10]

Although the Scottish Farm Servants' trade union was very weak before the First World War, they did not campaign for the removal of women workers. Neither did the Scottish miners campaign for the removal of women workers from the pit-heads. In 1885, the English miners began to campaign for the removal of the infinitesimal number of women workers. Barbara Drake describes it: 'The action of the Miners' Federation in promoting the Coal Mines Regulation (Amendment) Act of 1885, with a view of removing 4,450 women employed at the pit-heads, and again the strike of the Kidderminster carpet weavers, who paraded the streets, wheeling infants in perambulators, displaying placards of men cooking and turning mangles, and trying by means of ridicule to persuade the women from employment, brought forth similar protests from the Women's Protective and Provident League, whose action gained in each case the powerful support of the employers'. As a result of this famous — or infamous — controversy over the employment of women at the pit-heads in England, some of 'the pit-brow lassies marched proudly to Westminster to demonstrate their physical ability'.[11]

Despite the male chauvinism of the British trade unions, working-class women began to make real advances. Although between 1906 and 1910 the female membership of all British trade unions had only risen from 166,000 to 183,000, women's membership doubled between 1910 and the outbreak of the First World War. Indeed, in an editorial in the *Women's Trade Union Review* (the Women's Protective and Provident League had already changed its name to the Women's Trade Union League) in July 1912, it was asserted that: 'The last few months have been months of exceptional importance in the history of trade unionism, and particularly of the struggling and pioneer trade unionism among the poorer classes of women workers'.[12]

Although separate Scottish statistics for women's membership of the Women's Trade Union League do not exist, there were many spontaneous strikes of working-class women throughout Britain. In 1910, *Forward*, the Scottish socialist newspaper, described one such strike of women workers:

> The spirit of revolt among women workers seems to have found its way to Larkhall (which by the way is the home of Robert Smillie).
>
> A strike affecting some 64 women has taken place at D. C. Millar and Co Ltd, Avonbank Bleach and Dye Works, Larkhall. The women were not members of any trade union. . . .
>
> After a mass meeting and stirring addresses by Miss Macarthur and George Dallas, the masters caved in and a satisfactory settlement was carried out.
>
> The Larkhall branch of the National Federation of Women Workers intend to approach the girls employed at the local silk factory with a view to them joining the union.[13]

In Britain as a whole, however, some of the advances of working-class women were made as a consequence of working men's changing conceptions of women and the 'woman question'. Thus, the increase in women's membership of British trade unions was at least partly due to a change in the attitudes of male trade unionists, as Barbara Drake puts it: 'Men members were (after 1910) enjoined to persuade, or compel, their womenfolk to join the union; and some local associations went so far as to lay down that "no person shall be eligible for any official position, whose wife and children, if working, are not members of the union"'.[14] However, if social change was sometimes inspired by male officials, the trade union bureaucrats would not have championed the cause of women workers without pressure from the middle-class feminists. The agitation for equal pay, for example, developed out of the conflict in the Labour Movement between traditional patriarchal conceptions of women's role in society. This is explained by Sylvia Anthony, the

English feminist, in *Women's Place in Industry and Home*:

> During the 'eighties, the men's Metal Unions of the
> Midlands made great efforts to prevent the employment of
> women altogether, whose efforts met with determined
> opposition from the English women's representatives at the
> Trades Union Congress. As a compromise, a resolution was
> passed in 1888, to the effect that "where women do the same
> work as men, they should receive equal pay".[15]

In England, the years between 1910 and 1914 were marked by a
sustained revolt of working-class women. One feminist historian
described it: 'In August 1911 came a great uprising of underpaid
workers, and among them the women. The events of that month are still
fresh in our memories; perhaps their full significance will only be seen
when the history of these crowded years comes to be written'. In
Scotland women's militancy was sustained before and after these years
of 'labour unrest'.

This new self-activity of British working-class women was to play a
decisive role in the struggle for women's emancipation. Within the
patriarchal working-class culture of the time, however, it is difficult to
envisage the growth of these struggles without the initial stimulus and
impetus provided by the middle-class Women's Movement.

From the perspective of women's role in society, the general ethos of
Scottish society was quite liberal compared to many other industrialised
countries. This was seen in the total absence of the wife-sales which so
degraded social life in working-class communities in England and
Wales. It was also obvious in the different national attitudes towards
the question of divorce, as Cecil Chapman puts it in *Marriage and Divorce*:
'In England and Wales the ratio is 2:5, in Scotland it is 6 per thousand
marriages; and in Scotland the rule since the Reformation has been to
recognise sex equality in the matter of adultery, and to include
malicious desertion as a cause for divorce'.[16] Clearly, however, the
expensiveness of legal proceedings, together with working-class
cultural inhibitions, put divorce beyond the reach of working-class
women. While the Scots' comparatively liberal divorce laws did not
impinge directly on the lives of working-class women, they both
contributed to and reinforced the *comparatively* 'liberal' ethos in which
most Scottish women lived and worked.

Even within a patriarchal capitalist society, Scottish women,
whether middle or working-class, were tough, strong-minded and
relatively autonomous. The distinctiveness of the milieu in which

Scottish women lived and worked was well-known to a whole host of contemporary observers of the British scene. In 1905, in one of his rare acknowledgements of the different experiences of Scottish and English working-class women, Keir Hardie wrote: 'That there are various degrees of this feeling of subjection goes without saying, and I think it could be shown that the position of women, as of most other things, has always been better, nearer to an equality with man, in Celtic than in non-Celtic races. Thus in Scotland a woman speaks of her "man", whilst in Staffordshire he is always spoken of as "the master"'.[17] As a preliminary to understanding the distinctive national responses that were evoked by the Suffragette agitation and women's trade unionism in Scotland and England, we need again to relate these responses to their distinctive cultural traditions.

The distinctive experience of Scottish and English women has been discussed by historians, as Sheila Lewenhak explained in a paper she presented to a conference on British labour history in 1973: 'The interesting question is why it was that women did more in Scotland than in England. It may have something to do with the different religious and educational traditions'. However, while her fellow historians accept her identification of a major question in British labour history, Raphael Samuel challenges and refutes her answer to it by arguing: 'In Dundee there were many Irish whose militancy could not be attributed to any connection with John Knox. There was a big strike of women in 1894 and a strike of washerwomen in 1871'.[18] To answer the question of why the Scots were so militant, we need to reconstruct a picture of the total social context in which British women lived and worked.

In contrast to women in England, Scottish — and indeed American — women possessed an independent identity and a separate legal existence. In a description of the Women's Movement in Britain in the 1880s, Agnes Mure MacKenzie writes: 'The beginning of the movement came in England, for the position of women in that country, though high in the sixteenth century, had sunk badly, and now though a woman reigned there, was at its nadir'. Blackstone, in fact, the supreme authority on English law, had declared categorically that 'by marriage a woman's very being or legal existence is suspended'.[19] The national differences in relation to questions of property and status were significant. Throughout the period between 1880 and 1914, the Women's Movement in England persistently campaigned for a separate legal existence for women.[20] In an extended comment dealing with the different 'privileges' enjoyed by the women of the propertied classes in Scotland, in 1915 H F Normanton wrote: 'In that country (Scotland) a married woman is also not bound to maintain an indigent husband (Married Women's Property Act, Scotland 1881). An English woman is bound to keep an indigent husband'.[21] In Scotland, too, the custom of 'a married woman retaining her own name after marriage was the usual one',[22] thus symbolising the independent identity of Scottish women.

Before the outbreak of the First World War, the liberality of the Scottish divorce laws compared with those of many other countries was well-known in the international Women's Movement.[23] In every area of social life, the cultural force of the past and the effect of distinctive national laws on Scottish and English women played a major role in both motivating and inhibiting various agitations and protests. If the distinctive legal status of Scottish and English women reflected different national traditions and attitudes, the practical consequences of these differences in the development of the women's protest movements should not be overlooked.

Nationalist historiography sometimes obscures rather than illuminates the differences between the Women's Movement in Scotland and England, for example, in an essay on *Scottish Women in Politics*, Margaret Bain argues: 'Much of the literature of the period concentrates geographically on the South because the struggle was against the seat of power (in London) . . . But Scotswomen played a major role in the winning of votes; any idea that their right was won by hanging on to the petticoats of their English counterparts is unjustifiable and dishonest'.[24] This sort of comment conceals the paradox that the Women's Movement in Scotland, though it functioned in more favourable circumstances than existed in England, failed to muster as much support.

The major — and perhaps the only — aim of the Suffragettes in Scotland was to win the suffrage for the women of property. They did not take up any of the social problems and concerns with women's legal subjection which preoccupied their English sisters. Unlike the Labour Movement, the Women's Movement in Scotland was not an indigenous one. It was, in fact, an offshoot of the English one, without its own separate institutions. The paucity of Scottish literature on social questions facing women was not, however, a result of the Scots lack of national autonomy. It simply reflected the Scottish bourgeois élite's uncritical acceptance of the *status quo*. At the same time as the cultural traditions of the past gave Scottish women an independent identity, the Scots lacked a radical tradition of social criticism. The subtle interaction of this complex process within Scottish society was what shaped the peculiarities of the women's movement.

English feminist propagandists persistently pointed out that working-class women always referred to their husbands as their 'masters'. However, in a book entitled *The Vocation of Woman*, one feminist writer writing in 1913 denied that this provided any evidence of 'subjection'.[25] In any case, Scottish women did not refer to their husbands in the language of the 'master and servant' relationship. It was also generally accepted within the international women's movement that Scottish women did not suffer from the legal restrictions and impediments that were common in many other countries. The laws of Scotland in relation to women were comparatively more 'egalitarian'.

However, since it is now fashionable among some sections of the Left to deny the efficacy of legal attitudes in shaping social behaviour. Leon Trotsky's fairly orthodox Marxist comment on the relationship between the law and wife-beating in Russia in the 1920s is pertinent: 'Our marriage laws are permeated with the spirit of socialism — and physical violence still plays no small part in our family life'.[26] While he was aware of the impossibility of sustaining socialist relationships between men and women in conditions of severe economic scarcity, Trotsky did not abandon the important task of toughening the socialist laws against wife-beating.

In a whole host of books, for example, *Marriage* by Annie Besant (London, 1882), *Woman's Suffrage* by Mrs Ashton Dilke (London, 1885), *The Case for Women's Suffrage* by Brougham Villiers (London, 1909), *The Women's Charter of Rights and Liberties* by Lady McLaren (London, 1909), *The A.B.C. of Votes for Women* by Marion Holmes (London, 1910), *Woman's Suffrage* by Millicent G Fawcett (London, 1912), the English feminists sought to improve women's plight by campaigning for a reform of the divorce and property laws. The urgent need for such amelioration was transparent to most observers of English life. In contrast to the situation in Scotland, where most of the middle class accepted the *status quo* uncritically, the Suffragettes in England did not regard the campaign for 'votes for women' as an end in itself but as a means of improving the legal and social status of women as a whole.

The assumption that men actually owned their wives pervaded the whole of English society. The Women's Movement, therefore, was forced to develop a critique of the patriarchal attitudes that English women had to confront in their day to day lives. The right of a husband, for example, to 'restrain a wife's liberty may not be said to have become completely obsolete until the case of Reg. v. Jackson in 1891'.[27] The extreme patriarchal attitudes of the English (as distinct from the Scots) were well-known to Suffragettes in other countries. Thus, in *Women and Tradition*, A M B Meakin describes the attitudes of middle-class Englishmen towards the women of their own strata of society: 'In 1880 a well-known English clergyman preached a sermon on the subject of "Woman" at Philidelphia: "Wifehood" is the crowning glory of a woman. In it she is bound for all time. To her husband she owes the duty of unqualified obedience. . . . It is quite possible that this sermon, which continued to its close in the same strain, had often been preached to English congregations without evoking a single protest, for it contained nothing new or striking for the average English mind. But the word now fell on different soil. The women of America were pained, thunderstruck, and indignant. "Is this the sort of teaching that Englishwomen imbibe" they asked. "Why! According to the Rev. Knox Little, woman possesses no reponsibility; she is divorced of conscience, of intelligent thought, of self-respect: and is simply an appendage to man — a thing"'.[28]

The sense of ownership was very strong in English working-class communities. It was frequently asserted that working men's sense of owning their wives explained why wife-beating was 'still a flagrantly common offence in England'.[29] In *Grain or Chaff: The Autobiography of a Police Magistrate*, Alfred C Plowden describes working-class attitudes towards women in London: 'The sense of ownership still survives. With the wife it makes little or no difference. It is a privilege to be a wife at all. It satisfies the law of her being, to feel that she is under the care and protection of a man, and so long as she has this protection of a man she is willing to pay the price in undergoing a certain measure of physical suffering at his hands'.[30] Under English common law the husband had the right to inflict corporal punishment on his wife,[31] and in ascribing wife-beating to women's inferior legal status the Suffragettes frequently quoted the verbal responses of working men who were sometimes taken to court. In *The A.B.C. of Votes for Women*, Marion Holmes quotes one such case: "'Things have come to a pretty pass in this country", remarked one indignant husband recently, when ordered to pay a ten shilling fine for assaulting his young wife, "when a man can't thrash his own wife in his own kitchen"'.[32]

Such diverse figures as Ethel Snowden and H G Wells frequently criticised the assumption that English women were the property of their husbands.[33] In a reference in *Women, Marriage and Motherhood* to the plight of English women, Elizabeth S Chesser says: 'In England, as a woman is under guardianship, custody, and control of her husband, he has the right of regulating her mode of life, her domicile, and her domestic arrangements'.[34] Sometimes, English working men even described the black eyes that they gave their wives as 'love taps'.[35] While recognising the distinct differences in England and Scotland, Lady McLaren in *The Women's Charter of Rights and Liberties* attributes 'the numerous assaults on (English) wives and the brutality with which they are treated to the curious survival of the old legal theory that the wife was the chattel of her husband'.[36] The extremely low status of English women was also seen in the survival of wife-sales in the closing decades of the nineteenth century.[37] T Sharper Wilson describes the changes in the practice of wife-sales in England during the first decade of the twentieth century: 'In the modern transfers, the scene being the bar of a public-house, the halter is missing, and a few coins take its place'.[38]

In an essay dealing with the legal repression of English women written in 1913, Mrs J M Swanwick says: 'In England at the present day, a working man has almost absolute power over his wife'.[39] Because the English feminists wanted to mobilise the support of working-class as well as middle-class women, they repeatedly directed attention to the problem of wife-beating among the working classes. The problem of the 'aggravated assault' had already been raised by Frances Power Cobbe and other English feminists in the 1870s.[40] By the late nineteenth century any woman whose husband was convicted of assault could obtain 'a separation order with the custody of the children' and 'a weekly sum from her husband for maintenance'.[41]

The general impression within the international women's movement was simply that wife-beating was not a problem in Scotland.[42] A number of factors explain why diverse observers of the Scottish scene came to believe this. First, there was not an exact Scottish equivalent of the Matrimonial Causes Act of 1878 which covered England and Wales. Secondly, the Scots did not have a category of 'aggravated assault'. In England the 'aggravated assault' agitated enlightened police magistrates of all political persuasions, as well as the Women's Movement. While some police magistrates in England defended working men's right to beat their wives, there were a minority like Thomas Holmes who were appalled by wife-beating.[43] The latter played a small role in accelerating the social changes already at work before the First World War in raising the status of working-class women. Human agency is, after all, always a force in social change.

In Scotland, however, the Suffragettes did not even conceive of defining wife-beating as a social problem. This is a crucial point to bear in mind before we cast a critical glance at the statistical evidence relating to wife-beating. Clearly, criminal statistics cannot be taken as objective indicators of change (for example, wife-beating) without historians making known their awareness that social definitions and perceptions of 'crime' and disapproved activities change over time. Yet, they cannot be ignored. An examination of the statistics in the Parliamentary blue books on wife-beating in Scotland and England suggests that ordinary wife-beating was probably worse in the latter than in the former.[44] With the different Scottish and English legal definitions of wife-beating, statistical comparisons would not be illuminating.

English and American socialists as well as the international Women's Movement were particularly concerned with the problem of wife-beating in England. During the strike for the dockers' tanner in 1889, John Burns, then a leading member of the Social Democratic Federation, appealed to the dockers to stop beating their wives: 'I want to see some of your wives bear less evidence on their faces and bodies of your brutal ill-treatment. I want to see you men use this strike as a new era in your personal and domestic lives'.[45] By 1902, however, Jack London, the famous American socialist, offered a more economic based interpretation of wife-beating in working-class communities in London, when he wrote: 'The men are economically dependent on their masters, and the women are economically dependent on the men. The result is that the woman gets the beating that the man should give the *master*, and she can do nothing. There are the kiddies, and he is the breadwinner, and she dare not send him to jail and leave herself and her children to starve'.[46] However, the women depicted by Jack London were not always quite as helpless as he imagined. Social attitudes were already changing. Police magistrates had the authority to grant aliment for life. Women gradually began to understand the implications of the legal changes and this led to concrete improvements for the enlightened or militant minority. Nevertheless, a number of factors still worked against working women who sought freedom from violent husbands. Some police magistrates, for example, would not grant legal separations,[47] and notions of working-class 'respectability' often inhibited women from seeking separation orders, anyway. Furthermore, a legal separation could also make it difficult for English women to find employment, as one writer explained in 1911: 'They do suffer from public opinion when separated. "The disgrace" is dreaded, and we are told "it would go against you at the works" and be a hinderance in looking for employment'.[48] In Scotland, this particular fear dominated working-class consciousness.

By focusing on the problem of wife-beating in both Scotland and England, we come face to face with clear evidence of the cultural as well as the economic determinants of working-class culture. Before the First World War the Scottish legal profession including Sheriff Officers (the equivalent of the police magistrates in England) did not regard wife-beating as a serious problem. Yet it was a problem, though on a smaller scale than in England. The Scots' silence on the question can only be explained by reference to the Presbyterian 'respectability' that was woven into the social fabric of Scottish society as a whole.

The Suffragettes in Scotland did not raise the question of wife-beating because they did not want to criticise the existing social order. I have been researching in the archives of Scottish labour and socialist organisations for two decades now, and I have not found one example of wife-beating being discussed in working-class organisations between

1880 and 1914. Even John Maclean, a radical and perceptive Scottish socialist who campaigned against corporal punishment in the State schools,[49] did not say anything about wife-beating. The much greater depth or the more intense internalisation of the 'respectability' of the Scottish working class may have been partly responsible for their silence on the issue. Moreover, when we examine the difference in the pattern of legal separations in Scotland and England, we see yet again evidence of the distinctive cultures of the Scots and English. While the number of legal separations in England and Wales fluctuated between 7,007 in 1907, 4,539 in 1910 and 14,000 in 1912,[50] the Scottish statistics were 44 in 1900 and 7 in 1912.[51]

The relationship between wife-beating, legal separations and the capitalist mode of production were very complex. While the advent of capitalism played a positive role in the unionisation and protests of British working-class women, we should not ignore the cultural determinants of class-consciousness. It is, in fact, relevant to recall Antonio Gramsci's objections to all attempts to explain history only in terms of the 'economic factor'. In a penetrating study of *Gramsci's Politics*, Anne Showstack Sassoon shows that Gramsci explicitly rejected 'an economistic interpretation of historical development'. Far from assuming that historical conflicts are 'determined in any immediate sense by a development of the productive forces',[52] Gramsci urged historians to focus on the class struggle. So, if wife-beating and legal separations were much more common in England than Scotland, then such differences surely were shaped to some extent by the distinctive inheritance of the two countries.

Through their membership of such bodies as the School Boards and the Parish Councils, the Presbyterian clergymen were able to legitimise social inequalities and foster their repressive sexual morality. In the Highlands of Scotland, the customs and practices of 'primitive communism' were much closer in time and sharper in memory than in England.[53] There was also a constant influx of dispossessed Highlanders into the Lowlands. One result of this was a perennial conflict between the cultural values of the past and the Presbyterian clergy's attempt to sanctify private property and encourage a social morality suitable for a patriarchal capitalist society.

As Presbyterian morality and the cultural values of the past had an effect on the consciousness of Scottish women, an unending conflict raged around such questions as 'respectability', illegitimacy and sexual morality. If Presbyterianism could, as Hamish Henderson argues, 'both energise and hypnotise', there is concrete evidence of its psychological impact on working-class widows in Glasgow. William Mitchell sums it up in *Rescue the Children*: 'She (the working-class widow) will get washing or cleaning or sewing, but to turn pauper and be separated from her children, "No! No! rather let me die"'.[54] The much higher Scottish illegitimacy statistics that obsessed the civil and religious authorities were partly influenced by the 'irregular' and 'trial' marriages which had been so common in the Highlands,[55] yet, the Scottish socialists did not totally transcend the Presbyterians' narrow patriarchal mentality and critique of sexual behaviour. With the exception of some of the members of the Socialist League in Scotland, most socialists accepted bourgeois sexual morality in their day to day lives. The Scot did not, therefore, produce any Utopian socialist communities similar to the ones created in England by Edward Carpenter.[56]

The inherited cultural traditions of the past also influenced the distinctive attitudes of the Scots and the English towards sexual matters. Although sexual repression was general throughout Britain, the Scots did not begin to challenge the dominant sexual attitudes until after the First World War. It was otherwise in England.

An important index to the cultural class struggle in England was the changing of working-class women's attitudes to birth control propaganda. In objecting that the phrase 'birth control' is a tautology, A J P Taylor says: 'It only means that conception was restricted and does not explain how'.[57] Contraception was partly restricted as a result of the neo-Malthusians and the minority of socialists who rejected Marxist orthodoxy on the question of birth control. Ignorance of sex and basic physiology was very widespread. This particular form of ignorance is described by Margaret Bondfield in *A Life's Work*: 'Many street girls smoked and thought it would act as a preventive to conception. Sometimes girls were told that they must go out with as many men as possible to avoid conception'.[58] In a graphic account written in 1914 of how conception was sometimes restricted by a minority of women in English working-class communities, Ethel Elderton says: 'There is no doubt that restriction of the family has been publicly urged in Durham; men and women formerly stood like cheap-jacks on platforms in the market-place and openly sold appliances for preventing conception, and although through the influence of the clergy this has been stopped by the police, literature which advertises every sort of preventive, is still (in early 1914) exposed on a bookstall". In many other English working-class communities, Elderton described the work of socialists in circulating such literature in coal mines, workshops and factories.[59] There was no comparable development in Scotland. The Calvinist traditions of sexual repression still exercised an unquestioning influence over the minds of Scottish socialists.

Clearly, patriarchal attitudes were present in Scottish society before the advent of industrialisation. However, as the tentacles of the new capitalist mode of production spread throughout Scotland, the evidence of their impact on the behaviour of some working-class families became more visible. Male chauvinism was particularly evident in the Fife mining communities. Kellogg Durland was astounded by the widespread servitude of the Fife miners' wives, daughters and sisters within the home.[60] The servitude of the miners' womenfolk everywhere (except among the Finns in the American coal-mining communities)[61] might seem to suggest close and direct relationships between the capitalist mode of production and male chauvinism. History seldom operates so simply. In contrast to the miners in the English coal-mining communities,[62] the Scots militants seem to have been less prone to engage in brutal wife-beating.[63] Then, when we look at Scottish and English working-class families outside the mining communities, we soon realise that the relationships between the consciousness of working women and men and the capitalist mode of production were very complex.

In England the working-class mother was responsible for the running of the home. The role of the mother was described: 'The care of the children is delegated to the mother. It is she who chooses the school, interviews the teacher, the inspector or the magistrate. The father is only called in to administer punishment in its more severe forms'.[64] A similar pattern was discernible in the Scottish working-class home, except that the Scots were more authoritarian. Stanley Reynolds, who was a perceptive student of working-class life, also argues in his book, *The Lower Deck*, that English working-class children were not 'disciplined in the pastor and master sense of the word'.[65] By contrast, authoritarianism was deeply embedded in the cultural fabric of the Scottish working-class family.[66] The cultural inhibitions induced by Gradgrind Calvinism often meant that Scottish working men were even less directly interested in their children than their English counterparts. In Glasgow, for example, the artisan father 'would not for his life be seen (to) demean himself' by blowing 'the weans (children's) noses in the tramway car'.[67]

As well as suggesting that there was no simple economic mechanism determining every facet of the social behaviour of the working-class family in Britain, these important differences of degree between the Scottish and English working classes should stimulate questions about the connections between family life and militancy in the factory, mine, mill or farm. At the same time as the Scottish working-class family seems to have been more authoritarian than the English one, Scottish women in the factories, mines and mills were clearly more autonomous, militant and class-conscious. By glancing at some of the differences between Scottish and English working-class families, we are at least able to show that there were no *simple* causal relationships between degrees of economic deprivation and class-consciousness. The differences between the Scottish and the English experience raises the question, however, of whether there was a direct correlation between degrees of male chauvinism in the home and trade union militancy in the factories and mills.

It is not my intention to romanticise the Scottish working-class. Nevertheless, there is an abundance of evidence to suggest that the Scottish Labour Movement was much less patriarchal than its English counterpart. These differences were not innate or God-given, but rooted in the distinctive interaction between history and politics, culture and economics. The Scots were more sympathetic to the agitation for women's freedom and they were not hostile to the women in the factories and mills.

Perhaps the majority of socialists everywhere were more interested in struggling to build a unified movement of men and women to overthrow capitalism than in transforming sexual relationships in the here-and-now. In a comment on the situation before the First World War, Mari Jo Buhle writes: 'While most socialists vehemently decried "the slavery of the mother of the home" in their propaganda, they allowed the same conditions to exist in their homes'.[68] The same was true of Scotland, as Harry McShane puts it: 'Most of the (Scottish) socialists were just like other men in their attitudes in the home. Many of them had big families, and it was the women who carried the burden'.[69] But in contrast to the English socialists, the Scots were much less hostile to the notion of women's participation in the class struggle.

The Scottish socialists were also much more sympathetic to the concept of recruiting women to trade unions and socialist groups than were their English counterparts. From the early 1880s, the various socialist groups in Scotland had concentrated on enrolling women. In England, on the other hand, there was an unbroken continuity of keeping women out of labour and socialist organisations. In Bristol in 1886, for example, a sentence in a draft manifesto of the newly established Labour League declaring that female workers 'might become members was voted out after considerable discussion'.[70] In 1903 Christabel Pankhurst published an article in the *I.L.P. News* in which she argued: 'Working men are just as unjust to women as those of other classes'.[71] Moreover, it was the refusal of the Salford branch of the Independent Labour Party to admit women into membership which led Mrs Pankhurst to found the Women's Social and Political Union.[72]

The Scots' greater willingness to enrol and mobilise working women is of considerable interest for two reasons. First, it was an important agency of social change, in that it raised the status of working-class women. Secondly, it created the pre-conditions which made it easier for the militant socialists to mount a major anti-war agitation including the famous rent strike in 1915 on Clydeside. Besides, the Scottish socialists' tendency, before the outbreak of the First World War, to enrol and train working-class women as speakers and organisers was to have other important consequences later on. Socialists such as John Maclean on Clydeside and Lawrence Storione in Fife were somewhat hostile to the Suffragette Movement in Scotland precisely because they saw it as a diversion from the socialists' main task of agitating for the general social and economic emancipation of women.[73]

In early twentieth-century Scotland, there were sixty-three branches of the National Union of Suffrage Societies and, though the Scottish branches of the Women's Social and Political Union were not very numerous, the Scots opposed the Pankhursts' interference in the affairs of their Edinburgh branch. Here another paradox came into play. At the same time as the Scots operated within a much less hostile atmosphere than that of their English sisters, they were nevertheless not able to muster as much support. The reasons for the weakness of the Women's Movement in Scotland cannot, however, be reduced to a single cause, though the weakness of the Scottish middle class was probably a factor.[74] The provincialism of Scottish society was, as Stephen Maxwell argues, another cause. The major reason, however, was the timidity, conformity and acceptance of the *status quo* by the Scottish middle class.[75] Also, as happened in England, the Labour Movement was often divided over the question of supporting the Suffragettes' agitation for 'votes for women'.

Although the Scottish middle-class Women's Movement was numerically weaker than the English one, it did participate in British agitations for the vote. In depicting the Scots' participation in the British demonstration in London in 1906 after Campbell Bannerman became the new Liberal Prime Minister, Frances Balfour wrote in 1930: 'I remember so well the faces of the pioneers in that meeting, they came from all parts. Flora and Louisa Stevenson from Edinburgh, where they had won marvellous triumphs for education'.[76]

At the same time, a number of 'Scottish university women brought an action against the University courts of the universities of St Andrews and Edinburgh on the ground that their names being on the register of the University, they were entitled to have been served with voting papers at the general election. The case caused a great deal of interest in Scotland. Large funds were subscribed, but the judgment of Lord

Salveson was adverse to the pursuers'.[77]

The Women's Movement in Scotland left its greatest imprint on events through direct political agitation. Although the Women's Social and Political Union in England was born out of the patriarchal prejudice of members of the Salford branch of the ILP, it attracted much of its strength from socialists throughout Britain, Elspeth King explains: 'In many of the industrial towns of Britain, the WSPU drew its strength from the ILP. This was particularly true in Glasgow, where the office-bearers had difficulty in convincing the more conservative ladies of the non-militant Association for Women's Suffrage that the WSPU was not in fact an ILP organisation. Nevertheless, many ILP members were also WSPU organisers, the most notable being Helen Crawfurd, who later became a founder member of the Communist Party, and Janie Allan, whose father and brother, owners of the Allan Shipping Line, were notorious for their socialist principles'.

The Scottish socialists' attitudes towards the question of women's emancipation was sympathetic but complex. In *Scotland: 1689 to the Present*, William Ferguson argues that 'The suffragists' most consistent supporters were the socialists'.[78] Margaret Bain says something similar in her essay on *Scottish Women in Politics*. Because the Suffragettes in Scotland were mainly Liberals who did not want to endorse any criticisms of capitalism or the harsh, insensitive social policies of a grasping, tight-fisted bourgeoisie, they did not succeed in mobilising the Labour Movement's support for their cause. It is simply not true that, as Margaret Bain puts it, 'In Scotland links are found between the nascent ILP and Labour Party, and the bulk of male support for the cause in Scotland came from members of radical forces of change'.[79] In brief, the Scottish Labour Movement was sympathetic to agitations for women's social and economic emancipation, but hostile to the Suffragettes' narrow aim of securing votes for women on the basis of the existing property qualification.

Certainly the pre-conditions existed in Scotland for a strong, militant Women's Movement. In contrast to such English socialists as H M Hyndman and Ernest Belford Bax, the Scots were sympathetic to the agitation for women's rights. Such Scottish members of the Social Democratic Federation (SDF) as W J Nairne (Sandy Macfarlane), James Leatham and John Carstairs Matheson were exceptionally eloquent advocates of sexual equality, and Leatham came into conflict with the English leadership of the SDF in 1896 for suggesting that there was a specific 'socialist theory of sexual morality'.[80] But the emancipation of women was, from the Scots' particular perspective, impossible without the abolition of capitalism.

Such Scottish socialists as Archibald MacLaren, William J Nairne,

Archibald Muirhead, James Leatham, John Maclean and John Carstairs Matheson repeatedly raised the question of women's oppression. By sketching in the role played by capitalism in transforming the status of women from the early days of Christianity, Nairne sought to arouse working-class women against poor wages, intolerable working conditions in the factories and mills and domestic enslavement.[81] In an article dealing with *The Cleanliness of the Sexes*, James Leatham implicitly criticised the English leadership of the SDF for denying the existence of 'sex-subjection'. By the early twentieth century, both James Leatham and John Maclean were much more interested in strikes of working-class women than in the 'votes for women' agitation.

Ernest Belford Bax, a leading figure in the English leadership of the SDF attributed wife-beating to men's legal subjection. He also argued that what he called the 'sham equality' between the sexes really amounted to the subjection of men by women. The extraordinary bitterness of Bax's anti-feminism was shared by the whole of the English leadership of the SDF, and the Scots and the American De Leonites attacked Bax and Hyndman for not recognising the slavery of 'the proletarian of the home' — the working-class wife.[82] The question of the emancipation of working-class women was, indeed, a major issue leading to the formation of the breakaway Socialist Labour Party in 1903.

The Scots often remained Calvinistic in their attitudes to sexual questions. The few who were exceptional usually belonged to the Scottish branches of the Socialist League. In 1888, Archibald MacLaren wrote a note to R F Muirhead in which he announced his plans to address a street-corner meeting in a working-class district of Glasgow on free-love. He concluded with the cryptic sentence: 'Socialism and sex — dangerous'.[83] In Edinburgh, Andreas Scheu, an Austrian emigré, alienated working-class socialists by expounding his 'advanced sexual views' on free love, etc.[84] 'Respectability' and orthodox bourgeois attitudes towards sexual questions were commonplace in the Scottish Labour Movement.

In the late 1880s, James Leatham wrote articles exposing 'the conditions of the female workers' in Aberdeen, and in 1896 he challenged the bourgeois sexual attitudes of Bax and Hyndman.[85] By 1912, he was depicting the Suffragettes as 'hooligan elements' without abandoning his earlier agitations for women's emancipation.[86] Then, in 1913, John Maclean also criticised the Suffragettes in Glasgow for their acts of incendiarism.[87] However, in 1914, Maclean took part in organising general working-class support for a strike of women textile workers in Dunfermline.[88] What alienated socialists like Leatham and Maclean was simply the Suffragettes' lack of sympathy for the plight of working-class women.

If the De Leonites in Scotland and America were passionate advocates of the emancipation of women, they were also very critical of the middle-class Suffragettes. The clearest exposition of their opposition to this movement came from the pen of the American socialist thinker, Daniel De Leon, who argues: '"Woman suffrage" is a term that denotes liberalism. In the cards is the maneuver (sic!) of female and male capitalists availing themselves of the sound of liberalism, and, wrapping themselves in the colours of "woman suffrage", throw a tub to the whale; grant the suffrage to property-holding women; and, under the glow of such a seemingly liberal act, change radically the basis of the franchise reactionward'.[89] Though John Maclean did not join the Socialist Labour Party until after the death of De Leon, he shared the same antipathy towards the middle-class orientated Suffragettes, as he puts it in *Justice*: 'If these high-spirited women could only realise that not only women, but the whole working class — men and women — have no chance of justice in our country they would be with us in our utter contempt for capitalism as well as the evil outcome of vile domination'.[90] In any attempt to judge the attitude of the Scottish Labour Movement as a whole towards the Suffragettes' agitation, we must not lose sight of the socialists' practical objections to the Suffragettes' middle-class outlook.

What led the socialists like John Maclean to criticise the Suffragettes was their lack of radical objectives beyond securing the vote for middle-class women. However, as Maclean made clear, there was widespread sympathy for Scottish women who confronted the capitalist Establishment head-on. In Dundee in 1909, for example, the militant Suffragettes 'adopted the hunger strike, but in Scotland so great was the feeling against forcible feeding that in Dundee it did not take place'.[91] Once again Scottish and English responses to the tactics employed by the militant Suffragettes were distinctive, as Agnes Muir MacKenzie puts it: 'It is fair to add that Suffragettes of experience have declared that violent treatment was rare in Scotland, and mild compared with that of England and Wales'.[92] In both the Scottish and English Labour Movements, male chauvinism was undoubtedly an important factor inhibiting working men's support for 'votes for women'.[93] However, other factors were often at work, too, including principled socialists' opposition.

Although she was not as well-known in British labour circles as Emma Paterson or Mary MacArthur, Margaret Hardinge Irwin was, as Sheila Lewenhak suggests, 'the second major female personality to emerge in British trade unionism'. The daughter of a Broughty Ferry sea captain, information about her early life is simply non-existent. In

1891 Margaret Irwin was appointed by the Scottish branch of the Women's Protective and Provident League as its full-time organiser. She was a very effective organiser of women workers. In summing up one of her major achievements, Sheila Lewenhak says: 'By 1895 the National Federal Council of Scotland for Women's Trades claimed to have in affiliation 16 Trades Councils and 25 trade unions representing a membership of 100,000'.[94] Since she condemned strikes as 'uncivilised' because of the hardship they involved, some of her male trade union colleagues were, as Sheila Lewenhak puts it, able to 'rationalise' their patriarchal prejudices against her.

The Scottish Labour Movement took a much more active part than its English counterpart did in attempting to involve working women in its activities and government. The Scots did not express the same extreme patriarchal prejudice that Ethel Snowden documents in her extended comments on the English labour movement.[95] In a passionate and heated discussion of the votes for women agitation at the Glasgow Trades Council in 1912, the delegates were divided between those who supported 'votes for women on equal terms with men' and those who wanted an extension of the franchise to women on the basis of a property qualification.[96] What the Left clearly feared was that the votes of middle-class women would be used to strengthen the anti-socialist forces within Scottish society.

Nevertheless, before the outbreak of the First World War, there was considerable sympathy for the cause of women's suffrage within the Scottish Labour Movement. This was not, however, identical with sympathy for the middle-class Suffragettes or suffragists. In Scotland, the class lines were drawn much more sharply than in England and the Scots were already preparing themselves to struggle to obtain votes for women by engaging in direct action. By January 1914, Sylvia Pankhurst's East London Federation of Suffragettes had not made much impact on working-class women. This was acknowledged in the minutes of the meeting that took place on 27 January 1914: 'They had no objection to the "No Vote, No Rent Strike", but said it was impossible to work it through their organisation because it was only in working-class houses that the woman pays the rent'.[97] At roughly the same time, however, the Scottish socialist newspaper, *Forward*, was much more optimistic abut the 'No Vote, No Rent strike':

> The idea of the "No Vote, No Rent strike" is that when a
> sufficient number of householders are pledged to strike, it
> shall be that no more rent be paid until the vote is granted...
> It would not be possible to evict several thousand families in
> a city, and if any attempts were made to victimise a family
> the "Popular Army" would be brought in to help them.[98]

But perhaps the most powerful impact of the past on the consciousness of Scottish working women was seen in their militancy in the factories and textile mills.

Strikes of Scottish working-class women were frequent and they were *always* taken seriously by the employers and public opinion. The strikes of English working women however, were a 'laughing matter' and often a source of ridicule and amusement.[99] The strikes of English women also seem to have been much less frequent than those of the Scots, but they got greater press coverage. In contrast to the well-known and indeed legendary strikes of the London match-girls, the women chain-makers at Cradley Heath, the women at the Millwall food-preserving factory and the factory women at Bermondsey in 1911, the strikes of Scottish working women were ignored except for the relatively brief and obscure news reports in local newspapers.

Here again, a crucial difference in determining the peculiarities of the history of Scottish working-class women was the blindness of the indigenous middle classes towards social problems. A major reason for the much greater volume of contemporary and historical literature chronicling and analysing the strikes of English working women was the vociferous *activity* of a minority of wealthy and influential philanthropists who campaigned to improve the lot of English working-class women. In contrast to the situation in Scotland, the strikes of working women in England were supported by such bourgeois figures as Lady Beauchamp, Lady Dilke, George Cadbury and the Bishop of Worcester.[100] Not only did a substantial and influential minority of the English bourgeoisie support the strikes of the match-girls, chain-makers and factory women, but they also criticised the appalling working conditions of the women workers in the mills, shops, factories and sweatshops.

English bourgeois women who agitated for 'votes for women' were usually also evangelical advocates of wider social rights for women *per se*, and it is significant that Emma Paterson came to women's trade unionism via the Women's Suffrage Association. Paterson set up the Women's Protective and Provident League in 1873 and represented her organisation as a delegate to the British Trades Union Congress until 1886.[101] (In 1908 the Women's Protective and Provident League changed its name to the Women's Trade Union League.) In 1906, Mary MacArthur, a Scot who had done organising work in various Scottish towns, founded the National Federation of Women Workers and henceforth did most of her work of organising women in English towns and cities.[102]

The Scots certainly seem to have mounted more strikes than the English, though trade union membership amongst women was not any more impressive. Such British or really English organisations as the Women's Protective and Provident League, the National Federation of Women Workers and the Women's Trade Union League were represented in only a few Scottish towns and cities. On the face of it, the pre-conditions for women's trade unionism in Scotland were excellent. In an essay on *The Seamy Side of Trade Unionism for Women*, Lady Emilia F S Dilke wrote in 1890: 'I said, and I repeat, that those anxious to organise women's labour no longer met with the same determined opposition to their efforts as of old, and that the women themselves, in one or two of the districts of Scotland showed intelligence and enthusiasm. I wish I could have said as much for their English sisters, but I have nowhere found in England audiences of women as large and as well-informed on trade questions as I have met in one or two Scotch towns'.[103] But when the Women's Labour League was founded in 1908, they were almost pleased to acknowledge the difficulties that they faced in persuading Scottish working-class women to organise themselves. This was summed up in *The Woman Worker* of 26 June 1908: 'Scotland is usually supposed by its inhabitants to supply the brains and intelligence of every forward movement. But in our League we can, at any rate, claim that the English branches were well established before the sister country came to share the work'.[104] This paradox can only be explained by reconstructing the context in which Scottish working-class women lived and worked.

By the late nineteenth century, English working-class women were known as 'the white slaves of England'. During the strike of the women chain-makers at Cradley Heath in 1910 the President of the British TUC appealed to the delegates to 'help these poor white slaves of England to get their humble demand'.[105] But at least a section of the English bourgeoisie was prepared to engage in a crusade to improve the lot of women, including working-class women, by campaigning for better laws, easier divorce, women factory inspectors and better working conditions. In the process of doing so, they created an immense partisan literature in which they chronicled the appalling brutalities inflicted on working-class women at home as well as in the factories and mills.

Scottish working-class women were certainly oppressed. They did not live in the veritable paradise portrayed by such Kailyard novelists as J M Barrie and Ian MacLaren, but no-one would have dreamt of speaking or writing of 'the poor white slaves' of Scotland. Even so, the oppression of working women in Scotland was real and tangible. In both Scotland and England, for example, working women were frequently raped by foremen and overseers.[106] In 1886 the trial of a twenty-one-year-old Dundee factory woman led the Sheriff to comment: 'He believed from what he had heard of the worst affiliation cases before he came to Dundee, and from those he had seen since he came there, the case of the accused was not a solitary one. There were foremen in the factories who abused their position in a most abominable way, and indulged in practices which were assigned to the American slave-owners'.[107] Nevertheless, the Scots were exempt from some of the harshness which was inflicted on working women in England.

In England, women workers were treated very harshly by their employers, especially when they attempted to form trade unions, as Geoffrey Drage puts it in *The Labour Problem*: 'Two East End firms were mentioned in this connection, in one of which "the employer told his women distinctly that if they joined the union he would sack every one of them, if he had to shut up his shop". In the other case a newly-formed union was destroyed by the action of the employer, who "dismissed forty of his oldest and best hands merely because they belonged to it. The other girls remained in the union till they were watched to the union office and the girl's club by a man employed as a searcher to the factory and also to follow the girls to their club. The girls were at last afraid of being seen, and gradually dropped out of the union"'.

In an important and well-documented book, *Women's Work*, A M Bulley and M Whitley make a similar observation: 'But in many cases the attempt to form a combination among women meets with the open hostility of their employers. . . . The manager of a confectionery factory in a large provincial town recently attempted to turn away all those who had given in their names to a newly-formed union. Under these circumstance it is not surprising that women, especially in the worst paid trades, are afraid to join a trade union, and that even after joining they readily fell away from an undertaking which may possibly involve so serious a risk'.[108]

The same cultural attitudes which in 1909 prevented the forced-feeding of the Suffragettes in Dundee also thwarted the extreme brutality that was used to maintain discipline in English factories. Thus, in a large English factory a foreman 'had, nominally as a means of discipline, turned a fire hose on to a large group of young tenters and weavers. The water, drawn from the mill pond and filthy, was directed over a partition upon them while they were jammed in a narrow vestibule in which they took refuge. The girls (of whom forty were examined by the inspector) were then turned out on a cold March morning, dripping, to walk in some cases several miles to their homes'.[109] This, of course, was an extreme example of the sort of discipline that was imposed in English (as distinct from Scottish) factories. However, patriarchal attitudes existed in Scottish society, too, and this was particularly so in the attitudes of the large employers of female labour.

The conditions in the Scottish factories, mills and sweatshops were primitive and female labour was exploited by the native employers. Some employers who were questioned by Margaret H Irwin about why they paid such low wages to females frequently replied: 'It takes so much less, you see, to keep a woman than a man'.[110] Certainly poverty was much worse in the Scottish towns and cities than it was in the English ones. In his book, *The Child Slaves of Britain*, Robert H Sherard describes the poverty of working-class women in Glasgow: 'The wages of the women are so miserable that even the small sums that their children earn for them are indispensable additions to the resources of the family'.[111]

By 1913, the local Liberals in the industrial town of Falkirk were beginning to acknowledge the links between female wages and the growth of prostitution. One writer put it at the time: 'Indeed, as a well-known local worker amongst the poor pointed out to our representative, it is to be wondered at that there is not more prostitution in view of the fact that there are 1,500 women workers in Falkirk and district, whose average wage is only seven shillings per week'.[112]

In the rural areas, women's wages were kept down by traditionalism and a reluctance to leave home, as George L Bolen, an American student of working-class life, puts it in *Getting a Living*: 'Women were so unready to leave home that their pay on one side of narrow Scotland is fifty per cent lower than on the other side'.[113]

The experiences and behaviour of Scottish working-class women were extremely varied, and the intensity and inconstancy of their militancy in the factories and textile mills can only be understood within the context of the culture and social values of the working class as a whole. The literature chronicling Scottish (as distinct from English) women's militant activity is very scanty, and what evidence there is has to be used imaginatively. If one is making a comparison with England or America, it is very striking that Scottish novelists and social reformers refused to acknowledge the reality of the class struggle.[114]

A critical literature could only have come from the Scottish women and men of property and leisure and they were not critical of the savage social conditions engendered by capitalism. In England, Emma Paterson had taken it for granted that the Women's Protective and Provident League depended on the assistance of 'persons of wealth and leisure'. While she 'had it in her mind before she died to emancipate the women's societies from the middle-class tutelage of the League, trade unions in Britain were still middle-class-dominated in 1914.[116] The role of the Women's Trade Union League in England before the outbreak of the First World War is, in fact, summed up in *Mary MacArthur* by Mary Hamilton: 'The Trade Union League itself was an object lesson in social co-operation. Its members belonged to all parties, and to none. They came from all classes, though the middle class decidedly predominated. Differing on many points, they came together for practical work. With them in mind, tirades against the bourgeoisie became unreal: an idle interruption of the real task'.[117]

Here and there a few — a very few — Scottish middle-class philanthropists did try to organise working-class women into trade unions. This happened in the 1880s and 90s in the textile mills and factories in Arbroath, Montrose, Brechin, Forfar and Dunfermline. By 1892, fourteen trade union branches existed in these towns, and militant working-class women sometime received assistance from the committee members of the London-based Women's Protective and Provident (later re-named the Women's Trade Union) League 'on their grand tours through the east of Scotland'. Certainly, too, between 1880 and 1914, there were many strikes of women workers in Scotland. Some of them are mentioned in W H Marwick's book, *A Short History of Labour in Scotland* and in Sheila Lewenhak's book, *Women and Trade Unions*.[118] However, the growth of women's trade unionism in England owed a great deal to the middle-class philanthropists. Not only did they possess the wealth and leisure that allowed them to spend a great amount of time building up women's trade union membership, but they were also immune from the victimisation often suffered by working-class women who formed trade unions. The relative absence of such women within Scottish society helps to explain the paradox of extensive women's militancy and strikes and weak trade union organisation.

To understand some of the other aspects of women's trade unionism in Scotland, however, we need to at least glance at working-class culture and social values. In Scottish as in English society, trade unionism was not regarded as 'respectable'. Indeed the very existence of trade unionism and socialism was seen as antithetical to working-class 'respectability'. In 1892, Sidney Webb, who was gathering material for his book on the history of British trade unionism, was informed by Thomas Don, the secretary of the Dunfermline Trades Council, that 'the rule of the working-class "respectability"' was particularly 'inimical' to trade union organisation in a small industrial town where the labour force was predominately female.[119] But by 1912 the 'social pride' which had previously inhibited English working men and women from joining trade unions was 'diminishing'.[120] In their book, *Industrial Warfare*, Charles Watney and James A Little describe the decline of this particular form of 'respectability' as an important factor in the 'labour unrest'.[121] A similar decline was witnessed in Scotland, too, but it was still strong in some working-class communities.

The paucity of material describing women's strikes in Scotland is a problem the historian has to acknowledge. This is why the surviving evidence of Scottish women's involvement in strikes and trade unionism must be evaluated *critically* and seen *dialectically* in relation to their changing consciousness. When Margaret H Irwin said that 'the girls' and women employed in paper-bag making in Glasgow were 'indifferent' to trade union organisation,[122] she was being 'realistic'. However, a variety of factors could either foster or inhibit the confidence of women who were dissatisfied with their wages and working conditions. Fatalistic attitudes did exist in the minds of Scottish as well as English working women, but the growth of permanent trade unionism amongst women workers was not assisted by the action of the Independent Labour Party in discouraging a strike of women paper-bag-makers in Edinburgh in 1894.[123]

While their strong cultural traditions assisted Scottish women who tried to organise themselves, the difficulties they faced were nevertheless formidable. Just as they had to confront the notion that trade union membership was antithetical to working-class 'respectability', so they were often faced with male prejudice. Though male prejudice was less intense and less widespread in Scotland than in England, it did exist. A hint of male prejudice was seen, for example, in a comment made by Mr Hendry, an organiser of the Scottish Mill and Factory Workers, when he said: 'Women are kittle-cattle, and if anyone had lingering doubts on that point, which he desires to dispel, let him spend a few weeks in organising work amongst women, and his cure will be complete'.[124] What he forgot to mention was that the women workers in some of the Scottish textile towns were sometimes better organised than the men, and that women faced even more obstacles in attempting to organise themselves than male workers did.

Throughout Britain, women's — and indeed men's — trade unionism was very unstable. Women who were relatively well-organised one year could be without any organisation the next. This is why the surviving evidence must be used with particular care. In the *Report of the Royal Commission on Labour* a very bleak and dismal picture was painted by the Commissioners of the plight of women employed in the Scottish spinning industry: 'Thus, in Scotland, it was noted that in the spinning industry women's labour was both "cheap and unorganised", while in England, where women as well as men are highly organised, it is comparatively well-paid'.[125] What we must keep in mind, however, is that the Scottish women spinners were not always badly organised.

Also, labour in Scotland was generally cheaper than in England, and economic depressions usually forced down the wages of women workers still further.

The fluctuations in the strength and weakness of trade unionism amongst Scottish women arose from a variety of factors including the ups-and-downs of the trade cycle and the 'dialectic' of the class struggle. This pattern was especially noticeable in the 'she-town' of Dundee. The peculiarities of the social structure in such towns as Dundee and Norwich were shaped by the presence of a predominantly female labour force. Dundee was particularly well-known for attracting one-parent families. This contributed to the serious social problems of illegitimacy, cot deaths and high infant mortality rates. Besides, the impermanence of working-class social life vitiated most attempts to form stable trade unions amongst women workers. It is also important to realise that the Dundee and District Mill and Textile Workers' Union set up by the Rev Henry Williamson had been motivated by a desire to persuade women workers from striking to improve their wages. Indeed, Williamson's motive in organising the women was 'because women and girls were the only kind of workers who came out on strike and threw a whole town out of employment'.[126] In a descriptive paragraph written in 1912, Charles Watney and James A Little alluded to the ever-changing consciousness of working-class women in Dundee, when they said: 'An industry in which trouble may be expected is the jute industry of Dundee. Here the majority of the employees are women who are badly underpaid, notwithstanding the fact that huge fortunes are made in the jute trade. At present the women are unorganised, but there are many signs that the desire for organisation is growing amongst women workers generally'.[127]

However, important inherited cultural values were to assist the growth of women's trade unionism in Scotland. At the same time as there were enormous difficulties involved in attempting to organise women workers, a gradual, if slow, process in building up women's trade unionism was also perceptible. Militancy and profound caution sometimes existed in the same heads. Nevertheless, the difficulties were, as we have seen, often formidable. In 1896, the President of the Falkirk Trades Council complained of the Council's failure to establish a branch of the Women's Protective and Provident League because they had begun 'too low down the scale'.[128] Fear of victimisation, 'social pride' or notions of what constituted working-class 'respectability' repeatedly thwarted attempts to organise women workers. In 1889, Emilia Dilke reported on the problems she faced in Dundee when she tried to organise women workers: 'But no-one would come forward either to promote or join a union, and yet they were visibly interested

124

and stirred by what I had to say, and a local reporter recorded that as he left the room, he heard a young lady declare to her companion: "I was just glad when Emilia Dilke left speaking, for I was afraid that before she'd done I would be rolled into doing something"'.[129] When strikes broke out in the textile mills and factories, Scottish women could quickly abandon their 'respectability' in the heat of class conflict with those who employed them for a pittance. This is why 'realistic' comments about women's indifference to trade unionism must be evaluated very critically.

While the strikes of the Scots did not go unrecorded, they did not give rise to anything at all comparable to the voluminous literature and comment about the strikes of English women. There is, in fact, only one adequate description of a strike of Scottish women during the years between 1880 and 1914. It is an oral account given by James D MacDougall, the closest friend and colleague of John Maclean, to Nan Maclean Milton over two decades after the strike took place. It is, therefore, worth quoting in full:

> One of the villages in the East Renfrewshire area where he carried on systematic propaganda was the mining village of Nitshill. Like many other mining villages and towns throughout the country, the men and boys found employment in the mines while the girls travelled to the nearest textile factories. These happened to be thread mills situated at Neilson some miles away. This was a very large factory employing thousands of girls, and of course they were on piecework. One or two of the Nitshill girls, daughters of socialist miners, worked in the Copwinding Department, and they put forward demands for better prices.
>
> When the demands of this department were refused, the whole mob of girls steamed out of the mill, shouting defiance of the management. Many of them were quite young; none of them had any experience whatever of organisation, but their fathers at Nitshill knew that to carry on strikes there had to be meetings, and so they went for John Maclean and his friends to come up to organise the girls.
>
> Maclean came and infused his own vigour and courage into these girls. He instructed them how they must act in order to win, not only this immediate wage demand, but to be able in future to protect themselves against the tyranny of the foremen or any unjust demand that might be made upon them. They must get into a Trade Union. Maclean himself took the initiative in writing to the Federation of Women Workers, and very soon a whole array of women organisers

and speakers, including the famous Mary MacArthur, were on the scene. Miss Kate Maclean, afterwards Mrs Kate Beaton, took a prominent part in organising the girls.

The manager lived many miles away in Pollokshaws, a "posh" Glasgow suburb. The most prominent incident of the strike was when it was decided to have a march from Neilson right through all the intervening towns and villages to Pollokshaws in order to interview the manager. It can be understood that to lead such a disorderly, undisciplined horde of young girls, to whom the thing was more of a joke than anything else (they were carrying effigies of the manager which were intended to be burned) was by no means an easy job, but Maclean was equal to anything of that kind. He was full of fun and chaff, and so took the hearts of the girls that they would have done anything for him, with the result that no serious trouble occurred.

The march, with a great banging of tin cans and shouting and singing pursued its noisy way from Neilson to Pollokshaws, where the respectable inhabitants were thoroughly disturbed. The meeting was held in a field adjacent to the manager's house, and then the weary strikers dispersed to find their way home as best they might. The wage demands were won. The whole of the girls in the factory were organised, and a great mass of virgin minds received a favourable impression of their first real contact with socialism.[130]

The narrative detail seems to be authentic, and it ought to persuade us to question the 'realistic' account of those contemporaries who said that women workers were not militant.

In Scotland, the fishing girls were among the most oppressed and exploited women within the labour force. If the 'Scottish fishing girls (saw) more of the British Isles than the average British woman',[131] they were sometimes difficult to organise. In contrast to the graphic picture of the harshness of the day to day lives of the herring girls sketched in by Archie Crawford,[132] in *An Old-time Fishing Town* the Rev Daniel M'Iver argues: 'One might think that the fisher-girls are a sorely distressed lot — but no. They are very happy, for they learn to take their sufferings philosophically'.[133] This description of the *alleged* docility of working-class women ignores the fact that profound discontents could be concealed from outsiders.

In 1910, the Scots were in the thick of the mass strike by the fishing girls at Grimsby against excessive hours of labour,[134] but discontent had already existed in 1906 when the Rev M'Iver spoke of them taking their 'sufferings philosophically'. In an account of a real strike as recently as

1978 in the textile industry in the American South, the heroine who inspired the film *Norma Rae* told a reporter from the *Chicago Tribune* of the smouldering resentments that went back a long way before the famous strike finally erupted.

> I got tired of being called cotton mill trash and lint head, said Mrs Sutton, 39, the heroine of one of the most difficult struggles of organised labour. I got tired of being poor and pushed around, said the fiesty millworker, who achieved national fame when she battled the South's bastion of anti-unionism — the J. P. Stevens and Co firm.
> I tried to weave a union into the fabric of the company back in 1972, and in 1973 I got fired, said Mrs Sutton, whose plight was depicted in the movie *Norma Rae*.

What was important in Mrs Sutton's biography was that she 'inherited' a job in a cotton mill, and a legacy of being looked down upon. 'But I also inherited something else from my daddy. I always spoke up for what I believed in just like he did.'[135] It is clear from James D MacDougall's account of the 1910 strike of the girls in the Nitshill thread mills that the socialist ideas of the girls' fathers played an important part in translating fatalistic 'apathy' into a fighting militancy.

An important feature of the strike described by James D MacDougall was that most of the girls regarded 'the thing' more as 'a joke than anything else'. This stands out in sharp contrast to the experience of English women workers who struck work. In 1908, in a biographical sketch of Mary MacArthur, J J Mallon described how most English working women viewed their employers. 'The *"master"* is to them a figure of myth and legend: a goblin who eats of those that anger him.'[136]

By emphasising the influence of the past on the *class struggles* of Scottish women, I do not wish to give the impression that I am engaging in Celtic romanticism.[137] Quite the contrary. In the 1920s, before the rise of Stalinism, a number of socialist thinkers recognised that the 'unsimultaneity' of history or 'the persistence of older forms of historical existence in contemporary society'[138] could be as important as the 'economic factor' in fostering class struggles, as Antonio Labriola, the Italian socialist thinker, argues in his *Essays on the Materialistic Conception of History*: 'Historic time has not marched uniformly for all men. The simple succession of the generations has never been the index of the constancy and intensity of the *processus*'.[139] Moreover, if the 'unsimultaneity' of history played a reactionary role in fostering the rise of German fascism, it also played a progressive role in Highland women's resistance to the infamous Clearances which took place throughout the nineteenth century. In a pioneering and path-breaking essay dealing with 'the hidden world of matriarchy' in the nineteenth-century Highland resistance to the capitalist modernisation, Hamish Henderson sums up: 'Surely it is only completely explicable as another hang-over from the mental world of the shattered tribal system. It was the women's world, which stood in, with all its spirit, courage, and resilience, when the man's world faltered'.[140]

In looking at the specific strike of the Scottish fishing girls at Grimsby in 1910, we have concrete evidence of how past traditions could foster the class struggle. By the early twentieth century, six thousand Highland women, who followed the herring north to Lerwick and south to Peterhead, Aberdeen, Lowestoft, Yarmouth and Grimsby, were employed at Lerwick in the Shetland Islands for four months during the summer season to gut and pack the herring catches. Just before the strike in 1910, they had been regarded as the most 'docile' and 'apathetic' section of the female labour force in Scotland. As the Highlands were increasingly drawn into what Archie Crawford describes as 'The Octopus Capitalism', a new mode of production was imposed on an essentially pre-industrialised labour force. What happened to the fishing girls at Lerwick was important in so far as it demonstrates that the women's latent militancy could not be eradicated by the imposition of a new mode of production. At a time when 'the overworked fishermen' molested 'girls whose wooden huts' offered them 'no protection' from sexual assault, and when 'the fingers of these herring girls suffer(ed) frightfully from bone cuts', the women were already well-known for their socialist sympathies,[141] but a crucial factor in the coalescence of the cultural sediments of the past with the potential militancy of pre-industrial women with no experience or tradition of trade union militancy may have been the active, flourishing and influential branches of the Social Democratic Federation and the Socialist Labour Party at Lerwick.[142]

One of the most unfortunate aspects of the English Suffragettes' historiography is the tendency to ignore some of the distinctive cultural traditions and consequences of the strikes of English, Irish and Scottish women. In her book, *The Cause: A Short History of the Women's Movement in Great Britain*, Ray Strachey lumps English, Irish and Scottish working-class women together without realising that Scottish women were less cowed by their menfolk than their English sisters: 'In the Midlands and the South, as well as in Scotland and Ireland, the women workers were in no position to stand out for their rights . . . the contributions of time and money which they could themselves give to the campaigns were pitifully small'.[143] However, English working-class women often lacked confidence in themselves. This lack of confidence was so strong that the fifteen thousand women who struck work in the Bermondsey factories in 1911 could not themselves believe what had happened, as Mary Hamilton explains in *Mary MacArthur*: 'Afterwards legends flew about as to the cause: a story was told of a fat woman who had appeared in many factories, called the girls out or threatened employers. No-one had seen her; everybody believed in her'.[144]

The Scots sometimes linked the agitation for better wages and conditions in the factories and mills to the demand for 'votes for women'. Soon after a strike of women textile workers in the Leven mills was called to protest against fines for being late, it quickly escalated into a demand for higher wages. The strike was supported by the local socialists, the Fife Miners' Union and the Methil Trades Council. Before the strike culminated in complete success, the employers conceded recognition of the Textile Workers' Union. When Mary Westwood, the local leader of the women strikers, told mixed audiences of men and women of the need for women's suffrage, she met with great enthusiasm.[145]

The spontaneous strikes of women in the Scottish textile factories in 1912 and 1913 were also successful. At that time when the women 'formed the majority of the operatives in the Forfarshire factories', the employers originally offered the men an increase of five per cent and the women only two-and-a-half per cent.[146] By staying out for several months, the women won their full demand. Also, in 1912 and 1913, women textile workers and female farm servants in Fife squeezed higher wages out of their employers by coming out on strike.[147] Elsewhere in Scotland, women workers took advantage of the booming conditions in the textile industry to push up their wages.[148] In common with the male workers, the women were at their most confident during an upturn in the trade cycle.

It would be a mistake, however, to convey the impression that Scottish working women were always successful when they struck work to improve either their wages or working conditions. Some strikes ended in failure. In 1898 a strike of women textile workers in Newmilns was crushed by the employers who took advantage of a trade recession to compel the women to sign a declaration repudiating their trade union. It read: 'I hereby acknowledge having been a member of the Newmilns Textile Workers' Union, but now declare truthfully that I am so no longer, and shall not again form any such connection as long as I remain in your employ'.[149] By 1910, the women textile workers at Newmilns were again members of their trade union.

The fear of victimisation, particularly after employers' repression, persuaded many women to keep aloof from trade unionism. Thus, in 1898 the Galashiels Textile Workers' Union found it extremely difficult to persuade women to play an active part in trade union affairs.[150] The problem of overcoming the fear of victimisation contributed to the particular instability of trade unionism amongst women. However, the Social Democratic Federation and the Socialist Labour Party toughened the resolve of working women to fight for their rights.[151] Yet, even where no socialist organisation existed, women workers frequently threw up their own leaders. Here is Mary Brooksbank's vivid description of a woman strike leader — a woman whose name she could not remember when she came to write her autobiography — who organised Dundee mill girls in 1911: 'It was during this strike that a young woman came into prominence as a leader of the strikers. She was known as "The lassie wi' the green felt hat". She blew her whistle and gathered the mill girls around her, and, with a half loaf of bread tied round her neck, marched the strikers around the rest of the mills seeking other support. Their united determination won them a rise of 15%'.[152]

Certainly, there is no evidence that Scottish working women ever regarded their employers as 'goblins'. Unlike English women, the Scots did not think of their employers as the living embodiments of the 'evil figures' they were perceived as within the folklore of factory women in England. In the agricultural districts of England, working women were, as Flora Thompson noted in *Lark Rise to Candleford*, taught to 'order themselves "lowly and reverently before their betters"'. In Scotland, 'the humblest' Presbyterian women workers were encouraged to think of themselves as 'equal' citizens. Clearly, the independent identity of Scottish women allowed them to come out on strike without creating the riducule or amusement that occurred in England when striking women workers confronted the 'goblins' who were their employers. Moreover, in contrast to the predominantly English-led British Trades Union Congress, the Scottish Trades Union Congress from its inception in 1897 was much more sympathetic to the cause of organising the womenfolk of the working classes.

A typical case of the prejudice of English trade union leaders towards women workers is quoted in Brougham Villier's book, *The Case for Women's Suffrage:*

> My opinion should have some weight, said the secretary at a Lancashire Trades Council meeting, for I represent by far the biggest union in the town. What's the good of your union said the Engineers' secretary, why it's all women: mine may not be large, but, at all events, they are voters.[153]

Since patriarchal attitudes in present-day Scotland are now frequently said to be worse and more intense than elsewhere in Britain, a historical perspective of the 'hidden history' of Scottish women's militancy and independent identity is particularly useful. Sheila Lewenhak sums up the distinctiveness of the Scottish Labour Movement's attitude towards women: 'One of the distinctive features of the trade union movement in Scotland has been the part women played in the Scottish Trades Union Congress leadership. This included the work of inaugurating the Congress in 1897 since when some women have been intermittently elected to its Parliamentary Committee and later its General Council. In contrast, in the British Trades Union Congress, established in 1868, no woman found her way to the Parliamentary Committee until 1918 when Margaret Bondfield headed the list of unsuccessful candidates in the election and later replaced Fred Bramfield who withdrew after his election'.[154]

In examining the distinctive experience of Scottish and English working-class women within British labour history, it is clear that there was not a necessary concordant between ideas or 'ideologies' and the social structures created by industrial capitalism. The force of cultural tradition was just as important as the capitalist mode of production in shaping the history of working-class women within the United Kingdom.

To recognise the important differences between the experiences of Scottish and English working-class women is not to engage in either chauvinism or criticism about the common heroism of working-class women. The heroism of British women was too real to require exaggeration. It should, however, assist us to appreciate the richness of the British historical experience of women by taking account of George Lichtheim's strictures on those historians whose economic reductionism ignores the complexity of human consciousness in the making of the militancy of working people. When working women in Scotland and England experienced their most confident moments in their struggles against patriarchal capitalism, they shared the assurance of the English poet Thomas Hardy:

> That the rages
> Of the Ages
> Shall be cancelled, and deliverance offered from the darts
> that were,
> Consciousness the Will informing, till it fashion all
> things fair!

5

British Women, Class Struggles and 'Emancipation', 1914-1927

> The war revolutionised the industrial position of women. It not only opened to them opportunities of employment in a number of skilled trades, but, more important than even this, it revolutionised men's minds and their conceptions of the sort of work of which the ordinary everyday woman was capable. It opened men's eyes to forms of work needing only very mediocre intelligence. It also opened their eyes to the national as well as personal values of ordinary domestic work of women which has been in their hands for uncounted generations.[1]

THE FIRST WORLD WAR radicalised both Scottish and English women who were employed in industry. This was observed by B L Hutchins as early as 1915, when she stated that 'women trade unionists, who have long been taxed with apathy and lack of interest in their trade organisations, are drawing from the women's movement a new inspiration and enthusiasm'.[2] In 1914, there were 358,000 women trade unionists. By 1918 there were 'well over a million'.[3] As a consequence of the Restoration of the Pre-War Practices Act in July 1918, and the onslaught of a serious economic depression in the early 1920s, there was a slump in women's membership of trade unions.[4] Nevertheless, women's trade unionism remained 'well above the pre-war figure' and was, as Mary A Hamilton argues in *Mary MacArthur*, 'to a new degree, active and conscious'.[5]

The First World War also had a big influence in changing working women's social values and attitudes. In most Scottish and English towns and cities, working-class women were much less deferential towards their so-called 'betters'. By 1919, government inspectors wrote that 'the stigma which formerly attached and should attach to the receipt of poor relief' was disappearing, and 'there was much less reluctance on the part of the working classes to accept relief than there had been formerly'. In London, many working people had rejected 'The principle of "deterrence" which was accepted without question by the majority of Charles Booth's contemporaries'.[6] The same thing was true in the Scottish coalfields.[7] In a discussion of how these new attitudes were impinging on the consciousness of the Welsh miners, in 1922 J J Astor and A L Bowley wrote:

> The Guardians are continually faced with the demand for "full work or maintenance", and cannot convince the "active" leaders of the workless that full maintenance does not incline men to look for work. This is the old, familiar demand, of which notice would not be taken here were it not that "full work or full maintenance" explains the readiness of many otherwise independent-spirited men to apply to the Guardians. It is a political creed to which thousands in the mining valleys subscribe in all sincerity, and it has no less forceful adherents in Cardiff.[8]

By 1920, most British working-class women were accused of adhering to a 'smouldering, irrational and intemperate socialism'.[9] Certainly the radicalisation produced by the First World War made 'a return to the worst conditions of sweated labour impossible',[10] but, by 1926, the proportion of wage-earning women to the total female population was 'the same as it was in 1911 and in several previous Censuses'.[11] While it is clear that many British working-class women had not been radicalised by the war, a large minority of 'the young and the labouring classes will not accept what once was sufficient'.[12] There was a decline of male chauvinism amongst the men who belonged to the co-operative movement.[13] Certainly, too, the 'rules of sex were greatly relaxed';[14] and there was a diminution of 'the power of the churches and convention'.[15] The 'intemperate' socialism of working-class women was, however, much more evident in Scotland than in England.

The see-sawing elements of continuity and discontinuity in British working-class culture shaped the militancy — and sometimes the lack of militancy — of working-class women. While male trade unionists in England 'demanded the restoration of the monopoly of men in the old traditional trades, they could not succeed with the new ones'.[16] In contrast to the pre-war practice in the mills in the north of England, in the early 1920s, 'there was a growing tendency in the mills not to engage married women'.[17] In 1921, the High Court in England upheld an employer's right to impose fines on factory women who were caught singing at work.[18] Nevertheless, the system of imposing fines on women workers in Scotland and England for singing or bad work was almost extinct.[19]

After the First World War, in Britain as a whole, working-class attitudes towards strikes, birth control, women's role in society, wife-beating and abortion were much less uniform than they had been before the war. There were important differences between the responses of Scottish and English working-class women towards the war itself. Some of these differences were almost certainly reflected in the much greater anti-militarism of the womenfolk of the Scottish working class.

However, if Scottish working-class women were often more aggressive and self-assertive than their English counterparts, the Scots were also prisoners of a more extreme 'respectability', but whether they were 'respectable' or not, they were often viewed unsympathetically by the middle classes. In 1907, T F Henderson and F Watt, unsympathetic authors of a book on contemporary Scotland, described working-class women in Glasgow:

> A large proportion of the occupants of the High Street are women and they are nearly all slatternly. Most of them are comparatively young — even of those that look hopelessly middle-aged. As a rule they are bare-headed, except when their head is covered with a dirty shawl; and if it be summer, and even when it is not summer, some are bare-legged. A few coquettishly sport a fringe. They saunter mostly in twos or threes, or stand gossiping aimlessly in small groups. When the shawl — as often as not of faded tartan — is not made use of as a head-dress, it is thrown around the shoulders, and, more often than not, from the ege of the shawl emerges the dull, dirty, sickly, unsmiling face of a puny infant. . . . Many are quite respectable. The faces of a few are sodden, or rosy and pimpled, with drink. The majority show the discoloured pallor conferred by the crowded slum. Their voices have usually a rusty and raucous tone, whether the accent be touched with the Irish brogue, or the Highland lilt, or the tinker twang of slum-bred Glasgow; and their talk is occasionally spiced with mild womanly oaths.[20]

By the 1920s, Gilbert McAllister, a socialist journalist, was focusing on the new militancy of women in Glasgow in the midst of the most terrible poverty. In spite of women's 'heart-wearing, body-wasting battle against poverty', McAllister was impressed by their 'heroism'.

The class-consiousness of the Scots was certainly heightened during and immediately after the war. This 'dialectical' leap in class-consciousness occurred in a context where Calvinist attitudes were embedded deep in the cultural fabric of Scottish society. The bourgeoisie in Scotland was constantly unsympathetic to investigative journalism and social research. The Scots had not produced a Gramsci or a Labriola and the heightened radical consciousness of the working women was not matched by the sort of critique of society being formulated by Antonio Gramsci in Italy. This contributed to the social and intellectual climate in which 'even the (Scottish) socialist working class had a feudal respect for its "betters"'.[21]

Traditionalism and the cultural 'dominance' of bourgeois ideas over working women were certainly weaker in Scotland than in England. While, before the First World War, the miners had been the most socially conservative and culture-bound group in Britain, Bob Selkirk had no doubt that 'The post-war strikes displayed new features which indicated fundamental changes in the outlook of the (Scottish) miners'.[22] By the end of the war a Birth Control League was active in the Fife coalfields[23] and working-class women throughout Scotland began to play a prominent role in the Labour Movement on a significant scale for the first time since the great days of Chartism. In the town of Armadale, for example, the minority of active women in the local branch of the Independent Labour Party were already agitating for the setting up of a distinctive women's branch.

Both Sylvia Pankhurst and Dora Montefiore had been advocates of women's emancipation before the First World War.[24] By the end of 1918, they were advocating contraception as a means of raising the status and easing the oppressive burden of women — particularly of working-class women — in circumstances where some socialists in the British Labour Movement were opposed to birth control. While John Maclean, the famous Clydeside socialist, did not make any public statements on birth control, he was not influenced by his friends, Sylvia Pankhurst and Dora Montefiore. He retained his orthodox Marxist views on birth control.[25]

Since there has been far too much of a tendency amongst some historians to praise, damn and mythologise the role of socialists in relation to the agitation for birth control and the sexual behaviour of working-class men, we must reconstruct the context in which socialists debated the arguments for and against birth control. In a gross oversimplification of the sexual consequences of the First World War, John Collier and Iain Lang wrote in 1932:

> For the first time expert advice on contraception became readily available to every young man and woman, and Dr Marie Stope's manual on *Married Love* abolished a major risk of unmarried love.[26]

However, at her birth control clinic in London in the early 1920s, Marie

Stopes 'received requests for procuring abortions, mostly from mothers who did not know that abortion was criminal'.[27] While many working-class women adhered to the traditional idea that abortion was a means of 'birth control', Stopes had already (in 1918) argued that 'medical methods of controlling pregnancy consist, not in destroying an already growing embryo, but in preventing the male sperm from reaching the unfertilised egg cell'.[28]

Even in Calvinist Scotland, working-class women in the Socialist Movement were now more interested in sexual questions than they had been before the war. When Margaret Sanger, the American radical, came to Glasgow in 1920 to lecture on birth control, she discovered the emergence of these new attitudes amongst working-class women whose husbands were active socialists. She described it: 'That evening I spoke in a hall under socialist auspices, Guy Aldred acting as chairman. One old-timer said he had been a party member for eleven years, attending Sunday evening lectures regularly, but never before had he been able to induce his wife to come; tonight he could not keep her at home. "Look", he cried in amazement, "The women have crowded the men out of the hall. I never saw so many wives of comrades before."'[29] But they were not representative of the majority of working-class women in Scotland or England. They were the 'vanguard' of the socialist minority who were developing new attitudes towards the question of sexual emancipation.

There was still a great deal of ignorance about sexual questions in most working-class communities in Britain. In some of the tenements in Glasgow incest was believed to be 'common and inevitable'.[30] In England there was much more tolerance for 'extra-marital sexual relations of a non-commercial kind';[31] and 'amateur prostitution' was believed to be 'one of the economic consequences of the peace'.[32]

The 'crimes' of abortion and infanticide were treated less harshly after the war than they had been in the late nineteenth and early twentieth centuries. In an article written in 1892 Henry Salt described the contemporary situation: 'Infanticide — i.e., the killing of an infant by its mother at time of birth. To this very day, to our shame be it said, unhappy girls, who, in the agony and excitement of childbirth, destroy their infants, are, by a Court full of men solemnly sentenced to death, which means — what is worse than death — years of penal servitude'.[33] However, infanticide was regarded as a very serious crime until the formal legal punishment was mitigated in 1922.

In an important book, *Women under the English Law*, written in 1925, Maud Crofts describes the situation: 'Before 1922, a woman, who was found to have wilfully caused the death of her newly-born child, had to be convicted of murder and sentence of death had accordingly to be passed on her. In practice, however, the death sentence was not carried out, and a period of imprisonment (frequently in a criminal lunatic asylum) was substituted'. Under the Infant Life (Preservation) Act of 1929 abortion was treated more leniently than in the past; and prostitution was looked upon with far greater tolerance than ever before. But instead of the ILP examining the economic causes of prostitution in the same detail as the first socialist pioneers had done in the 1880s, they simply asserted that 'Socialism strikes a blow at the very root of prostitution by asking from, and providing for, every woman honourable communal service, the nature of which she is free to choose'.[34]

But choice within a capitalist society always pre-supposes *knowledge* as well as economic freedom, so when Arthur Marwick argues that 'What the war did was to spread promiscuity upwards and birth control downwards',[35] he is simply ignoring the obstacles in the way of the widespread acceptance of birth control by the majority of working-class women. There was, in fact, a great deal of popular prejudice against birth control methods and the Catholic Church was an important source of popular ignorance. In 1918, for example, a Catholic priest accused Marie Stopes of 'experimenting with the poor and of advocating methods of birth control which were known to be physically harmful'.[36]

British socialists themselves were divided over the question of birth control. Elected in 1924, the first 'minority' Labour government was unsympathetic to the agitation for birth control. When a deputation of Labour Members of Parliament, doctors and representatives of the clinic movement asked that 'doctors at maternity and welfare centres should be permitted to give birth control information to mothers who desire it', they had to face the hostility of John Wheatley, the Minister of Health.[37] Wheatley was unrelenting in his opposition and 'until 1930 birth control provision remained in the hands of the voluntary associations which, by that date, had twenty clinics operating throughout the country'.[38]

In an accurate and perceptive assessment of the Scottish socialists' attitudes towards birth control, Eveline Hunter writes:

> Whilst it was actively sought by some of the women's labour organisations many of the socialists were suspicious of the implication that poverty was the fault of the working classes overbreeding rather than economic exploitation.
>
> This view was particularly strong in Clydeside where the famous revolutionary spirit was not matched by an awareness of the oppression of their women. James Maxton and Stephen Campbell as I.L.P. members of Parliament

refused to support the campaign for free contraceptive facilities.

They were right to suspect the motives of some of the campaigners but wrong to ignore the real need and desire for contraception among working-class women.[39]

But Maxton and Campbell (as distinct from Wheatley who adhered to patriarchal conceptions of women's role in society) were not opposed to the general emancipation of working-class women. Moreover, they should not be judged by the standards of the 1980s, especially since the technology for mass contraception did not exist in the 1920s.

Within the context of the international Socialist Movement, the Scots did not produce any advanced thinkers in relation to sexual ideology. They did not, as Eveline Hunter suggests, adopt a very radical stance on the question of birth control. However, it is important to understand why this happened.

Though the Marxists in Scotland had been sympathetic to the struggle for women's political rights since the late nineteenth century, they had always accepted the orthodox Marxist hostility towards such neo-Malthusians as Annie Besant and Margaret Sanger. The important distinction between the orthodox and the unorthodox Marxist attitude to birth control is described by David Kennedy:

> In 1913 Rosa Luxemburg in Germany and Anatole France in France proposed that workers undertake a "birth strike", a cessation of childbearing in order to stop the flow of exploited manpower into the industrial and military machines. Karl Kautsky and other orthodox marxists rebutted those heretical proposals with the classic marxist retort to Malthusian ideas: that a reduction of the proletarian birth-rate would harm socialism by dulling the revolutionary fervour of the working class and weakening its numerical strength.[40]

Since the Scots' Marxist orthodoxy in relation to neo-Malthusianism and birth control had influenced the wider Scottish Labour Movement, including the ILP, since the 1880s and 1890s, the agitation for birth control in the early 1920s was an entirely new development.

While James Maxton and Stephen Campbell were not progressive in relation to the controversial question of birth control, Maxton protested when Guy Aldred, the communist-anarchist already living in Glasgow, was jailed,[41] in 1923, for selling Margaret Sanger's book on *Family Limitation – A Handbook for Working Mothers*.[42] There is also reason to believe that Scottish socialists who were sympathetic to birth control propaganda were much more reticent about sexual questions than their English counterparts.[43] It is surely significant, too, that Aldred was an

Englishman, not a Scot. To make the picture even more complex than that offered by John Collier, Iain Lang and Arthur Marwick, the reader should also be aware of the tensions and opportunism within the birth control movement itself. Thus, Sylvia Pankhurst wrote in her newpaper, the *Workers' Dreadnought:* 'Our sympathy with Dr Stopes is lessened by her letters to *The Nation* defending the prosecution of Bradlaugh and Besant, Margaret Sanger, and the Aldreds for a birth control propaganda which, in effect, is the same as her own'.[44]

Miners in some of the English mining communities seem to have been exceptionally patriarchal in their attitudes towards their womenfolk. It was well-known that 'childless marriages were a source of disquietude in the Rows'; and miners despised those who did not add regularly to the mining population in case the pits should be 'denuded of the young to take the place of those who were killed, crippled or ultimately broken'.[45] These attitudes were commonplace in the English coalfields in the 1920s.[46] By contrast, the Scottish miners, though patriarchal in their attitudes towards women, seem to have modified their attitudes after the war.[47]

Sheila Rowbotham's superb books on women's history have sometimes been slightly vitiated by a tendency to romanticise the behaviour of English working men. She argues that 'It was not their unkindness or insensitivity but sheer ignorance which prevented them from understanding the women's attitudes to sex. It was the same with contraception'.[48] But English working men, whether they were artisans or unskilled workers, were still displaying 'primitive ideas on marital rights'.[49] Moreover, 'most (English) working-class men seem to think that the use of preventives is bad for them; the idea that it caused consumption is pretty general'.[50] Much of this comment by Eleanor F Rathbone and Margaret L Eyles was based on acknowledged oral testimony. But in their almost total indifference to the fate and experience of the Scottish working class, the bourgeoisie in Scotland could not produce any Rathbones, Eyles, Pankhursts or Montefiores. There is no reason to assume that most Scottish working-class men were any more sexually enlightened than their English counterparts.

One index to the improved status of British working-class women after the First World War was their much greater participation in trade unions and socialist organisations, but far from the war lifting English working-class women out of 'the anonymity of a species' and setting 'them free',[51] there was actually a considerable increase in the incidence of wife-beating and legal separations. Indeed, a report on civil and judicial statistics for England and Wales asserted that working-class 'women who were ill-treated by their husbands often formerly went no further than applying for their husbands to be bound over, or at furthest prosecuting for assault, they are nowadays more inclined, or are more often advised, to go at once on similar facts for separation and maintainance orders'.[52] While the correlation between wife-beating and legal separations in England was probably not as simple and uncomplicated as those who compiled the civil and judicial statistics believed, the statistics do at least throw doubt on the argument that working-class women were *emancipated* as a result of the war.

It ought to be pointed out that the increase in the incidence of wife-beating in England occurred within a context in which there was a decline in 'the number of crimes of violence'.[53] In an interesting essay dealing with *The Facts of Poverty in England*, H A Mess argues that wife-beating and cruelty to children are largely due to drink',[54] but it was being increasingly recognised that drunkenness was only one factor among many. In a report of a conference on Christian Politics, Economics and Citizenship held in 1924, the authors of the conference report argue:

> Bad housing conditions contribute to many offences — assaults on women and girls, incest, cruelty. Drink too is responsible for many assaults and other offences against the person, though drunkenness is often a symptom of underlying causes rather than itself a cause.[55]

In Britain as a whole, the causes of wife-beating were very complex. Cultural factors were probably more important than economic ones in explaining the differences in the status of Scottish and English working-class women. There was a tendency for some observers of the English scene to exaggerate the extent of the *emancipation* of working-class women in the 1920s. Sometimes the *class* dimension of the experiences of English women was ignored. In 1923, for example, Arnold Bennett wrote thus:

> But something has been accomplished; and the husband had lost some of the tyrannic power by virtue of which he used to be master in his own house. He cannot, for example, now beat his wife with impunity, nor can he lay hold on her private property, and in sundry other ways his claws have been clipped.[56]

Some police magistrates in England, however, persisted in displaying the extreme patriarchal attitudes that were so prominent in their pre-war courtrooms.

In a study of the English police court and its work, one English police magistrate said he was 'perplexed to know what on earth he should say' to working-class women who were beaten by their husbands. Even so, he had no hesitation in refusing them legal separations.[57] In 1932, in a book dealing with *The Case Against the English Divorce Law*, Alfred Fellows lamented the fact that a working man had no redress against an incompetent wife 'apart from beating her'.[58] It is within this context that the role of drink as a cause of wife-beating is sometimes exaggerated. Some police magistrates and many working-class men in England believed in the male's inalienable right to punish his wife. Drink was often a factor, but women could be — and were — beaten by husbands whose sobriety was not in question, as Hermann Mannheim puts it: 'Whilst for the Welsh district of Pontypridd and Rhondda it was stated before the Royal Commission that a high percentage of assaults on women and children had been committed under the influence of drink, a comparison between the rates of drunkenness convictions and those persons prosecuted for assaults in various other districts (of England) shows that the figures do not always move in the same direction'.[59]

By examining the problem of wife-beating in Scotland during the 1920s, it will become clear that a crude 'economistic' analysis of wife-beating is not very helpful. Such an analysis cannot illuminate, for example, the distinctive militancy and experiences of Scottish and English working-class women. In the first place, the Parliamentary volumes of Scottish civil and judicial statistics no longer gave details of the incidence of wife-beating (as distinct from general assaults). Secondly, the bourgeoisie in Scotland was still unwilling to investigate social problems on a significant or adequate scale. However, one consequence of the First World War was that wife-beating in Scotland was beginning to be recognised as a social problem. In an article written in 1923, James Leatham commented on the widespread problem of wife-beating in working-class communities in Glasgow before the war,[60] but this was a retrospective comment, probably influenced by the new social and intellectual climate of opinion in the early 1920s. It is very important to recall the fact that wife-beating was not discussed in the Scottish (as distinct from the English) Labour Movement before the First World War.[61]

In *The Children of the Unskilled*, a careful study of the families of unskilled workers in a Scottish, a Welsh and an English working-class community after the war, E Llewelyn Lewis observes that the problem of wife-beating had to be tackled by means of 'the tactful interference of police-officers, Salvation Army men and others'.[62] He did not discover any evidence to suggest that wife-beating was any worse in Glasgow — an area of severe unemployment — than in Middlesbrough. This is particularly interesting in the light of Stuart Macintyre's unconvincing assertion that wife-beating was a major social problem in the Fife coalfields. While arguing that wife-beating was much worse in Lumphinnans and the Vale of Leven than in Mardy, Macintyre also articulates a more general impression that 'Domestic violence was therefore one more symptom of the increased incidence of marital breakdown that observers noted among the depressed areas'.[63] On the basis of the existing evidence, it is simply not accurate to make this sort of generalisation about wife-beating in British mining communities. Though it is true that divorces in Scotland increased after the war, the cultural inhibitions induced within the Scottish working class by the Presbyterian ethos was the reason for the fact that there were only forty-two legal separations in 1920.[64] It is, therefore, clear that 'marital breakdown' was not prominent in the Scottish mining communities. Yet the lives of the women in the Scottish mining communities were not rosy.

The distinctive cultural traditions of the Scottish past continued to impinge on the consciousness of working-class women in conditions where women generally were more radical and self-assertive than ever before. While there was still evidence of Scottish working-class women being 'strong personalities and characters',[65] women were frequently obsessed with 'Keeping Up Appearances'.[66] Bob Selkirk, the veteran Fife socialist miner, had no doubt that there was a marked decline in patriarchal authority in miners' families after the First World War. There is also evidence that at least one Scottish Sheriff did not regard repeated wife-beating as grounds for legal separation,[67] and that the pre-war socialist Left in Fife coalfields was much more critical of miners who beat their wives than the communists were in the 1920s.[68] The firmest evidence of the higher status and greater self-assertion of the Scottish than English working class was displayed during and after the war at the point of production in the factories, mills and workshops.

Moreover, Stuart Macintyre's argument that 'the vigorous hostility of the Communist leaders' in Lumphinnans, the Vale of Leven and Mardy towards wife-beating actually mitigated violence against women ignores the differences in the cultural attitudes of the pre-war and the post-war socialist Left in the coalfields.[69] The different socialist attitudes towards personal relationships before and after 1917 are described by Sheila Rowbotham in Beyond the Fragments.[70] This was particularly evident in such Fife mining communities as Lochgelly, Lumphinnans and Cowdenbeath.

Before the First World War, the Socialist Movement had actively campaigned against wife-beating. Members of Fife socialist groups were expelled for beating their wives. With the advent of the Communist Party, there was a new tendency for 'socialists' to depict wife-beating amongst the miners as, in Macintyre's own idiom, 'simply misplaced antagonism arising from work conditions' in the pits.[71] By contrast with such pre-war socialist activists as Lawrence Storione and Bob Selkirk,[72] the communists were actually much less critical of working men who assaulted their wives. How far these changed socialist attitudes towards wife-beating contributed to any increase in the incidence of assaults on wives is a matter for speculation.

While it is sometimes suggested that the British suffrage organisations did not disintegrate under the impact of the First World War,[73] no-one has convincingly refuted Martin Pugh's argument to the contrary.[74] With the disintegration of the suffrage organisations in Scotland and England, the pre-war leaders of the agitation for 'votes for women' became increasingly polarised between those who were pro-war and those who were anti-militarists. At the very beginning of the war, Helen Crawfurd joined forces with John Maclean and soon played a major role in the famous rent strike on Clydeside.[75]

In contrast to what happened in England, the Labour Movement in Scotland became even more sympathetic to women's agitations for equality than they had been before the outbreak of the war. This was admittedly only a difference of emphasis. However, the role of the Scottish working-class women during and after the war helped to reinforce the general image of *Red Clydeside*. With the increasing evidence of working-class women's militancy and the disintegration of the middle-class suffrage organisations, the Scots now gave much greater attention to the 'woman question' than ever before. In an article on *The Position of Women after the War* published in *The Vanguard* in 1915, James D MacDougall wrote:

> As women enter into production in huger and huger numbers; as they take their place alongside of men, their importance to society will come to be more fully realised. Not merely as producers of wealth but as producers of men. Women themselves will become more conscious of the decisive part that they play in human development, and will no longer be content to sit at the feet of the male sex, or should we say remain under the heel? They will arise in their power and demand their rightful position as equal friends and comrades of men. Then there will be no question of treating women as inferiors by refusing them the vote or in any other way.[76]

In the major Scottish towns and cities — and not just on Clydeside — working-class women became increasingly active and vocal in trade unions, socialist organisations and housing committees. In various English towns and cities working-class women also agitated over such issues as appalling housing conditions and high rents. Discontent over housing in England was a major factor in radicalising working people of both sexes.[77] The Scottish women were more militant and self-assertive than their English counterparts. Thus, the first women's branch of the Independent Labour Party in Britain was formed in the small Scottish industrial town of Armadale.[78]

Nevertheless, Scottish working-class women were much more integrated into the Labour Movement than English women were. Anti-militarism dominated the Scottish Labour Movement from the beginning of the war at a time when the Glasgow suffragists began to visit 'babies in a whole ward of the city and in other towns started day nurseries'.[79] What gave anti-militarism in Scotland a mass popular base was the vocal opposition of working-class women. In an acknowledgement of this important difference between what happened in Scotland and England, Helen R Vernon says that 'The traditional Scottish distrust of British institutions and English rule may have had something to do with this'.[80]

The contrast with the activities of the militant socialist women in London was very marked. While it is true that Sylvia Pankhurst's East London Federation of Suffragettes 'showed a great ingenuity in organising',[81] they were remote from the lives of ordinary working-class women. They were doing the same work as the suffragists in Glasgow, but they did not have a single delegate who 'was born and bred in East London'. As a friend of John Maclean, Sylvia Pankhurst became very aware of the differences between the Labour Movements in London and Glasgow. In January 1916, she had spoken at various meetings of radical working women on Clydeside and she and Miss Smyth reported to their organisation:

> Miss Pankhurst said that when she was in Glasgow she found that the Independent Labour Party took a big theatre every Sunday, charged for admission and made enough out of the meetings to run the whole branch. . . . Miss Smyth pointed out that in addition the I.L.P. were able to pay a speaker's expenses from London and it was only a working class organisation.[82]

Even in 1919 Sylvia Pankhurst's Women's Suffrage Federation was still 'gathering cast off clothes for children' in London.[83]

In 1915 a growing number of working-class women in Britain were determined that they were going to secure the right to vote in Parliamentary elections,[84] but there was much more male chauvinism in

England than in Scotland. Margaret L Eyles, who was well-informed and sensitive to the nuances of English working-class behaviour, wrote in 1922:

> Dr Marion Mackenzie, writing in "Time and Tide", quotes the case of a Yorkshireman who argued that women should not have the vote because men did all the work. She asked him if he were married — he was and had twelve children; his wife did all the sewing, washing and nursing for the fourteen of them. But she could not make him see that his wife earned anything.[85]

The Scots had already taken the lead in agitating for the full equal suffrage. This demand was again supported at a Scottish miners' conference on women's rights.[86] Soon afterwards the Scots (in March 1917) pushed for this demand to be adopted as Labour Party policy at a British conference on women's suffrage. The Scots were defeated, because most of the English delegates wanted women's suffrage to be based on age and property qualifications.[87] The unevenness in the class-consciousness and 'egalitarianism' of the Scots and the English was also witnessed after the war.

Scottish and English women were radicalised by the complex processes unleashed by the First World War. However, there was much more *mass* disaffection amongst the Scottish than the English working-class women. This was already evident in Glasgow during the women's mass *political* strike against exorbitant rents. As resentment against landlords became intermingled with anti-war feelings, mass disaffection forced the authorities in London to introduce emergency legislation in the form of the Rent Restriction Act of 1915.[88]

The many rent strikes that occurred in Scottish and English towns and cities in 1915 are carefully documented by Ann and Vincent Flynn,[89] but the fact remains that no other major city in England was as disaffected as Glasgow between 1914 and 1922. Before the war was over, many other Scottish towns were just as radical and disaffected as Glasgow. Not only were there 'little Moscows' in such Fife coaltowns as Cowdenbeath and Lochgelly. There were other such Scottish towns as Motherwell,[90] Coatbridge, Hamilton, Airdrie, Falkirk,[91] and Dundee. Glasgow, however, was undoubtedly the spearhead of revolutionary socialism in Britain during the early phase of the war. The reasons for the distinctiveness of organised — and, indeed, unorganised — the labour on Clydeside, therefore, need to be analysed.

The lateness and the abruptness of the process of industrialisation on Clydeside and the constant influx of dispossessed Highlanders before and during the war were important factors in the disaffection of working-class women.[92] In a very perceptive comment on the first of these reasons, Walter Kendall argues:

> Yet the growth of industry was sufficiently novel for its arrival to be remembered, its growth checked and annotated. To the Clydeside workers industrialism did not appear as the God-given and inevitable environment of mankind but rather as one phenonemon amongst others, changing and changeable, fit to be moulded by their hands, as it has been by others. Large-scale industry, growth of population, a proletariat still in the process of training for new processes, all these factors were also to be found in St Petersburg, and like Russia's capital, Glasgow, too, began a revolutionary wave.[93]

One need not accept the late C Wright Mills' argument that a proletariat is only revolutionary during its formative period of evolution to see the relevance of Kendall's insight. But an equally important reason was the role of *socialist educators* both inside and outside the factories, mills and workshops.[94]

The process of radicalisation was not, however, an uninterrupted one. By the summer of 1916 'the militant Labour Movement on the Clyde reached its lowest ebb'. The extensive repression and the reasons for the revival of militancy by the summer of 1917 are summed up by Helen R Vernon:

> Socialist agitators had been either imprisoned or deported from the trouble centre, and Glasgow sank back into industrial and political apathy. But in the long-run the Governments reliance on strong-arm tactics did more for the socialist movement in the west of Scotland than years of revolutionary propaganda, for it caused a deep-rooted resentment amongst many sections of the population and reinforced the ingrained suspicion of authority.[95]

By 1917 there was a national strike of women who were employed in the Scottish dressmaking and millinery trades.[96] Occurring as it did during the war itself, it was viewed by the authorities as another expression of the disaffection of many Scottish working-class women.

The mass support for the May Day demonstration in Glasgow in 1917 was also a precursor of what was to come. What happened in the west of Scotland was unique. In 1918, the Labour Movement in London decided to combine a celebration of May Day on the first Sunday of the month with a recognition of the centenary of the birth of Karl Marx. The proposed meeting in London was banned by the Home Secretary, although three hundred people turned up to defy the ban before they were brutally attacked by mounted policemen.[97] However, in the midst of the war, the Labour Movement on Clydeside decided to abandon their traditional practice of celebrating May Day as a day of international solidarity on the first Sunday in May. In contrast to the Labour Movement in England, the Clydesiders decided to celebrate May Day on the glorious first of May.

At a time when the newspapers were censoring news reports of socialist industrial or political activity, the Establishment conducted a systematic campaign against working women, who were proposing to take the day off work without pay, and as a result halting war production, to celebrate May Day, the Russian revolution and the struggle for socialist internationalism. Even the hostile *Glasgow Herald* was forced to admit that over 100,000 working people took part in the procession through the streets of Glasgow.[98] In a note of triumph, the editor of the Glasgow socialist newspaper, *Forward*, argued that despite 'the appeals to "patriotism", working-class women as well as the men came out on strike'.[99]

Before the First World War, the Labour Movement on Clydeside had really been unrepresentative of working people as a whole. Such factors as the behaviour of rapacious landlords and employers, the impact of the war, the Russian revolution and systematic socialist education in the factories and communities were behind the colourful radicalisation of the Labour Movement in the west of Scotland and beyond the Highland Line. There is a marked similarity between what happened on Clydeside from 1914 onwards and Eric Hobsbawm's description of the experience of the French Labour Movement:

> The impact of the war and the Russian revolution must be traced by parallel enquiries into the evolution of the working class and the loosely organised and sometimes unrepresentative minority which made up the French labour movement. The distinction is important, because the very fragility, instability of the French labour movement may have made the appeal of the revolutionary parties after the war greater in countries in which the labour movement was more representative of the masses.[100]

In any case, such Scottish newspapers as the *Glasgow Herald* continued to be struck by the mass participation of working-class women in May Day parades and demonstrations in Glasgow in the early 1920s.

In contrast to the working women in England who accepted the Restoration of the Pre-War Practices Act in 1918, the women of the Red Clyde took part in a huge march in Glasgow to protest against their dismissal from the munitions and other factories and workshops.[101]

Since this struggle was, like the struggle against excessive rents in 1915, a women's struggle, it is clear that the Clydeside women were acting as independent, autonomous human beings rather than as mouthpieces for a patriarchal Labour Movement. May Day was, moreover, celebrated on the first of May until 1924 when the traditional pre-war practice of celebrating May Day on the first Sunday in May was reverted to.

In 1919, 1920 and 1921 the *Glasgow Herald* noted that working-class women and children were in the forefront of the May Day celebrations.[102] By 1920, there was also a general stoppage of work in such Scottish towns as Greenock, West Calder, Falkirk and Hamilton.[103] By 1923, much of the revolutionary fervour of the previous years had gone and the *Glasgow Herald* gloated over what it depicted as the 'poor turn out' of the dissident elements in working-class communities. Even so, the *Glasgow Herald* noted that a number of 'unemployed women' played a prominent part in the May Day demonstrations.[104] From 1921, the Labour Movement on Clydeside and elsewhere in Scotland was engaged in a struggle against the problems imposed on working people by mass unemployment. While the Scottish Labour Movement was now much less optimistic than it had been during and immediately after the war, it would be a mistake to assume that it became apathetic.

Organised labour was militant in England, too. In London in 1922 'a crowd of thousands of unemployed had rioted and fought with police in Whitehall'.[105] C F G Masterman, a Liberal politician who was by no means particularly sympathetic to organised labour, argued in 1920 that 'the unprecedented power' of English trade unionism 'has made more impression than ever before on the middle classes and women'.[106] Nevertheless, there was much more hostility to the notion of organising women workers in England than in Scotland.[107] While patriarchal attitudes were most certainly present in the Scottish Labour Movement, English socialists and trade unionists seem to have been more élitist in their attitudes towards women.[108]

While patriarchal attitudes were prevalent in both Scottish and English towns and cities, they were more extensive and intense in England. The radicalisation of the Red Clydeside had a profound effect in raising the status and expectations of working-class women. There was much more of 'a "matriarchal" strain' in Scottish than in English working-class communities. The attitude of working men in the towns and cities of England was described in 1926 by Leonora Eyles in her stimulating book, *Women's Problems of Today*:

> I have heard it said by working men that they have no
> pleasure in life but "beer and the missus", and this, I think, is

> typical of most working men except true socialists. Most
> wives seem to be domestic drudges, wage-earners, child-
> bearers and ministers to their husbands' physical appetites.
> They are not loved for themselves, but for their usefulness.[109]

Patriarchal attitudes were even worse in the English mining communities. Most English miners believed that women were only 'worth keeping because of their craft'.[110]

After 1922, as the revolutionary socialism that had strengthened the Labour Movement on Clydeside began to weaken, the whole of the Labour Movement in Britain increasingly focused its attention on the problems arising from mass unemployment. Once again the previous radicalisation of working-class women in Scotland gave a new impetus to the agitation against unemployment and for 'work or full maintenance'. While these agitations occurred in a wide variety of Scottish and English towns and cities, the Scots seemed to have attracted more support from women than their English counterparts. Miners' wives in Fife and factory women in Dundee were particularly active in the unemployed agitations.[111] When Jock Thomson, the leader of the Dundee branch of the National Unemployed Workers' Committee, died in 1923, '100,000 people followed him to the Eastern Cemetary'.[112] The new dimension of the class struggle in Scotland was the greater prominence of rank-and-file women such as Mary Brooksbank in Dundee and Mary Docherty in Cowdenbeath.[113]

With the onslaught of the economic depression, employers were in a much stronger position to intimidate working women than they had been during the war. One consequence was that there were fewer strikes of working women in Britain as a whole in the 1920s, than during the decade before 1914. Nevertheless, strikes did take place in Scottish factories and mills. In 1921, for example, there were prolonged strikes of women textile workers in Dunfermline and Tillicoultry.[114] Instead of coming out on strike women — and men — concentrated on go-slows, ca'canny working practices and mass demonstrations against unemployment.

Descriptions of the new mood of militancy and discontent in the factories, mills and workshops abound in the literature produced by working people. In an analysis of a strike in a factory in Newcastle in 1920, R M Fox describes the new attitudes of women and men before the strike was 'killed' by a trade union organiser:

> They were sick of the monotony. Individually they often
> went "on the booze"; collectively, they wanted to strike.
> Work pressed too heavily on their lives; they wanted some
> change, any change, no matter what it might be.[115]

Even 'uneducated and ignorant (sic!) workers' who passed their 'lives groping in darkness' were much more willing to resist management speed-ups and factory discipline than ever before.[116]

Throughout the 1920s, women workers articulated their conscious opposition to the 'monotonous routine' of factory life imposed by the technique of scientific management.[117] The level of militancy of working women in the factories and mills was to some extent dictated by the presence — or absence — of militant socialists. Certainly, discontent was widespread in factories and workshops even in those where trade unionists were numerically weak and politically inarticulate. In an extremely interesting book, *The Woman in the Little House*, Margaret L Eyles ascribes the 'labour unrest' in most of the English factories to apolitical, vaguely discontented and inarticulate workers.[118] In contrast to Margaret L Eyles, who was describing social tensions from the outside, Mary Brooksbank subsequently wrote about her experience in a chocolate factory in Dundee:

> Of course, I got my books that afternoon. I heard one of the
> girls in passing with her tray of chocolate remark "Hear!
> Hear", Mary, "English Rats". I did not understand this
> remark at the time, but learned later that many of the
> overseers had been displaced and Englishmen had been sent
> in their places. They were not popular with the workers.[119]

Moreover, working-class women played a major role in the General Strike of 1926. They were particularly active in the committee rooms and regional Councils of Action and Trades Councils. While most of the surviving photographs of the General Strike portray women in the subservient role of those who served tea, sandwiches and soup, women were often just as militant as men. The militancy of the women in the Scottish coalfields was especially constant, forceful and angry.

In the 1920s, poverty was much worse in the mining communities than it was in other working-class communities. This point was made, in 1925, by A L Bowley, and M H Hogg when they concluded that 'The general reduction of poverty, evidenced in the industrial towns, has not taken place in the coal districts'.[120] During the General Strike itself, Lesley Baily observed miners' children going to the elementary schools in the north of England with 'gaping holes in their boots'. Yet, they were 'not the worst cases'.[121] In *Women and the Miners*, a touching and compassionate description written in 1927 of the poverty of the mining families in Britain as a whole, Marion Philips wrote:

> Occasionally a woman was found wearing her husband's
> coat, and in one case between them they had one pair of
> boots. At the beginning of the winter a little girl in

> Derbyshire was attending school in a thin cotton dress
> without sleeves, as these had been taken out to patch the skirt.[122]

But much of the militancy of the miners and their womenfolk was
motivated by deep socialist convictions as well as desperate poverty.

The General Strike of 1926 was of decisive importance in the history of
British working-class women. An increasing number of working
women were being pushed out of the trade unions by the end of the war
and the situation was not improved by Mary MacArthur's decision to
incorporate the National Federation of Women Workers into the
National Union of General Workers. She also arranged for the
remaining functions of Women's Trade Union League to be taken over
by the new General Council of the British Trades Union Congress.[123]
This happened in England at a time when male trade unions believed
that 'women should not be allowed to remain in most of their new lines
of work'.[124] And working-class women's activity in the Labour
Movement was increasingly challenged by male trade unionists who
tried to impose their own patriarchal conceptions of women's role in
society on the Labour Movement.

The tendency to revert to traditional patriarchal perceptions of the
women's role was even articulated in some of the Fife branches of the
Communist Party; but, in Fife, socialists like Bob Selkirk and Mary
Docherty, who had been influenced by militant libertarian socialist
ideas before the war, agitated for women's right to participate in the
activities of the Labour Movement as equals. Elsewhere in Britain,
there was a marked tendency for working-class women to lose some of
the rights that had been won before 1914. After the failure of the
General Strike, women trade unionists were only allowed a fringe
meeting during the proceedings of the British Trades Union Congress.
Miss Ellen Wilkinson, MP, protested against the disbandment of the
Women's Trade Union League and Miss House, a prominent trade
unionist, said 'the agenda savoured of a happy evening for the poor'.[125]
This was the context in which it was asserted in a Communist Party
pamphlet that 'The idea of "strikes" and "politics" is very obnoxious to
the women and especially the girls of the (English) working class'.[126]

A simplistic Marxist interpretation of the history of the British
working-class women must inevitably obscure the important and
distinctive cultural differences in the status, expectations and militancy
of the Scots and the English. What Arthur Gleason wrote about English
women in 1920 when he asserted that 'Inferior status has been and
continues to be the position of women'[127] was less true in Scotland when
viewed from a less narrowly economistic perspective. The famous

Clydeside radicalism contributed to the process of drawing increasing numbers of women into such organisations as the Socialist Labour Party, the Independent Labour Party and the Scottish Workers' Republican Party. Without the mass involvement of women on Clydeside and in other parts of Scotland, the Labour Movement would not have been so radical and outward-looking.[128]

Working-class women were very prominent in the General Strike. With the disbandment of the National Federation of Women Workers and the Women's Trade Union League, women's distinctive feminist interests were abandoned. While it is true that 'The completeness of the stoppage (in 1926) was a remarkable tribute to the strength and discipline of the movement',[129] working-class women in Britain as a whole, though less oppressed than before the First World War, were again being forced to fit into the needs of a patriarchal, capitalist economy. R M Fox was soon to whistle in the dark by asserting that 'Today no-one on the side of the working class doubts its coming victory. The only question is how and when the victory will come'.[130]

By 1927, the tragic reality was that 'After the collapse of the General Strike political conservatism was higher in prestige and authority than it had been for twenty years'.[131] The real lesson of history is that defeats are often a necessary pre-condition for the ultimate emancipation of the oppressed, whether they are women, national minorities or colonial peoples, under the heel of an iron dictatorship or of a Parliamentary democracy vitiated by such legislation as the crippling Trade Disputes Act.

6

Images of Women

DESPITE SCOTTISH WOMEN'S persistent role in popular struggles, they did not make any permanent imprint on the dominant culture. In an important essay on *Peripheries and the Core* (or the historical relationship between Scottish and English culture), Cairns Craig says:

> To live on the periphery of a major culture or on the periphery of Europe is almost inevitably to be parochial. And the consequence is self-hatred. . . . And the self-hatred is not just a psychological phenomenon: it is projected outwards upon the whole cultural field. In Scotland our cultural analysis is obsessed with images of self-hatred.[1]

By offering this sharp insight into the condition of the Scotland question, Craig identifies at least some of the reasons for the dominant images of Scottish women as largely passive victims of fate.

By comparison with their English counterparts, Scottish women have played an inordinately prominent role in popular struggles since the Reformation. Yet, the gap between Scottish women's place in the continuum of popular struggles and the images of their 'docility' in the dominant culture since at least the mid-Victorian years prompts the question, why? The major reasons were: the relationship between the periphery and the core; the absence of a radical tradition of social criticism; the comparative weakness of the middle-class Women's Movement; and the images of women fostered by Kailyard novels.

Moreover, from 1850 to the 1930s, there was a large hiatus between Scottish women's role in popular struggles and their portrayal in imaginative literature. In acknowledging this problem in Kailyard and anti-Kailyard novels, Ian Campbell says:

> Something else is missing in (George Douglas Brown's novel, *The House with the Green Shutters*); sympathetic women are woefully few in Brown's novel, the baker's wife who makes an all-too-brief appearance being almost the only

case. . . . Here there is more parody of Kailyard values, but
the relative absence of women characters from the Kailyard
is typical certainly of Ian Maclaren's sketches; even J. M.
Barrie's engaging Leeby and Jess rule the roost at home, but
outside are subservient to a Henry whom privately they
henpeck mercilessly. In such a society change comes slowly.
Patriarchal figures hold sway . . .[2]

But, despite the considerable advances made between 1880 and the early
1920s by British women towards the goal of emancipation, a reaction
soon set in. By the mid-1920s, there was throughout Britain, as Gail
Braybon suggests, 'much propaganda about the joys of domesticity and
the role of the housewife'. Although between 1915 and the early 1920s
the British Labour Movement was more sympathetic to new
conceptions of women's role in society, it soon accepted the dominant
patriarchal view that 'women's duties and interests lay in the home'.[3]

During the years between 1915 and the early 1920s, the Scottish
labour movement did not adopt the view that 'the woman's place was in
the home'. Indeed, it broke completely with such patriarchal
conceptions of women's role in society. It was, in fact, very progressive
in supporting the struggle for women's liberation — except in relation
to directly sexual questions.

Unfortunately, Willa Muir did *not* portray the rich history of Scottish
working-class women betweeen 1915 and 1925 in her writings on 'the
woman question' — a period when working-class women played a
particularly conspicuous role in the Labour Movement as the equals of
men. As a passionate socialist feminist, who wanted to rouse women to
struggle for their own liberation, she tried to expose the historical roots
of male chauvinism in Scottish society by focusing on the negative (as
distinct from the positive) features of 'Knoxian theology'.

By the 1930s, the oppression of British women was probably worse
than it had been in the 1920s. In Scotland a resurgent patriarchal
capitalism and the advent of Leninist dogmas from the mid-1920s
destroyed the previous liberal-socialist culture in which working-class
women had played a role as equals. There is no reason to doubt the
accuracy of Willa Muir's comment about the position of Scottish
women in 1936:

> Scotland, taken by and large, is, I suppose, a socialist
> country. Yet it is difficult to speak of women's movements in
> Scotland, since most Scottish working-class women — and
> men, too — are dominated by the belief that outside the
> home men have all "the say". But a Scotswoman who is too
> timid to utter a word in public may tongue-lash her family in
> private with great efficiency.[4]

Moreover, the relative passivity of British working-class women in the 1930s was partly a consequence of political defeats and the advent of Stalinist attitudes towards women.

In recent years the legacy of Kailyard literature and the absence of a radical tradition of social criticism within a society basically hostile to women have had a strong influence in weakening the confidence of potentially radical women. Although Stephen Maxwell claims that 'the absence of a more assertive movement for women's rights in Scotland remains a mystery', Sally O'Sullivan has produced a more searching analysis of why women's liberation is 'passing Scotland by'. One of the most interesting comments in O'Sullivan's essay is Chris Aldred's remark that 'Scotland has always been a relatively poor country, hence when it comes to the women's movement, we are behind'.[5] This echoes the analysis developed in 1935 by Eunice Murray in her book, *A Gallery of Scottish Women*.[6]

It is, however, paradoxical that women in 'backward' countries have usually been inordinately militant and conspicuous in popular struggles. But after the mid-1930s British women ceased to play a major role in political struggles. In Scotland women's agitation was largely restricted to the minority of working-class women who participated in strikes.

In recent years, Scottish socialist-feminists have faced distinctive problems. In contrast to the resurgence of women's literature and other writings in England, Scottish women could not get published. In the 1950s and 60s, when Helen Crawford tried to get Lawrence and Wishart to publish her autobiography, it was rejected on allegedly 'stylistic' grounds.[7] In the 1960s, Mary Brooksbank had similar difficulties in finding a publisher for her autobiography. In 1974, she published a thin volume of autobiography, *No Sae Lang Syne: A Tale of This City* and a volume of poetry, *Sidlaw Breezes*, at her own expense. Mary Docherty, the veteran Fife Communist, has not yet found a publisher for her fascinating autobiography.

When the well-documented, best-seller, *The Red Paper on Scotland*, appeared in 1975, it did not contain one essay on feminism or women's role in Scottish society and not one of its twenty-nine contributors was a woman. The Scots also failed to produce anything comparable to the collection of essays entitled *Beyond the Fragments: Feminism and the Making of Socialism* by Sheila Rowbotham, Lynne Segal and Hilary Wainwright. From 1979-1981, *Beyond the Fragments* was a best-seller in England.

The hiatus between the dominant images of Scottish women and their actual historical role in popular struggles reinforces contemporary women's sense of powerlessness; but it was not always like that.

In Scottish journalism, imaginative literature and historiography 'lower-class' women have been repeatedly portrayed as more passive, oppressed, downtrodden, abused and 'slatternly' than their English counterparts. In the dominant contemporary and historical literature, the images of Scottish women are images of women as the largely *passive* victims of a vicious witch-hunting, Calvinist misogyny. This witch-hunting, Calvinist misognyny has allegedly enjoyed an unbroken continuity within Scottish society from the sixteenth century to the present. It is, however, a major paradox that these widely-fostered images of Scotland as an almost uniquely misogynistic nation within modern Europe co-exist with a vague consciousness of the much greater militancy of Scottish than English 'lower-class' women.

These erroneous images of women in Scottish history were not invented by ruling-class conspirators. They were the outcome of the interaction of diverse and disparate social, cultural, intellectual and historical forces in Scottish life and letters. Whether Scottish historians, sociologists and other commentators have belonged — or indeed belong — to the right or the left, or whether they are nationalists or anti-nationalists, they have usually portrayed 'lower-class' women as the total victims of an oppressive Calvinistic misogyny.

Although the struggles of British plebeian and working-class women have been hidden from history, the struggles of Scottish women were less fragmented and episodical than those of their English counterparts. However, the popular struggles of English women have received much more attention from British labour historians, dramatists, poets and feminists.

Before I return to analyse the reasons for the virtual disappearance of the struggles of Scottish 'lower-class' women from imaginative literature, investigative journalism and historiography, it must be emphasised that the considerable intellectual achievements of middle-class women have also been largely ignored. Moreover, Scottish intellectuals of a *nationalist* persuasion have often fostered the most condescending images of women's role in history. Thus, Stephen Maxwell contributes to the process of reinforcing the hidden history of Scottish middle-class women by stating: 'In the eighteenth and nineteenth centuries the failure of Scotswomen to match the intellectual and literary achievements of such English women as Jane Austen, George Eliot or Mrs Gaskell might be attributed to the untimely survival of Scottish theocracy'.[8]

Scotland was in quite significant ways more liberal than England in relation to women's long-drawn-out and unfinished struggles for emancipation throughout the eighteenth and nineteenth centuries. What the Reformation did was to initiate a complex historical process

— a long process interrupted by persistent starts and stops — in which Scottish women acquired a higher legal status than their English sisters. It also created a passion for education amongst Scottish women in all social classes.

Although they did not function within nineteenth-century Scotland, such important socialist-feminists as Frances Wright and Helen Macfarlane came out of a liberal Scottish milieu. The Scots also produced Catherine Sinclair, of whom Eunice G Murray said: 'She was a bright and witty writer, and showed skill in characterisation and description. She was interested in the beginnings of the demand for education for women, a subject beginning to rouse thought amongst the more advanced minds of the time. She wrote *Modern Accomplishments, or the March of the Intellect*, a study of female education, 1832'.[9] Though Catherine Sinclair did not display the same powerful talent as the English women novelists cited by Stephen Maxwell, it is clear that Scottish theocracy did not suppress women's literary and intellectual activities.

The major factor in Scottish intellectual history was, in Christopher Harvey's view, the lack of a *national centre*. Consequently, the Scottish intelligentsia was divided between two loyalties — 'the red' and 'the black'. In contrast to 'the cosmopolitan, enlightened red Scots', the 'black Scots were demotic, parochial and reactionary'. In endorsing this characterisation of Scottish intellectual history, Tom Nairn has contrasted 'the red outward-bound strain in the Scottish intelligentsia' with 'the black stay-at-home one'. Though these insights should not be used without some qualification, they help to illuminate some of the puzzling questions about the virtual absence of the 'middle-class petticoat rebellion' in Scottish (as distinct from English) imaginative literature and historiography.

The major problem facing literary and intellectual women in Scotland was not 'Scottish theocracy' or 'Knoxian theology'. It was the absence of a national centre or milieu in which women could function at a high intellectual level as doctors of medicine, novelists, journalists and scholars. However, if Christopher Harvey's imaginative concept of 'the red outward-bound' and 'the black stay-at-home' Scots was applicable to the male intellectuals, it was somewhat less applicable to some of their female counterparts.

From what we know about the careers of such progressive women as Sophia Jex Blake, Mary MacArthur and Jessie Stephens, they were 'red' intellectuals whether they struggled for justice and women's rights in Scotland or in England. While such women as Helen Crawfurd, Mary Brooksbank and Mary Docherty were stay-at-home Scots, they were also, in Harvey's imagery, 'reds'.

157

The brilliant career of Sophia Jex Blake illustrates the difficulty of dividing Scottish middle-class women within the intelligentsia into 'reds' and 'blacks'. Because of the available historiography produced by the English Women's Movement at various times from the late nineteenth century onwards, the achievements of the English feminist, Elizabeth Garrett Anderson, are much better known than the accomplishments of the Scottish feminist, Sophia Jex Blake.

Although Blake won her struggle to study for the degree of MD at the University of Edinburgh, the English universities refused to admit Anderson as a student. Instead, she studied medicine at the University of Paris and she got her MD degree in 1870. What defeated Blake was the absence of a national milieu in which she could function properly as a doctor, Margaret Cole explains:

> Meanwhile the long fight of Sophia Jex Blake for recognition from the Scottish medical schools was nearing its end; and deciding on a change of scene she came to London, and in 1874 founded the London School of Medicine for Women. Elizabeth Garrett joined the staff as a lecturer.[10]

However, it was Elizabeth Garrett Anderson who received the recognition of posterity — not Sophia Jex Blake.

In the late nineteenth century, Margaret Harkness emerged as both a socialist novelist and a prolific labour journalist. Although I have not yet been able to find out anything about the details of her biography, she was known to have had a Scottish upbringing. A close personal friend of Frederick Engels, Margaret Harkness wrote under the pseudonym 'John Law'. Far from being, in Tom Nairn's phrase, 'almost as difficult for a Scots intellectual to get out of the Kailyard as to live without an alias', Margaret Harkness published her novels under her own name and her journalist pieces under her pseudonym.

Margaret Harkness published a considerable number of novels between 1883 and 1917 including *A City Girl* (London, 1887), *In Darkest London* (1890) and *Captain Lobe* (London, 1915). She published articles on "A fear of my life," "The Children of the Unemployed" and "Railway Labour" in such diverse journals as *Nineteenth Century, New Review* and the *National Review*. Her formative years were spent in Scotland, but she lived in London during the period of her literary creativity. Far from 'Scottish theocracy' or 'Knoxian theology' stifling her talent, they probably provided some of the stimulus for the early intellectual growth of Margaret Harkness.

Just as Frances Wright and Helen Macfarlane could not create enough space for themselves as intellectuals and writers within Scotland in the early and mid-nineteenth century, so did Margaret

Harkness have to face the same problem later on. What made it particularly difficult for progressive women in nineteenth-century Scotland was the weakness of the bourgeois feminist movement. In England, in 1881, for example, the first Women's Liberal Association was formed in Bristol by Margaret Priestman. Then, in 1887, an English Women's Liberal Federation was formed. In Scotland no-one made any attempt to organise women into Liberal Associations.[11] On the other hand, the Scots made much greater efforts to integrate women into the political Labour Movement than their English counterparts.

Nevertheless, Scottish and English working-class women shared some elements of a common British identity and experience. Both Scottish and English working-class women produced far fewer autobiographies than male workers. In his study, *Bread, Knowledge and Freedom: A Study of Nineteenth-Century Working-Class Autobiography*, David Vincent suggests that the major reason for this was 'the absence among women of the self-confidence required to undertake the unusual act of writing an autobiography'.[12] Class and gender differences were accompanied, however, by the quite distinct experiences of middle-class women in Scotland and England.

Although Scotland had provided Frances Wright, Helen Macfarlane and Margaret Harkness with initial stimulus and education, it could not offer them the literary and intellectual climate they needed for their creative work. Also, they went to England and America to gain the kind of success and reputation which would have been denied to them if they had remained at home. Such Scottish women as Catherine Sinclair and the Stevenson sisters attracted very little subsequent attention from historians. The same thing happened to the outstanding Scottish women who devoted their energy and talent to the cause of women's trade unionism.

In her brilliant study, *Women and Trade Unions*, Sheila Lewenhak depicts Emma Paterson, Margaret Irwin and Mary MacArthur as the three most outstanding personalities in the history of British women's trade unionism before its demise in the early 1920s. But, although Lewenhak describes Margaret Irwin as 'the second female personality to emerge in British trade unionism', Irwin has not yet made any impact on Scottish historians. However, a great deal has been written about Emma Paterson, the English founder of the Women's Protective and Provident League. This was not an arbitrary development. Living in London and being connected to the middle-class Women's Movement and ruling-class circles, Paterson already attracted a lot of attention in her lifetime. It was otherwise with Margaret Irwin — an outstanding woman trade union leader who, in 1940, died 'unnoticed by the Scottish Trades Union Congress'.[13]

The third of the outstanding personalities in the history of British women's trade unionism was, as Sheila Lewenhak says, 'another Scot'. This other Scot was Mary MacArthur (1880-1921). MacArthur has been largely ignored by Scottish historians apart from a biography published in 1925 by Mary Agnes Hamilton, the daughter of a Scottish professor of philosophy and herself a prolific writer and labour journalist. Indeed, MacArthur was basically remembered for her sustained work in organising English women into trade unions. The Scottish aspect of her work even after she became the British secretary of the Women's Protective and Provident League has been neglected.

The daughter of a well-off owner of a drapery store in Ayr, Mary MacArthur had a Scottish upbringing. Although her father was a right-wing member of the Primrose League, he believed in education for women. In 1894 he sent Mary to study in Germany for a whole year. In explaining the significance of the year MacArthur spent in Germany, Mary Agnes Hamilton said:

> Home sickness rent her, and a longing for "Scotland and
> liberty"; her diary continues to record the passionate
> resolves and intense, if transient, miseries of an ardent
> concentrated young heart and some of its natural pleasures.

The turning-point in Mary MacArthur's life came in 1895 when she accepted a journalistic assignment to report a meeting of women trade unionists in Ayr for the local Conservative newspaper:

> I went to a meeting at Ayr to write a skit on the proceedings.
> Going to scoff, I remained to pray. I became impressed with
> the truth and meaning of the labour movement.

The Scots in the Women's Protective and Provident League were in 'close touch with the local socialist societies'. Mary MacArthur was soon influenced by the Scottish socialist women she met in the late 1890s. Moreover, she was just as 'red' during her activity in Scotland between 1895 and 1903, when she went to London, as she was later on.

Mary MacArthur spent eight years in Scotland organising working women into trade unions and engaging in socialist propaganda, but conversations and discussions with her 'new associates in Edinburgh and Glasgow, and elsewhere, gave her a sharp and troubling awareness of bigger movements whose surge could only be faintly felt in Ayr'.[14] In summing up the factors which led her to move to London, in *Women of Today* Margaret Cole says:

> But it was not long beore she began to feel that she could not
> stay in Scotland. It was partly because her new avocations
> were bound to bring her more and more into disagreement

with her family . . . But even more than that, she was anxious
to try her wings in a wider field than Scotland.[15]

MacArthur had not escaped the perennial dilemma facing progressive
middle-class women living in the Kailyard.

In contemporary journalism, imaginative literature and
historiography, Scotland has usually been perceived as being a much
more male chauvinist country than England. In the dominant images
Scottish women have always been portrayed as being more subordinate
and passive than their English sisters. A major reason for this is the
unsupported *assumption* that between 1880 and 1914 the bourgeois
Women's Movement made greater gains in England than in Scotland.
Yet, the English historian, R S Neale debunks this well-known
assumption when he says:

> At the end of their careers as militants, Christabel and
> Emmeline Pankhurst were no longer concerned with the
> wider "liberation" issues involved in the women's
> movement nor aware that a necessary condition for the
> emancipation of women was the "liberation" of men.
> Consequently militancy led to a great misdirection of energy
> dividing women from women and women from men instead
> of uniting them for concerted action to attack the roots of
> women's subjection in the family, economy and society.[16]

Although Scotland did not provide sufficient space for progressive
middle-class women, the legacy of the Scottish past stretching back to
the Reformation and from the early nineteenth century the growth of
relatively liberal laws in relation to women highlights the *relative
autonomy* of *cultural change*. Because Scottish culture and the law created a
degree of autonomy for themselves within a patriarchal society, most of
the important differences in the historical experiences of Scottish and
English working-class women were not themselves economic ones.[17]

In fostering the dominant images of the unparalleled degree of male
chauvinism throughout Scotland between 1880 and 1914, Rosalind
Mitchison says: 'Keir Hardie gave his blessing to the movement for
women's rights, but this did not go far in Scotland. The combination of
a dominance of heavy industry, a high birth rate, social conformity, and
Knoxian theology was against it. The network of socialist organisations
combined with the economic pressures of the First World War to
produce a militant labour movement on the Clyde'.[18] The clear
implication of this statement was that Scottish women were more
oppressed than their English counterparts. But it was not true. Between
1880 and 1914 male chauvinism was in fact much worse in England than
in Scotland, as the English feminist, Dr Frances Elizabeth Hoggan, put

it: 'Other nations have gone astray in this particular and that; the unrepresented sex is *everywhere* at a legal disadvantage, but in no civilised country in the world are such barbarous enactments still to be found on the Statute-book as those which determine the legal position of wives and mothers in this *boasted free England* of ours'.[19]

In focusing on the extreme *degree* of male chauvinism in England before the First World War, August Bebel glanced back to 1872: 'Married women are in virtue of a court decision, rendered in 1872, excluded from the suffrage, because in English law woman loses her independence by marriage'. But he saw the origins of this intense male chauvinism in England in the late-eighteenth-century hostility towards Mary Wollstonecraft. In looking for the reasons for the continuity of patriarchal attitudes in England, he said: 'Mary Wollstonecraft met in England with even less response than her sisters in France. Ridiculed and insulted by her contemporaries, she went under after trying ordeals'.[20]

If the oft-repeated assertion that Scotland has been a *peculiarly* misogynistic nation since the Reformation is obviously in need of revision, the sexual behaviour of 'lower-class' women was certainly distinctive. Whatever the origin of this behaviour (or sexual relationships between women and men), the dominant contemporary image of sexual behaviour is captured by Eveline Hunter when she says: 'Because of their cultural backwardness, many Scotsmen are like little boys who have just found a forbidden bag of sweets'.[21] This image reflects something of present-day reality; but the historian's task is to try to locate *the roots* of such attitudes and behaviour.

By the early eighteenth century, Scottish women were, as Eunice G Murray said, 'adepts at hiding their feelings'.[22] The place of Scottish women in the continuum of tactility or touching was probably distinctive from English behaviour before the Industrial Revolution got underway. Ashley Montage's comments on touching are particularly interesting: 'National and cultural differences in tactility run the full gamut from absolute nontouchability, as among upper-class Englishmen, to what amounts to almost full expression among peoples speaking Latin-derived languages, Russians and many non-literate peoples'. Moreover, he says that 'In general it seems possible to say that the higher the class, the less there is of tactility, and the lower the class, the more there is'.[23] Nevertheless, the cultural differences between peoples belonging to different nations were just as important as the class differences within them.

While there is some evidence to suggest that there was probably less tactility in Scotland than in England after the Reformation, we simply do not know whether such a pattern of behaviour existed in the two nations before the Reformation. Henry Buckle, who had an anti-Scottish axe to grind, insisted that the sixteenth-century Calvinists were responsible for the first attempts in Scotland to eradicate 'human affection'. In documenting his argument, he showed that in St Andrews no husband was allowed to kiss his wife and no mother was 'permitted to kiss her child on the Sabbath'.[24]

There is also some evidence in the labyrinth of Scottish imaginative literature suggesting that this process probably began in the eighteenth century. Thus, in James Hogg's novel, *The Three Perils of Woman*, set in eighteenth-century Scotland, the father of a 'lower-class' girl was upset by his daughter's lack of tactility:

> Why, daughter, ye hae neither taken the little dear bairn on
> your knee, nor kissed him, after a' the fraze you made. That's
> unco stepmother-like wark, an' I dinna like to see it.

The fact that she soon relented might suggest that the eighteenth century was the crucial period in the genesis of some of the sexual attitudes which went into the making of Scottish working-class culture.[25]

The scarcity of evidence relating to the degree of tactility amongst the 'lower orders' in the eighteenth century makes it difficult to offer any confident judgments. By the mid-nineteenth century, the evidence of distinctive patterns of tactility amongst the Scottish and the English working class was unambiguous. In 1860 in an anonymous essay on the Scottish national character in *Blackwood's Magazine* it was suggested that women were not demonstrative with their children or menfolk. In any case, the anonymous essayist perceived the enormous strength of the 'female character' as a vital component in the national character. Despite the presence of tough-minded women in the eighteenth and nineteenth centuries, however, a 'Scottish bride was expected to show reluctance and require a certain degree of violence, which was neither thought unbecoming in the man, nor a hardship to the woman'. An article in the *North British Review* also discussed the hostility of some Scottish working-class women to 'the English notion' of touching or being affectionate.[26]

By the second half of the nineteenth century, the expression of tactility in Scotland was seen as something peculiarly English. In a biographical study of his mother, Margaret Ogilvy, James M Barrie writes that 'The kissing of the hand was the one English custom she had learned'. Although there is little recorded evidence of resistance to the development of less tactility amongst the 'lower orders' in the nineteenth and twentieth centuries, Scottish working people, whether Protestant or Catholic, developed an 'obsessive puritanism'.

The Scots also increasingly perceived of tactility as being something inherent within English culture, but it is important to remember the comment by the American sociologist, Harry M Johnston, that although 'members of the same class "speak the same language"', no 'two persons have exactly the same culture'. In the novel, *Highland River*, Neil Gunn writes: 'None of the mothers in that land kissed their sons. If it were known that a boy had been kissed by his mother, not a dozen school fights would clear him of the dark shame of such a weakness'.[27]

Although from the mid-nineteenth century onwards Scottish and English 'lower-class' women shared elements of a common British working-class culture, distinctive differences also developed. In Britain as a whole there was a deep chasm between the dominant political attitudes, social values and spiritual outlook of the majority of working-class women and those of the radical and socialist minority. This was most obvious in sexual relations. With the collapse of Utopian socialism in Scotland in the late 1840s and its advocacy of 'free love', the minority of progressive women were increasingly influenced by the dominant sexual *mores* of a Calvinistic capitalist society.

Because mid-Victorian Scotland did not provide enough space for 'the cosmopolitan, self-avowedly, enlightened, red Scots' depicted by Christopher Harvey, modern Scottish socialism was to be shaped by this legacy of conformity to the dominant sexual *mores*. At a crucial period in the history of mid-Victorian Britain, when the Establishment in England was compelled to drop their charges against Annie Besant and Charles Bradlaugh for circulating Charles Knowlton's pamphlet on birth control, neo-Malthusianism simply failed to develop in Scotland.

In the sensational trial of Annie Besant in 1877, the neo-Malthusians went over to the offensive. The neo-Malthusians, therefore, recovered all their seized pamphlets and continued to sell them until 'the prosecution and the threat of prosecution were definately surrendered'.[28] From then on, neo-Malthusian advocacy of birth control began to influence the behaviour of a growing minority of English working-class women.

The failure of neo-Malthusianism to develop in mid-Victorian Scotland was determined by the cultural legacy of the past. In contrast to the red outward-bound Frances Wright, whose propaganda for birth control in the early nineteenth century was confined to America, the Scottish advocates of Malthusianism who remained in Britain did not practise birth control. Despite his support for the ideas of Thomas Malthus in relation to the restriction of population, James Mill had, for example, 'begotten more children than he could afford on a female whom he despised'.[29]

The distinctive responses of Scottish and English socialists to the neo-Malthusians' agitation for birth control between 1880 and 1914 was probably a factor shaping the apparently different pattern of the birth rate in the two countries. What Rosalind Mitchison depicts as 'the high birth rate' in Scotland probably owed something to Scottish socialists' uniform opposition to abortion and birth control. By the early 1880s, socialists and neo-Malthusians in England were already carrying birth control information into working-class communities. The evidence of this progressive activity was documented by Ethel Margaret Elderton. Being sympathetic to the dominant sexual *mores* of their own society as well as to traditional Marxist hostility to Malthusianism, Scottish socialists were, as Andreas Scheu recorded in his diary, hostile to 'free love', abortion and birth control.

Although it could, in one sense, be argued that Scottish socialists were conformists in relation to the dominant Calvinistic attitudes to abortion and birth control, the source of their conformity was the orthodox Marxism of German social democracy rather than 'Knoxian theology'. The Marxist orthodoxy in Scotland in relation to the 'woman question' was developed in the 1880s. By 1905, Daniel De Leon's brilliant translation of August Bebel's book, *Women under Socialism*, was already circulating throughout the Scottish Labour Movement.

With its critique of 'abortion and the artificial prevention of conception',[30] Bebel's arguments were very acceptable to the dominant patriarchal culture with which Scottish socialists had comfortably co-existed since 1880. In contrast to Scotland, where official *and* socialist opinion remained implacably hostile to abortion and artificial prevention as a solution to poverty, in 1893 Annie Besant described the change in official attitudes in England:

> During the last few years public opinion has been gradually coming round to our side, in consequence of the pressure of poverty resulting from widespread depression of trade, and during the sensation caused in 1884 by *The Bitter Cry of Outcast London*, many writers in the *Daily News* — notably G. R. Sims — boldly alleged that the distress was to a great extent due to the large families of the poor, and mentioned that we had been prosecuted for giving the very knowledge which would bring salvation to the sufferers in our great cities.[31]

While the Scottish Labour Movement was often more sympathetic to women's agitations and political claims, it did *not* oppose Grundyism. Though in the late nineteenth century large sections of the Labour

Movement in England also accepted the assumptions of Grundyism, a significant minority of English socialists challenged Grundyism root-and-branch. E P Thompson states: 'If many of the Yorkshire young people had in fact got socialism "inside of them", then something of its quality — the hostility to Grundyism, the warm espousal of sex equality, the rich internationalism — owed much to Tom Maquire'.[32]

Although the double-standard of sexual morality existed amongst the English as well as the Scottish working class, the Scots greater hang-ups about sexual matters have been well-known since the nineteenth century. Bruce Glaiser, who in the 1880s went with a Clarion van to Maybole in Ayrshire committed the following observation to his diary:

> Evening meeting disturbed by drunk men. Am shocked at the filthiness of their remarks. One old man, said to be a capable workman, was asked in a bantering way by one of the crowd, "Where did you get that hat?" "It did not come from down your mother's petticoats where you came frae" was the nasty retort. This tendency to constantly refer to sexual matters by Scotsmen when provoked is a very ugly fact.[33]

There was also a long tradition of anti-Irish sentiment in working-class communities in Scotland. This anti-Irish sentiment was an important factor in the acculturation of the Irish immigrants into what was probably the dominant Scottish working-class sexual culture. In contrast to 'the plump and genial' English working-class male, the Scot was 'a spare, reserved, sardonic person who would not for his life be seen "demean himself" by blowing the weans' noses in a tramway car'.[34] In 1888, in a well-researched essay on the Scottish miner, Robert Haddow, a socialist pioneer, described the pressures to which Irish immigrant women were subjected:

> Between the womankind of the Scots and those of the Scoto-Irish there is hardly a line to draw, but when we come to look at the female companions of the newly-arrived Irish the contrast is most marked. Dowdy and slovenly, the Irish women seem to take neither pride nor interest in their husbands, their children or themselves. They look perfectly happy in the midst of an amount of dirt and degradation that would drive their Scottish sisters mad. These women are in the rows exactly what their husbands are in the pits — a danger to those they are amongst.[35]

As successive waves of Irish immigrants were assimilated into the dominant culture, they probably became even more 'obsessively puritanical'. It is, however, important to realise that working-class socialists in Scotland were even more 'respectable' than the majority of unorganised workers.

However, the hidden 'matriarchal' feature of Scottish — and, indeed, Irish — working-class culture identified by Frederick Engels and Hamish Henderson was still evident in the early twentieth century. In an important essay on working-class women in England between 1890 and 1914, the American labour historian, Peter Sterns, offers an interesting portrait:

> Autobiographies by workers covering the period rarely mention women. Although it is often assumed that working-class children until recently had much warmer relationships with their mothers than with their domineering fathers, this is not apparent in the autobiographies of the time, where normally only fathers are given space. . . . The Ragged Trousered Philanthropist makes the image even clearer. Women appear only rarely in the novel but those who do are faultless, though in one case a woman is led astray by a man appropriately if unsubtly named Slyme.[36]

Moreover, the English trade unions seem to have been more patriarchal than their Scottish counterparts.

Robert Tressall's portrait of English working-class women is significantly different to the portrait of Scottish working-class women depicted in Lewis Grassic Gibbon's classic, A Scots Quair. Although American and Australian feminists in contemporary Scotland frequently project an image of the nation as being an unceasingly misogynistic one from the sixteenth century onwards, there is little evidence to support this view. There is, as Joyce Macmillan suggests, 'a matriarchal strain in Scottish working-class life that is not adequately dealt with by a brand of feminism that has been so heavily influenced by the experience of middle-class Americans and Australians'.[37] In an interesting essay on the politics of 'Red Clydeside', R J Morris makes some penetrating comments on this 'matriarchal' strain in Scottish working-class life:

> The importance of the mother is also clear in many of the Clydeside autobiographies. William Gallacher's early memories included his mother's grey-faced exhaustion, and his own pleasure when his sister's and his own earnings enabled her to stop work. John Maclean was also influenced by watching his mother's struggles to bring up a family. To counter this were Kirkwood's memories, which he admits were rather "Kailyard" in manner: "She never counted and took care of the scanty wages. She planned out the week's needs. We never wanted . . . To her my father's

will was her will . . ."[38]

So although this 'matriarchal' feature of working-class life was not universal in Scotland, it did exist. It did not exist in English working-class life.

Therefore, the reality of Scottish working-class life was at odds with the image of working-class women in Kailyard novels. Despite the images of patriarchal figures in Kailyard literature, reality very occasionally broke through elsewhere in their writings. In a biography of his mother, J M Barrie describes the impact of ongoing industrialisation in the small town of Kirriemuir. In *Margaret Ogilvy*, he sketches in an authentic picture of what happened in many Scottish towns:

> Another era had dawned, new customs, new fashions sprang into life, all as lusty as if they had been born at twenty one; as quickly as two people may exchange seats, the daughter, till now but a knitter of stockings, became the breadwinner, he who had been the breadwinner sat down to the knitting of stockings: what had been yesterday a nest of weavers was today a town of girls.[39]

Industrial capitalism offered women 'a much greater measure of independence and of equality with men than had previous class relations'.[40] In Scotland, the new opportunities opened up by capitalism merged with the older 'matriarchal' strains in 'lower-class' culture.

It is particularly interesting that R J Morris explains the women's rent strike in 1915 in terms of women's importance in working-class social life. Clearly, the dominant images of Scottish women are at odds with the historical reality of their role in day to day working-class life.[41] There was, however, nothing romantic about life in industrial Scotland.

Although *Lancet*, the medical journal, was already complaining in the 1880s about the practice of abortion in Glasgow, Scottish socialists, whether they were Marxists or not, were just as critical of abortion and birth control as the Presbyterian clergymen. In this specific area of social life, they were very close to the attitudes of ordinary apolitical working men. Lawrence Storione, a remarkably knowledgeable and highly cultured French anarchist, who lived, worked and agitated in the Fife coalfields between 1901 and his death in 1921, was criticised by the miners in his socialist group in Cowdenbeath for circulating an American Syndicalist pamphlet which advocated 'race suicide'.[42] Most other Scottish socialists, however, accepted the dominant patriarchal attitudes about sexual matters.

In England, many working-class women were hostile to birth control rather than abortion. In Bradford and Leeds 'the practice of abortion was fairly widespread in low-wage groups'. Although working-class women in Salford 'took abortifacients sold by vets for use with domestic animals', birth control 'continued to be looked upon as a sin against the Holy Ghost'. It was the same in the poorer working-class communities in London. Such socialists as Caroline Nelson, an American nurse who worked in London before the First World War, however, joined with the neo-Malthusian Liberal radicals in carrying birth control information into working-class communities. In 1914 Caroline Nelson stated: 'Neo-Malthusianism has nothing to do with drugs or abortion. . . . We must do the next best thing, and that is to acquaint them with a harmless preventive means so that their burdens shall not increase and be laid at innocent lives'.[43]

Although the Marxian socialists in the English Labour Movement were also opposed to abortion and birth control, they could not escape a great deal of criticism from within their own ranks. In developing a socialist counter-culture including a more libertarian attitude to sex, the less orthodox English socialists began to influence sexual behaviour. Furthermore, between 1890 and 1923, there were at least six English socialists who were prosecuted for selling pamphlets dealing with birth control.[44]

While most Scottish socialists were probably, in Harry McShane's phrase, 'just like other men in their attitudes in the home', they began to develop more progressive attitudes before the First World War. The Scots' more progressive attitudes towards women were influenced by the growing self-assertiveness of working women in the factories, mills and elementary schools. Besides, the Scottish Socialist Teachers' Association played a vital role in the struggle for greater sexual equality.

No-one ever spoke about Scottish working-class women as 'the white slaves of Scotland', though there was more than enough slavery. Unlike what happened in England, no-one described Scottish female domestic servants as women who donned 'the badge of servitude'. While the English middle class was more sympathetic to the idea of trade unions for domestic servants, English domestic servants were less self-assertive and militant than their Scottish counterparts.[45]

Although the cultural sediments of the past gave Scottish working-class women greater space within which they could conduct their struggles,[46] socialist women played an important role in the struggle for sexual equality. There were strikes of fisherwomen in Fraserburgh and Peterhead, for example, in communities where socialist propaganda had been conducted since the 1880s. The Scottish Socialist Teachers'

Association raised the question of equal pay for equal work within the branches of the Educational Institute of Scotland (EIS).[47]

Jessie Stevens, the daughter of a tailor and a domestic servant, describes the great moment in her life in 1906: 'When I was a girl of twelve I remember one night I was selling the *Labour Woman* outside St. Andrews Hall, and Keir Hardie was speaking. When he came out, he saw me selling the paper and he said, "That's right, my lassie, you'll be a credit to the movement yet". I was so proud: I could hardly wait to get home to tell my dad he had actually spoken to me. Eventually I worked for the ILP. We went on different missions each week round the country'.

In England working-class women were less involved in the agitation for sexual equality. According to R S Neale, the women's movement in England captured 'the enthusiastic support only of the smallest minority of working-class women'.[48]

By the eve of the First World War a significant minority of Scottish working-class women were politically active. One contemporary described the rent strike on Clydeside as 'the largest and most important in Britain'. Sylvia Pankhurst said: 'Numbers flocked into the Women's Housing Association, formed by the socialists to focus agitation. Sustained by appeals of sisterly kindness and mutual aid, and by visions of a better future for working people, to be won by present effort and solidarity, women kept watch all night on the common stair of the barrack dwellings, their neighbours heartening them with tea in their cold vigil'. Under the influence of socialist propaganda, the Clydeside workers were, as Helen Crawfurd put it, 'up in arms, and the women especially, were seething with a militant unrest'.[49]

As early as 1915, James D MacDougall championed the cause of sexual equality in the pages of John Maclean's newspaper, *The Vanguard*. By 1917, Maclean could report that his classes on Marxism were now being attended by working-class women. He explained: 'One significant feature is the growing number of women attending these classes, although the growth is not as quick as some of us would like'.[50]

In 1924, the first women's branch of the ILP in Britain was formed in the Scottish town of Armadale; in 1925 Minnie Dick became the chairman of the Airth branch of the ILP; and in 1926 Mary Bruce became the chairman of the Bainsford branch of the ILP in Falkirk. In 1927 Mary Brooksbank organised working-class women in Dundee. She described it: 'On my release from Perth Prison in 1927, we women got together and formed the Working Women's Guild, and we numbered three hundred strong. We sent deputations to the town council, and to Maryfield Hospital on behalf of the aged and poor inmates. We held meetings outside what was then the Poorhouse. . . . Our women began to chair meetings and to speak on behalf of working women'.[51] In Cowdenbeath Mary Docherty organised women for the Communist Party, although she was often discouraged by the Party's male chauvinism.

Although the war was an important catalyst in shaping the intensity of the struggle for women's rights and sexual equality, older mental attitudes persisted in working-class consciousness, too. In Dundee in 1906, for example, male workers would not allow the forced-feeding of the imprisoned Suffragettes. Mary Brooksbank described similar attitudes in Dundee in 1918: 'Meetings were held in Dundee to support the Russian Revolution. We must pay tribute to many Dundee women and men who took part in this support. . . . Our women were also very active, and would have been even more so but for the protective attitude of our men comrades. It was not apparent at the time but I now see the wisdom of that, as our impetuosity might have led us into unnecessary suffering'.[52]

Mary Brooksbank and Mary Docherty were Communists. But the women in the ILP were no less active, outspoken and determined advocates of sexual equality. Before the ILP succumbed to Stalinist images of 'the valorisation of the Scottish male industrial worker' ILP women played a prominent and equal role in strikes and political struggles. Moreover, ILP women in Glasgow were so effective in their propaganda work that the authorities were sometimes prompted to answer them in public proclamations, as Fenner Brockway reported in 1930: 'The Director of Public Assistance has recently published a special report, on the instructions of the Glasgow City Council, to meet the arguments urged by a deputation of I.L.P. women for the abolition of the Means Test'.[53]

In Scotland, traditional Marxist hostility to free love, abortion and birth control were not challenged effectively until 1918-1923. Although the critique of orthodox Marxist attitudes towards sexual questions came from such outsiders as Guy Aldred and Margaret Sanger, it met with a very sympathetic response from a minority of working-class women on Clydeside. However, throughout the 1920s Marxist orthodoxy in sexual morality remained the dominant ideology in the Scottish Labour Movement. As this aspect of traditional Scottish Marxist ideology merged in the 1930s with Stalinist images of women, the Scots were increasingly influenced by patriarchal conceptions of women's allegedly innate 'inferiority'. This latter development was a historical 'accident'. It owed more to what was happening in Stalin's Russia than to 'Knoxian theology'. Outside the sphere of sexual politics, Scottish socialists were originally quite progressive towards the 'woman question'. By the late 1920s, the earlier progressive culture was

171

in the process of being destroyed.

In an important essay, *Women in Scotland: Scotch Reels and Political Perspectives*, Douglas and Quaine Bain blame the media for not portraying the real history of women in Scottish history. In reinforcing this point, they argue: 'Not until *The Cheviot, the Stag and the Black, Black Oil* was there any acknowledgement of women's part in the Clearances; features on the Red Clyde rarely focus on the rent strikes among the women of the time'. But the media reflects the dominant culture in Scotland, and, as the Bains at least implicitly recognise, Scottish socialist culture is now just as patriarchal as the dominant culture.

In identifying and characterising contemporary Scottish socialist culture as 'Clydesidism', Douglas and Quaine Bain focus on the continuity of male chauvinism from the 1930s to the present without hinting that it might have been progressive before then. They sum up: 'Elementalism and giganticism are the setting for these sons of toil — the stage props of male chauvinism. Clydesidism has found expression in progressive and socialist culture: *Seaward the Brave, The Brave Don't Cry, Willie Rough*, etc'.[54] By unintentionally obscuring the self-activity of working-class women in Scotland between 1880 and the early 1920s, they make it easier for the Establishment to either ignore or to portray the Scottish women of the past as passive, apathetic and docile unpersons.

In the 1930s the emergence of Clydesidism as the new socialist ideology in Scotland represented a break in the continuity of political development. Although the origins of Clydesidism were at least partly a by-product of Stalinist industrialisation in Russia in the late 1920s, British socialist culture was previously liberal in relation to women. In attacking male chauvinism in the British Labour Movement, Dora Montefiore said:

> These old, ingrained ideas of sex and class dominance have helped to enslave women industrially to a degree that is more degrading than is the industrial slavery of men; and no reform, no amelioration, no palliation of existing conditions can be of any real help to the woman who seeks free and equal conditions with men. Nothing but a social and economic revolution, in which women themselves take a conscious and active part, can make for their complete emancipation. For this reason, we militant women strongly protest against the idea that socialism can be *given to us by men*.[55]

But, although Scottish socialists were more sympathetic to women's political involvement than their English counterparts, they were probably influenced indirectly by middle-class feminists. In Glasgow, for example, Jessie Stephens, a working-class socialist feminist, subsequently recalled discussions with working-class and middle-class women in her local branch of the Women's Social and Political Union on 'a wide range of questions which affected women including divorce'.[56]

Moreover, although working-class women were active in the Labour Movement in the north of England, the Scots were more active and self-assertive, as Harry McShane explains in *No Mean Fighter:* 'Most of the women in the movement were housewives, some widows, and there were a few teachers. There seemed to be more women in the movement in Lancashire and Scotland than in the south of England, and more in the British Socialist Party and the I.L.P. than in the Socialist Labour Party'.[57]

This important historical development was interrupted by the 'success' of the Russian Revolution. In discussing the outcome of this discontinuity in British working-class women's struggles for liberation from patriarchal oppression, Sheila Rowbotham says:

> Historically many radical movements in the past have raised the connection between changing our consciousness and making a new culture with opposing values. This was a vital aspect of Owenite socialist feminism, for example. In attacking the hold of religion the Owenites began to make their own marriage ceremonies. In contesting the values of capitalism they created their own schools.
>
> Discussion of the quality of relations was common in the early British socialist movement. Becoming a socialist meant for many people a spiritual rebirth. Socialist culture, particularly in the Socialist League, the Clarion cycling clubs and choirs and the Independent Labour Party, but even at a local level in the Social Democratic Federation, was a means of sustaining the faith as well as transmitting socialist values . . .
>
> These understandings of the personal, spiritual meaning of becoming a socialist was quite alien to Leninism. The growth of the Communist Party as the revolutionary party meant that such discussions were no longer central to the socialist experience.[58]

Because Stalinism in the 1930s was much stronger in the Scottish than in the English Labour Movement, Clydesidism emerged and suppressed the previous liberal attitudes towards women.

However, as a euphemism for describing the dominant male chauvinist character of Scottish socialist culture from the 1930s to the present-day, the word 'Clydesidism' has become irreplaceable. In recent years there has been an abundance of evidence illuminating the dominance of Clydesidism alongside the process of de-industrialisation. Although Scottish women were again more militant than their English counterparts in the 1970s and early 1980s, they made less impact on the socialist intelligentsia's consciousness.

Moreover, if the rediscovery of the hidden and distinctive history of Scottish and English women is a necessary pre-condition for the rebirth of an effective socialist Feminist Movement in Britain, so is the utter rejection of Leninist concepts of women's role in the Labour Movement. Despite recent 'socialist' criticisms of the Women's Movement past and present, a cultural critique of male chauvinism is just as valid now as it was in the early years of the present century when Dora Montefiore said:

> In order to secure this progress and development, much, very much, will depend on socialist mothers of the present day giving right thought and right teaching to their boys and girls. What I mean is that they must, above all, teach that *equality* is not something that is *given*, it must be deserved and won; and that women will conquer their equality with men just as soon as they are inwardly freed from the feeling of inequality of sex dependence, and not one hour earlier.[59]

Afterword

Throughout history the struggle of the generations has, like that of the sexes, formed a counterpoint with the struggle of the classes, and at certain moments even taken priority over it.

Victor Kiernan

Socialism is about abolishing the domination of people by other people, about collectivism which is nobody's prison, about social equality and justice, about making people conscious of their power and able to control their destinies here and now.

Teodor Shanin

ALTHOUGH BETWEEN the 1560s and the mid 1920s there were important differences of degree in the history of Scottish and English working-class women, orthodox 'Marxist' historians have subsequently refused to recognise this distinctive experience and history. What was also unacknowledged was the role of intra-class conflict between working-class women and men in helping to spread comparatively 'egalitarian' social relationships within the working class. Before Leninist orthodoxy gripped the British Labour Movement in the 1920s, Frederick Engels, Daniel De Leon and Rosa Luxemburg argued that intra-class conflict between working-class women and men was a progressive force in ameliorating the oppressive conditions of working women within capitalist society.

The explanatory device of intra-class conflict as *a motor force* in working-class history was abandoned in the mid-1920s. It was only revised in the late 1960s with the reappearance of a new women's movement.

In a particularly fine and sensitive book, *Wigan Pier Revisited*, published in January, 1984, Beatrix Campbell argues that the interaction between the present and the past was the crucial thing in

175

explaining the contemporary history of English working-class women in the 1980s. Unlike many left-wing commentators, she depicted the 'hidden history of intra-class conflict' between working-class women and men as the missing dimension in recent accounts of the history of the contemporary British working class. This helped to explain, in Campbell's idiom, 'the conservation of our (British) class struggle and its failure to mature into socialist struggle'.[1]

In a recent book permeated with the spirit of Leninist orthodoxy, *Class Struggle and Women's Liberation*, Tony Cliff dismisses the challenge presented by the women's movement — present and past — by pummelling the past of the British Labour Movement into shape. Conceiving of the woman's movement as a 'bourgeois' deviation from the real class struggle of a unified working class against capitalist society, he attributes the male chauvinism of such British socialists as Ernest Belford Bax to an 'intellectually backward' and conservative Labour Movement. Because Leninist orthodoxy in Britain since the mid-1920s has been so alien to the Promethean spirit of classical Marxism, Tony Cliff's book deserves more than a passing glance. Rather than acknowledge wife-beating and rape as social problems within the British working class, he argues:

> But, many feminists argue, the actual oppression of women is carried out by men. Men are rapists, pornographers, wife-beaters, and so on, they say. But while feminists correctly point to individual men as the agents of these forms of oppression, they are wrong to identify these as the main ways in which women are oppressed. Moreover, these are the actions of individuals and are small compared to the way the capitalist system structures and perpetuates women's oppression through its institutions. . . .
>
> This is not to deny, however, that men behave in certain ways which are oppressive to women. To pretend otherwise is to fall into the idealist error of denying that social relations are always relations between real people. But the blame should be placed squarely on class society, *not on its individual agents*.[2]

In contrast to Elizabeth Fox-Genovese, the American Marxist historian, who argues: 'Women did develop discrete values, frequently in conflict with those of the men of their own group and frequently in common with the specific sensibilities of women of other groups',[3] Cliff simply ignores the existence of intra-class conflict within the British working class before the collapse of the Women's Movement in the mid-1920s.

Although Sheila Rowbotham criticised Tony Cliff's chauvinist ideas in some of her books in the 1970s, he articulates so many ahistoric and un-Marxist ideas that they deserve further comment. If Cliff's male chauvinist ideas about the history of British women were not a hinderance to the spread of socialist enlightenment in the 1980s, they could be left to the judgment of posterity.

Unlike the Leninists in the British Labour Movement, Frederick Engels and Karl Marx always acknowledged the presence of intra-class conflict within the working class. In *The Origin of the Family, Private Property and the State*, Engels said: 'In an old manuscript written by Marx and myself in 1846 I find the words: "The first division of labour is that between man and woman for the propagation of children". And today I can add: The first class antagonism that appears in history coincides with the development of the antogonism between man and woman in monogamous marriage, and the first class oppression coincides with that of the female by the male'.[4]

Furthermore, Marx *did blame* the 'individual agents' of oppressive behaviour, whether they were workers or intellectuals, just as much as he criticised the social structure of capitalism. In a brief, though authoritative, essay on Marx's years in London, Wilhelm Liebknecht revealed that Marx criticised working men who beat their wives:

> He would have enjoyed having a man who beat his wife — which was common at the time in London — flogged to death. In such cases his impulsive nature often got him and us into trouble. One evening he and I were going to Hampstead Road on top of a bus. At a stop by a public-house there was a great hubbub and a woman could be heard screaming: "Murder! Murder!". Marx was down in a trice and I followed him. I tried to keep him back but I might just as well have tried to stop a bullet with my hand. We immediately found ourselves in the middle of a tumult with people pressing behind us . . . Only the arrival of two stalwart constables saved us from paying dearly for our philanthropic interference.[5]

By totally ignoring intra-class conflict between working-class women and men in British working-class history, Tony Cliff cannot acknowledge the tangible changes in workers' consciousness and sexual relationships before the collapse of the Women's Movement in the mid-1920s. Just as the late Engels argued that it was 'fatuous' to deny that ideas have 'any effect upon history',[6] so did such British socialist women as Dora Montefiore emphasise the role of progressive ideas in women's struggle for liberation within the context of capitalist society. With characteristic perspicacity, she said: 'Working women know very well that there are other burdens and grievances under which they as women suffer more than do men. In times of unemployment, the pregnant or suckling mother, who has either to starve at home or do heavy and ill-paid work outside the home, suffers more than the unemployed man. . . . The working woman is *more sweated, more despised, more downtrodden* in the last resort than is the working man, because, though under capitalism the working man is the wage slave, yet his *wife is the slave of the slave*; and if our gospel of socialism is to be fruitfully preached, we must kindle a spark in the gloom of the soul of enslaved motherhood, so that she may be able to bring forth intellectually free children, and teach them the gospel of discontent and of rebellion'.[7]

Before the collapse of the Women's Movement in the mid-1920s, the middle-class Women's Movement often assisted working-class women to challenge and modify male chauvinist behaviour within the Labour Movement. Although there were significant social and cultural differences in the historical experience of Scottish and English women, the partial 'emancipation' of British women in the early 1920s was largely the outcome of *the uprisings* of working-class women at various moments before the First World War.

The period between 1880 and 1914 was of crucial importance in outlawing some of the more extreme forms of male chauvinism in the British Labour Movement. This was the period when women were first encouraged to join some of the socialist political parties and groups, though the pattern was geographically very uneven. Moreover, the trade union bureaucracy did, in response to rank-and-file pressure, force male trade unionists to recruit women into trade unions. And with condescending patriarchal prejudice, the trade union bureaucracy also came out in favour of the women's agitation for 'equal pay for equal work'.

Although the major progress in the agitation for egalitarian socialist relationships between working-class women and men did not emerge on any significant scale until the early 1920s, when distinctive women's branches of the Independent Labour Party were formed, socialist women played a major role in this development by criticising male chauvinism. In a remarkable passage in *The Position of Women in the Socialist Movement*, Montefiore wrote:

> Nothing but a social and economic revolution, in which women themselves take a conscious and active part, can make for their complete emancipation. For this reason, we militant women strongly protest against the idea that socialism can be given to us by men. This is as false and deluding an idea as ever kept back a great movement.

Socialism given us women would be only an added slavery.[8]

They were, of course, encouraged and assisted by enlightened socialist men.

But, because he ignored the role of progressive ideas in the socialists' struggle for women's emancipation before the mid-1920s, Tony Cliff seems unable to either acknowledge the achievements, or to account for the collapse, of the Women's Movement. In *Class Struggle and Women's Liberation*, he was not only sceptical of the role of ideas in the working-class struggle, but also rejected out of hand the notion that middle-class women might have played a progressive role in weakening male chauvinism within the British Labour Movement. None of the socialist women, who were active in the British working-class movement before 1927, have succeeded in forcing themselves into the pages of Cliff's book. This was not at all accidental. Because the class struggle — an abstract, ahistoric class struggle of men against men— was narrowly conceived and conceptualised, there is no room for the crucial human activities of Dora Montefiore, Lily Gair Wilkinson or Helen Crawfurd.

Since Dora Montefiore's analysis of the woman question has been revived by such American Marxist-feminists as Linda Gordon, it is a pity that Tony Cliff did not address himself to the sort of criticism raised by Gordon and Rowbotham. In a direct comment which applies to Cliff's conceptualisation of the present and the past, Gordon insists:

> What marxists have seen as peripheral or superstructural — the gender order of society — is actually fundamental to the entire social, economic, and political order. When you start to talk about altering traditional gender relations, you are getting at part of the material base. Gender is not cultural as opposed to material. It is part of the fundamental economic and social organisation of society, and change will produce enormous resistance and backlash.[9]

With their dismissal of the role of ideas and socialist critique in history and contemporary society, orthodox Leninist historiography seems unable to account for either the fall of the Women's Movement in the mid-1920s or its subsequent rebirth in the late 1960s. Tony Cliff has had no difficulty in explaining these two major historical developments. He puts it with an almost awe-inspiring simplicity:

> But after the 1920s the question of women's liberation was swept aside under the hammer blows of economic crisis, Nazism, Stalinism and the resurgence of right-wing Social Democracy. Only half a century later did a new women's movement reappear in the deepening crisis of world capitalism in the late 1960s and early 1970s.[10]

179

In his analysis the 'economic crisis' was responsible for both the *fall* and the *resurrection* of the Women's Movement in Britain as elsewhere.

But the middle-class Women's Movement was mortally wounded by the Suffragettes themselves at the end of the First World War. At the end of the war, a whole host of factors convinced them that they had won their long struggle for women's liberation. Indeed, one of the great myths of British social history is that the First World War emancipated women *per se* and lifted them out of 'the anonymity of a species'.[11] If there was a much greater tendency after the war of 1914-1918 to question 'ancient sanctions',[12] many working-class women remained the 'slaves of slaves'. Nevertheless, sociologists and others including the middle-class advocates of women's rights argued that women's status and role in society had been transformed as a result of the enormous demand for female labour.

In 1920, Millicent Fawcett claimed that the beginning of the First World War found women 'serfs and set them free'.[13] Mrs Alex Tweedie asserted that a crucial subjective factor in the emancipation of British women was men's changed conceptions of women induced by the experience of four years of world war. Moreover, Ray Strachey, the feminist historian, concluded that 'what more than three-quarters of a century of persistent agitation had failed to accomplish was effected within four years of catastrophic upheaval'.[14] The Women's Movement, therefore, had written its own obituary some years before the factors identified by Tony Cliff came into play.

But just as orthodox Marxist historians have found it difficult to account for the collapse of the Women's Movement in the mid-1920s, so they have been even more puzzled by the reappearance of a new Women's Movement in the late 1960s and 1970s. Far from the new Women's Movement being the outcome of the deepening crisis, it represented the new confidence of women who had enjoyed greater economic freedom than ever before. Identifying the common causes underlying the rise of the middle-class women's movement in Britain and America, Peter Worsley says:

> The generation of women who had gone through the experience of mass higher education for the first time in human history only to find themselves back in that extra-mural world where their new skills and knowledge were still discounted, needed no other, specific cause, like Vietnam or the Bomb, to cause them to translate that common frustration into a movement for women's liberation.

But, although he criticises the traditional left for labelling such 'primordial concerns as gender or ethnicity' or 'the survival of humanity' as single-issue campaigns, Worsley seems to be somewhat remote from the grass roots of the Left when he concludes:

> Hence though they have often conflicted with what C Wright Mills called "Victorian" marxists and others for whom class was the only form of meaningful inequality and the politics of gender or race a "deviation", in the end, most of the Left has come round to accepting that ethnic self-determination, women's liberation, nuclear disarmament, and even ecology, are issues it has to take up, even if they have still not developed the theoretical categories with which to express the overlaps and contradictions between class exploitation and exploitation based on gender or ethnicity.[15]

Despite Worsley's admirable championship of socialist humanism and women's liberation, this particular description of the Left's response to the agitation for women's liberation really represents a somewhat facile optimism.

While Tony Cliff's somewhat élitist disdain for the Women's Movement in the present and past was born out of the narrow practical politics of a Marxist sect, university intellectuals have had no such excuses. Reflecting the dominant male chauvinist attitudes towards women in the Labour Movement as well as in the wider society, British socialist intellectuals have been as conservative, traditional and unimaginative in interpreting the world as busy trade union activists. Instead of helping to rediscover the world of labouring women and men in the times when social relationships were much less patriarchal before the collapse of the Women's Movement in the mid-1920s, most male historians have often reflected their own patriarchal prejudices. This has been particularly evident in their allegedly socialist conceptualisation of working-class history. When Eric Hobsbawm published an article on socialist iconography in the Marxist journal, *History Workshop*, in 1979, he quickly attracted the justified criticisms of socialist-feminists.

In a very effective critique of Hobsbawm's article, Sally Alexander, Anna Davin and Eve Hostettler said:

> A study of the content of different labour and socialist ideologies is a line of inquiry which Hobsbawm gestures towards in the last part of his article, and which we would suggest is a much more fruitful approach to the understanding of socialist iconography than the search for direct reflections of social reality . . . The relationship between industrial capitalism, class struggle and sexual division is treated as unproblematic, questions which should

be the proper concern of labour and socialist history are
unasked, and the effect is to foreclose discussion and to blunt
curiosity.[16]

But the strongest criticism was made by Ruth Richardson when she
said:

> What angered me so deeply about Professor Hobsbawm's
> article, then, was that it purported to offer a non-sexist
> examination of socialist iconography. Instead it reproduced
> at least one profoundly sexist image, which cannot even be
> called socialist. Not only was this image reproduced
> uncritically, but the commentary on it compounded its
> sexism. My anger, and that of other women who have read
> the article, stemmed from our awareness of the insidiousness
> of sexism, even amongst those who pretend to an awareness
> of it.[17]

Hobsbawm's sexism was fairly typical of the 'enlightened' sexual
attitudes of the British male socialist intelligentsia before the eruption
of the coal miners' strike in January, 1984.

Although the history of working-class women in Scotland and England
was disparate in terms of the force of distinctive cultural heritages and
responses to gender and the sexual division of labour once industrial
capitalism emerged, between 1927 and the late 1960s male chauvinism
ruled supreme in the British Labour Movement. With the reappearance
of the Women's Movement, intellectuals and activists in the Scottish
and English Labour Movements have had to confront the challenge
presented by militant women liberationists.

Though in the 1970s and early 1980s male chauvinism was challenged
within the Scottish and English Labour Movements, feminism did not
have any substantial impact until the outbreak of the miners' strike. The
perennial problems chronicled in the earlier chapters of *Women and
Popular Struggles* have continued to assert and reassert themselves in the
Scottish Labour Movement — for example, a numerically weak and
powerless socialist intelligentsia, the Scottish crisis of national identity,
university history departments' indifference to Scottish history,
cultural insecurity, etc. Although Scottish and English working-class
women have had to face common problems, socialist intellectuals from
outside Scotland frequently assert that wife beating and other aspects
of male chauvinist behaviour are much worse in Scotland than in
England. Without serious and much-needed sociological research, it is
just not possible to offer any *useful judgements* on these important

questions.

But what was clear in the early 1980s was Scottish working-class women's militancy in the factories, workshops and offices. Although the middle-class Women's Movement was once again very weak in Scotland by comparison with the movement in England, the concept of women's liberation did begin to shake male dominance in the Labour Movement. In spite of the suffocating male chauvinism within Scottish society, the new social atmosphere induced by the ideology of women's liberation was conducive to the women's role in the factory occupations and sit-ins.

With the election of a very right-wing British government under the leadership of Margaret Thatcher in 1979, a sustained effort was made by the forces of the right throughout the country to put women back into their traditional place in 'the home'. By then the predominantly middle-class Women's Movement had already had some influence on the national culture as well as on the thought-processes and social behaviour of working-class women. This was the most crucial development in the struggles to come in the 1980s.

Meanwhile, the Tories in Westminster were determined to turn back the clock by recreating a form of *laissez-faire* capitalism much more appropriate to the early nineteenth than to the late twentieth century. Demoralised by a vicious Thatcherite ideology and a world-wide economic depression, working-class women and men seemed to have abandoned labour politics and to be turning in on themselves.

The middle-class women's movement began to disintegrate under the impact of the economic depression. Working women were often the first victims of redundancy programmes; and sexist, racist and other reactionary attitudes began to find an outlet within working-class organisations. But, although women workers were increasingly subjected to a new and more intense form of exploitation as casual workers, they remained a significant group within the labour force, as Sarah Benton explains in an article in the *New Statesman* in March, 1984:

> Meanwhile, the peculiar exploitation of women's labour —
> the steady growth of casual and part-time work —
> continued unchecked. Between such women workers — in
> 1981 22.4 per cent of all 20-60 year-old women, compared
> with 5.2 per cent in 1951 — and traditional trade unions
> there are almost no points of contact.[18]

With the disintegration of the Women's Movement and the crisis of the Left itself, demoralisation soon appeared to set in. Despite the popularity of the best-selling book, *Beyond the Fragments*, which sets out the case for a more modern, humanistic socialism relevant to women as well as men, and despite its criticisms of Leninist attitudes, the Left as a whole remained locked into the 'conservative', backward-looking male chauvinist attitudes of 'the days of hope' in 1926 and 1927. Unsympathetic to women's liberation, the Left became more and more defensive. In any case the post-1927 traditions of what Beatrix Campbell calls the 'magic of masculinity, muscle and machinery' were inherently inimical to women's liberation agitations.

Then things began to change, though very slowly, in 1981. By then Sarah Benton was reporting an important factory occupation in Leyton. Although this short-lived factory occupation of 'the men and women of Staffa, an engineering firm in Leyton' soon ended in defeat, the workers did at least challenge the new American owners.[19] While there were many important factory occupations in England between late 1981 and early 1984, when the prolonged miners' strike began, women workers were not particularly prominent in them.

By the beginning of 1982, Scottish working-class women were putting the agitation against Thatcherism back on to the agenda of British politics. Writing in the *New Statesman* in February, 1982, Ron Edwards said:

> Scotland's recent wave of factory sit-ins, mainly dominated by women, has taken the male establishment by surprise. The occupation of the Lee Jeans factory at Greenock set an important precedent. Since it ended last August, half a dozen industrial disputes have involved similar actions. Two of these, at Plessey and at the Lovable factory in Cumbernauld, Strathclyde, are still under way. None of the others has ended in outright victory, but in each case the organisers have considered the effort worthwhile — not least because the women themselves, forced into desperate action by the threat of their jobs, have begun to feel their own strength.
>
> The closest parallel to the Lee Jeans sit-in is the action which was taken by 300 women at Lovable ladies' underwear factory, where the workers have been involved, since 8 January, in a round-the-clock "policing" operation to prevent the removal of stock or machinery. The women are all facing redundancy unless a last-minute buyer can be found for the business.

Furthermore, in one of its seemingly 'funny' advertising slogans, the American Lovable company informed the world that: 'Underneath, they're all Lovable', but they suddenly and surprisingly became much less lovable when they decided to challenge the male dominance of capital, power and property.

In January, 1982, 40 women workers in Glasgow threw their defiance in the face of the Tory Establishment, as Ron Edwards explains:

> In a similar protest last month, over 40 part-time cleaners
> occupied the headquarters of the National Savings Bank at
> Cowglen in Glasgow for a week, until they were forced out
> by a court order — and hunger. The women managed to
> close down one of the bank's main computers, while food
> and supplies had to be thrown to them over the fence or
> passed through the windows (a task made more difficult
> when the management removed all the window handles).
> They had been put out of work when one set of cleaning
> contractors lost out to another who employed cheaper
> labour.

Despite sexist criticism and abuse from the media, more and more
working-class women discovered that they could begin, in Shanin's
phrase, to 'control their destinies here and now'.

Although the women's sit-ins were remarkable for creating the
opportunities in which ordinary women could produce first-rate trade
union leadership and express their own creativity and talents, the
Scottish universities have not encouraged anyone to record their stories
and experiences. Considering that so many of the Scottish universities
are staffed with individuals who are hostile towards the native culture,
this is not very surprising, but what did surprise many commentators
and observers was the quiet determination and stubbornness of Scottish
working-class women at a time when so many left-wing intellectuals
were so apathetic.

A notable feature of the women's strikes and factory occupations in
the present and in the past has always been the release of suppressed
working-class creativity, poetry, enthusiasm and passion. In a
description of the strikes of American working women in 1915, Alice
Henry, the American historian, noted:

> In strikes of such magnitude, where whole groups of the
> participators themselves lived for months in a white heat of
> idealism and enthusiasm, life-stories are no longer dragged
> out of shy retiring girls, but are poured out in a burning flood
> by those very same girls, now quite transformed by the
> revolution through which they have passed, and by the *new
> ideas* of *liberty and sisterhood* with which they are possessed.

When allowances are made for the Scots' reticence, Ron Edwards
caught the essence of their similar responses in his fine article,
'Underneath, they're all redundant':

> "Apart from doing your shopping lists, I don't suppose any
> of you were ever organisers like this before, were you?"

queried the man from the BBC with a chuckle. The chief
organiser of the women's illegal occupation, Mrs Ina Scott,
replied with gentle sarcasm: "We never knew we could be
so clever".

The pawky Scottish humour was, of course, alien to the experience of
the commentators educated in Edinburgh private schools and Oxbridge
colleges.

Moreover, during the struggle over the future of the Lee Jeans
factory at Greenock, a woman worker uttered the plaintive cry of many
working-class women in Britain when she said: 'I don't want to retire at
22 years old'. Although the media focused their attention on such
outstanding women as Sadie Lang at Cumbernauld, Helen Monaghan at
Greenock and Ina Scott at Bathgate, the most important aspect of these
struggles with the forces of capitalism was the rank-and-file women's
discovery that women's liberation and socialism are essentially do-it-
yourself movements.[20] In challenging the power of their employers,
they also rearranged their lives at home. As the seven months' struggle
developed, they increasingly told their husbands: 'I am busy. You go
and make the tea and look after the children'.

The cultural force of the past has often reasserted itself within
contemporary history at given moments, particularly during economic
depressions. Marx always insisted that 'In conditions of economic
scarcity all the old crap comes to the top'. What he meant by all the old
crap was the revival of sexism, racism, intimidation, hierarchical
principles and authoritarianism. But, although economic depressions
often initiate a process of de-radicalisation in working-class
communities, they sometimes provoke sustained resistance, too. While
I am not aware of any tangible relationships between the distinctive
historical experiences of Scottish working-class women and their
recent role in factory occupations and sit-ins, this does not mean that
they do not exist. Moreover, in conditions where socialist intellectuals'
questions about the Scottish identity crisis and 'the radical dislocation'
of the British working-class identity have been pushed into the
background by the British miners' strike, perhaps the really important
factor in contemporary politics is the possibility of a unified British
working class re-emerging to cope with the immense problems created
by the right-wing Tories.

Whether this does in fact happen, will depend to a large extent on the
sensitivity of the English, Scottish, Welsh and Irish socialists' response
to the major problems confronting British socialism for the rest of the

1980s — for example, ethnic self-awareness, class conflict, racism, sexism and democratic praxis. Despite the legendary sexism of the British Labour Movement, the miners' strike and the Tories' attacks on working women and men have forced ordinary people to question, challenge and reject the patriarchal practices of the past.

Although such Liberal newspapers as *The Guardian* and *The Observer* feigned surprise over the male chauvinism of many of the younger miners during the early phase of the miners' strike, there was actually nothing at all surprising about this development. In a well-written book, *From a Pitman's Notebook*, published in 1925, Roger Dataller observed that women 'were only worth keeping for their craft'. In *Easingden* published in 1926, J G Sinclair reported that the miners feared that the coal mines might be denuded of labour. Therefore, the marriage bed was 'child-rearing bed' and childless marriages were a 'source of disquietude in the miners' Rows'.[21] But the present development of a new collective consciousness in working-class communities often merges with the past in strange and unpredictable ways.

Before the miners' strike was called by the National Union of Mineworkers in March, 1984, male chauvinism and patronising, paternalistic attitudes towards women workers were commonplace. In a perceptive, socialist-feminist critique of male chauvinist attitudes in the Labour Movement in the 1970s, Beatrix Campbell says:

> But women's right to earn as much as men on the grounds of their economic equality with the men of their community had not prompted an earlier campaign. The very argument that had supported the miners' own rise in the wages league during the 1970s — that the work was difficult and dangerous — counted against an egalitarian measurement of women's skills. The image of the miners as gladiators for women during the Grunwick strike by Asian women in London in the late seventies and the hospital workers' strikes during the early eighties veiled their reservations about the rights of women in general, which have been entrenched in the culture of their community. The sexual apartheid has been reinforced in the assumptions about men's social rights and women's domesticity.

The fact that so many of the Liberal newspapers were surprised by the male chauvinism of the younger miners conveys much more about the remoteness of Establishment journalists from the workaday world of everyday life than anything else. This was simply another confirmation of the observation made by Peter Worsley in 1958, when he said:

> Half-a-century ago Karl Kautsky remarked that the gulf

between the classes in modern society had grown so great
that the ruling-class, in order to obtain information about
working-class life, had to send out fact-finding expeditions
into territory every bit as unknown as Central Africa.

If such a gulf had not still existed in the 1980s, the British ruling class
would not have been so taken aback by the miners' wives, daughters and
sisters unyielding support for the strike of their menfolk.

Although the English — and, indeed, the Scottish — miners' militant
socialist sympathies have not extended during the years since 1945, in
Beatrix Campbell's phrase, 'to a radical philosophy of personal life', the
'loyalty of the women of the mining communities is, of course,
legend'.[22] But within a few weeks of the miners' strike, the women in
the mining communities began to intervene in the dispute
independently of their men. This very recent development in British
labour history would seem to confirm Royden Harrison's view that the
present period of 'discontinuity' represents 'the return to life' of
seemingly ossified working-class organisations at *a higher level* than
ever before.

Although the solidarity and *existentialist* humanism of the miners'
strike was initially marred by the male chauvinism of some of the
younger miners, this was eventually overcome by the leadership.
Moreover, if the force of cultural tradition in mining communities
counts as a factor in current trade union struggles, then the continuity of
the miners' male chauvinist attitudes about the pits being denuded of an
adequate supply of labour has reinforced the miners' resolve to resist
Margaret Thatcher's attempts to destroy their industry.

Yet, within a few weeks of the commencement of the miners' strike,
the women in the mining communities began to play an independent
role. In an article in the *New Statesman* on 27 April, Chris Burkham
reported a conversation with a miner in Brampton: 'Our wives are 100
per cent behind us. If my wife saw me crossing a picket line she'd leave
me'. He also reported the remarkable fact that miners' wives were
producing their own poetry about the strike.[23]

With the prolongation of the strike, the miners' wives and daughters
have become increasingly interested in political questions. In an article
entitled 'Women and the pit strike', Jane Ingham says:

Women are just not blindly backing their men. In the rallies,
on the marches, at the meetings, they have spoken and shown
that they understand only too well what they are fighting for
and against. They have gone on the picket line and learned,
at first hand, whose interests, the police are protecting.

Moreover, in some of the mining communities, miners' wives and daughters began to discuss such questions as the role of the Greenham Common women and the plight of the South African miners.[24]

As the strike developed, working-class women, who had been denied a decent education, discovered their hitherto suppressed talents as speakers, organisers and writers. In challenging the male chauvinism in the mining communities, they also discovered their latent power to 'control their own destinies', as Vanessa Loraine reports:

> Heather Woods is starting to write a book about the strike. She is fully aware of the politics behind it which she will be including as well as impressions, anecdotes, and stories funny and sad throughout the strike.
>
> Many of the women, including Jackie, Joan and Lorna, have written marvellous poems and songs that will become part of the community's history.[25]

This description of what was happening in Stockton was true of many other mining communities, too.

At the time of writing the Afterword to this book, *Women and Popular Struggles*, in November 1984, it might appear that working-class women and miners' wives support groups were involved in the miners' strike from the very beginning. Writing in July in the *New Statesman* in a brilliant article on 'The other miners' strike', Beatrix Campbell observed that Tony Benn's by-election in the north of England marked the real turning-point in the women's involvement:

> Tony Benn's Chesterfield by-election galvanised women. A Labour Club opened which provided a base and Caroline Benn suggested the idea of a women's canvass — by women among women — which had already been tried in London. The women involved kept their nucleus together, mobilised during the overtime ban and went on to hold afternoon meetings in villages during the strike. Now they have 30 groups in the county.

But, at first, the process was very uneven. Besides, although the women's initial role seemed to be spontaneous, it really required considerable organisation. Also working-class women's autonomous self-activity in the miners' strike clearly owed a great deal to the middle-class feminists' agitation for women's liberation. But whether women's role in the strike was spontaneous or organised, it could not have developed at all without the previous existence of anger, frustration and alienation from the *status quo*. In a vivid account of the situation amongst women workers before the First World War, Ray S Baker describes the links between moments of deep demoralisation and apathy and moments of mass militancy:

189

> Some years ago I heard deaf and dumb Helen Keller describe
> how, as a child, she tried to express herself and could not
> speak, could not even make motions that, conveyed any idea,
> could do nothing for herself. She described the wild fits of
> rage she went into. She was suppressed, inhibited.
> Something of the kind goes on among the masses of women
> who are not allowed self-expression.[26]

In emphasising the *universality* of this experience in all industrialised
countries, he noted that prolonged strikes have always had a profound
influence on working-class women's consciousness.

In her brilliant article on 'The other miners' strike', Beatrix
Campbell was much less pessimistic about the miners' traditional male
chauvinist attitudes. By contrast with the skillful and accurate picture
that she paints in her book, *Wigan Pier Revisited*, she is now describing the
new political attitudes and human relationships in the mining
communities in England:

> In ten years time, this miners' strike will be remembered as
> the one in which women emerged as an unprecedented force
> in the community. It's a memorable presence because the
> women were so absent as a collective force before, though
> the dangers associated with that absence are part of
> conventional wisdom in miners' politics . . .
> A "normal" miner's wife's life is a life of exclusion and
> isolation, welded to a culture of solidarity and support,
> though that culture has no clear organised form for women.
> Yet women's lack of organisation is a disaster in a strike of
> this duration and scale. The mobilisation of women also
> involves the *demobilisation of men's resistance*.

By August this resistance was broken when more than 20,000 working-
class women marched through the streets of London in support of the
strike, and Mrs Ann Scargill 'handed in a petition with 20,000 signatures
at Buckingham Palace, urging the Queen to support miners' families
suffering from the strike'.[27]

Moreover, the concept of women's liberation had already influenced
miners' wives long before the miners' strike began. Ideas do shape
working-class history, as Beatrix Campbell explains:

> In hard-pressed Derbyshire, the women's network also had a
> long history. Betty Heathfield went to Skegness, the miners'
> resort, every year for the miners' weekend school. "I used to
> get cheesed off because the miners had their school and we
> were left traipsing around with the kids. But we started to
> sort things out, we had a creche so we could do what we
> wanted, and then we'd have a women's thing and the men

could look after the kids. We never managed to keep our
group together because we came from all over Derbyshire.
But a lot developed from that, we were encouraged to be
something for ourselves.

In Scotland, too, the Women's Movement has had an important impact
on male trade unionists' chauvinist attitudes towards women. In
November, for example, the Edinburgh District Council's committee
for women organised an important exhibition in the City Art
Centre in Edinburgh: 'Not Just Tea and Sandwiches: An Exhibition of
the Miners' Wives Support Groups'. By organising this almost unique
event, Val Woodward provided working-class artists, painters and
photographers with an opportunity to record a new outburst of the
people's creativity. In the various leaflets produced to accompany this
exhibition, the comments and changed and changing attitudes of the
miners' wives, sisters and daughters have been quoted and preserved for
posterity.

Some of these emancipatory developments in the British mining
communities, however, have not always had the maximum impact on
post-1927 orthodox socialist attitudes towards women. Although some
of the miners' wives who participated in putting on the exhibition in the
City Art Centre are now aware of 'the positive aspects' of poverty
and hardship in creating more humane social relationships between
women and men, some socialist journalists have responded to the
women's role in an unconsciously patronising manner.[28] For example, a
journalist in the *Morning Star* was carried away by what he had seen in
some of the miners' welfare clubs without glancing at the actual
relationship between women and men within them:

> The welfares, and the people who run them, are like little
> islands of socialism ahead of their time, where people run
> their own affairs.[29]

Unfortunately, workers' self-activity and democratic relationships
between women and men have never developed automatically out of
existing trade union structures. In any case, male chauvinist attitudes
had not disappeared from the miners' welfare clubs, and some miners'
leaders in local communities have found it very difficult to transcend
their traditional attitudes towards women.

Furthermore, and despite the important developments weakening
male chauvinist attitudes within the mining communities and the broad
Labour Movement, socialist intellectuals have often lagged behind
working women and men. In some of the miners' support groups

191

composed of women and men, socialist intellectuals have sometimes refused to criticise male chauvinist attitudes in case they would alienate the 'heroic miners'. At one Labour Movement meeting in Scotland, a socialist intellectual told me: 'It will be difficult for the miners when the strike is over — the women will never be the same again. It will be difficult to recreate the old relationships'. This whispered comment was made with a strange mixture of sadness and wonderment.

But, although all the women who have participated in the miners' strike have already written a new chapter in the history of British working-class women, it will not be possible to write an epilogue to this particular episode of HERSTORY in Britain for many decades to come. Working-class women and men are now living through a period of crisis and creativity, uncertainty, anxiety and potential redemption and resurrection. Yet, historians are no better equipped than anyone else to predict the outcome of women's present struggles for liberation from oppressive social relationships, unemployment and poverty. Nevertheless, the struggles which began with the agitations leading up to the Reformation in Britain several centuries ago are unlikely to be silenced by such a woman as Margaret Thatcher.[30]

The consensus politics of the past four decades have been shattered beyond repair, and working-class women are again playing a major role in British politics. The last word on the significance of the role of women in the miners' strike ought to be left to Beatrix Campbell:

> For sure, the women have organised as women, they now have a sense of their own strength and without a doubt they have created the infrastructure of a working-class women's movement within the coal communities. But its very existence is contingent on it being a movement in support of men, and it has the support of men because it is for them.
>
> But the future of this women's movement lies in its commitment to women and changing the relationship between women and men. In decades to come, when we come to write and reflect upon the history of this strike as a watershed in working-class politics, the real test of change will be whether this women's movement is allowed to survive — for the women themselves.[31]

References

1 Calvinism and Scottish and English Women, 1560-1690

1   Christina Larner, *Enemies of God: The Witch-Hunt in Scotland* (London, 1981), p197
2   Archibald Robertson, *The Reformation* (London, 1960), p172
3   Christopher Hill, *From Reformation to Industrial Revolution* (London, 1967), p90
4   Willa Muir, *Mrs. Grundy in Scotland* (London, 1936), passim; Thomas Johnston, *History of the Working Classes in Scotland* (Glasgow, 1920), p113
5   Charles Roger, *A Week at Bridge of Allan* (Edinburgh, 1853), pp10-11
6   Rev Thomas Thomson, *A History of the Scottish People* (London, 1894), Vol IV, p535
7   Hill, op cit, p90
8   Larner, op cit, pp99-102
9   Elspeth King, *The Scottish Women's Suffrage Movement* (Glasgow, 1978), p4
10 Eveline Hunter, *Scottish Woman's Place* (Edinburgh, 1978), p2
11 Larner, op cit, p197
12 Michael Walzer, *The Revolution of the Saints* (New York, 1973), p138
13 George Lichtheim, *A Short History of Socialism* (London, 1970), p205
14 Kark Kautsky, *Thomas More and His Utopia* (London, 1927), pp70 and 182
15 G R Elton, *Reformation Europe, 1517-1559* (London, 1963), p53
16 M Philips and W S Tomkinson, *English Women in Life and Letters* (Oxford, 1927), p38
17 Jenny Wormald, *Court, Kirk and Community* (London, 1981), p131
18 George Lichtheim, *Lukacs* (London, 1970), p90
19 Kautsky, op cit, p160
20 Ibid, p190
21 James Napier, *Folk Lore* (Paisley, 1879), p155
22 Quoted in Philips and Tomkinson, op cit, p34
23 David Daiches, *The Paradox of Scottish Culture* (London, 1964), p38
24 Robert Chambers, *The Domestic Annals of Scotland* (Edinburgh, 1858), Vol 1, p6
25 Robert Wodrow, *The History of the Sufferings of the Church of Scotland*, edited Rev Robert Burns (Glasgow, 1828), pxii
26 Chambers, *Domestic Annals*, Vol 2, op cit, p54
27 A D Hope *A Midsummer Eve's Dream* (Edinburgh, 1971), p218
28 Chambers, Vol 1, pp8-9
29 Sheila Rowbotham, *Hidden from History* (London, 1974), p13
30 Hill, op cit, p112
31 Lawrence Stone, *The Family, Sex and Marriage in England, 1500-1800* (London, 1977), pp627-628
32 King, op cit, p15
33 Bob Scribner, 'Religion, Society and Culture: Reorientating the Reformation', *History Workshop*, No 14, 1982, p15

34   Edwin Muir, *John Knox* (London, 1929), pp132 and 309
35   John Langdon-Davies, *A Short History of Women* (London, 1938), p199
36   Stone, op cit, p196
37   Sheila Rowbotham, *Women, Resistance and Revolution* (Harmondsworth, 1972), p3
38   Charles Roger, *Scotland Social and Domestic* (London, 1869), p357
39   David H Fleming, *The Reformation in Scotland* (London, 1910), p475
40   Robertson, op cit, p171
41   Thomson, op cit, Vol 3, p264
42   Ibid, Vol 4, p513
43   Fleming, op cit, p475
44   Alan Macfarlane, *Witchcraft in Tudor and Stuart England* (London, 1970), p187
45   Thomson, Vol 5, op cit, p286
46   Stone, op cit, p80
47   Robert Chambers, *The Picture of Scotland* (Edinburgh, 1828), Vol 1, p198
48   Thomson, Vol 5, op cit, p286
49   Ibid, p287
50   James King Hewson, *The Covenanters* (Glasgow, 1913), Vol 2, pp111-112
51   Chambers, *Domestic Annals*, Vol 2, op cit, p277
52   A Beatrice Wallis Chapman, *The Status of Women under English Law* (London, 1909),
      p51 and *Encyclopaedia of the Laws of Scotland* (Edinburgh, 1929), Vol 8, p492
53   Barbara Ehrenreich and Deirdre English, *For Her Own Good* (London, 1979), p31
54   George Murray, *Records of Falkirk Parish* (Falkirk, 1887), Vol 1, p39
55   James Paterson, *Kay's Edinburgh Portraits* (Glasgow, 1885), p224
56   Alexander Barty, *The History of Dunblane* (Stirling, 1944), pp79 and 97
57   Johnston, op cit, p115
58   Patrick Tytler, *History of Scotland* (Edinburgh, MDCCCXLL), Vol 4, p35; James
      Anderson, *The Ladies of the Covenant* (Edinburgh, 1850), Vol 1, p514
59   James Anderson, *The Ladies of the Reformation* (Glasgow, 1854), p520, Hewson, Vol 1,
      p7
60   Anderson, *Reformation*, op cit, p515
61   Ibid, p577
62   Anderson, *The Ladies of the Covenant*, Vol 1, pxix; Robert Chambers *Traditions of
      Edinburgh* (Edinburgh, 1868), p119
63   Anderson, *The Ladies of the Covenant*, op cit, pxxi
64   Thomson, Vol 5, op cit, p138
65   Frederick Engels, *The Peasant War in Germany* (New York, 1926), p63
66   'But the Scottish masses had always been curiously docile. It was the only country
      in Europe which never had a serious peasant revolt' — Letter from Victor Kiernan
      to the author, 20 December 1979.
67   Chambers, *Domestic Annals*, Vol 2, p213
68   G H Williams, *The Radical Reformation* (London, 1962), pp184 and 862
69   Richard Evans, *The Feminists* (London, 1977), pp17-18
70   Christopher Hill, *The World Turned Upside Down* (Harmondsworth, 1975), p308
71   Christopher Hill, *The Century of Revolution, 1603-1714* (London, 1963), p308
72   Hewson, Vol 2, p182
73   Anderson, *The Ladies of the Covenant*, Vol 1, pxii
74   James Aikman, *Annals of the Persecution in Scotland* (Edinburgh, MDCCCXLII), p70
75   Robert Wodrow, *The History of the Church of Scotland* (Glasgow, MDCCCXXXIX),
      Vol 2, pp268-270
76   Anderson, *The Ladies of the Covenant*, pp360-362
77   *Memorials of the Rev Law*, op cit, pp186-192; Chambers, *Domestic Annals*, Vol 2, p415

78 Aikman, op cit, pp488-489
79 Quoted in Ibid, pp364 and xxv
80 Hewson, Vol 2, p464
81 Aikman, op cit, pp488-490
82 *Memorials of the Rev Law,* op cit, pp186-192; Chambers, *Domestic Annals*, Vol 2, p327
83 Thomson, Vol V, p296
84 Ibid, p293
85 Hamish Henderson, 'The Ballad, the Folk and the Oral Tradition', *The People's Past*, edited E J Cowan (Edinburgh, 1980), p96

2 *Popular Culture and Women's Struggles, 1770-1850*

1 A L Morton, 'French Revolutionaries and English Democrats', *Labour Monthly*, No9, 1939, p536; Robert Palmer, *The Age of Democratic Revolution* (Princeton, 1959), p82
2 Lawrence Stone, *The Family, Sex and Marriage in England, 1500-1800* (London, 1977), p156
3 Ibid p631
4 Robert Chambers, *The Domestic Annals of Scotland* (Edinburgh, 1858), Vol 3, p626
5 *Glasgow Mercury*, 31 July 1778
6 A C Chitnis, *The Scottish Enlightenment* (London, 1976), pp47-48
7 An important consequence of industrialisation in England and elsewhere was, in Shorter's view, 'the historic shift towards individualism and affection'. Edward Shorter, *The Making of the Modern Family* (New York, 1975), p108 and passim.
8 Stone, op cit, p667
9 I B O'Malley, *Women in Subjection* (London, 1933), pp18-19
10 Erna Reiss, *Rights and Duties of Englishwomen* (London, 1934), pp6-7
11 Janet Dunbar, *The Early Victorian Woman* (London, 1935), p25
12 Alfred Waddilove, 'The Law of Marriage and Divorce in England, Ireland and Scotland', *Transaction of the National Association for the Promotion of Social Science*, 1861, p196
13 Patrick Fraser, *Treatise on the Law of Scotland as applicable to the Personal and Domestic Relations* (Edinburgh, 1846), Vol 1, p241; Patrick Fraser, *Treatise on Husband and wife according to the Law of Scotland* (Edinburgh, 1876), Vol 1, p512 and Vol 2, p883
14 Winifred Holtby, *Women in a Changing Civilisation* (London, 1934), p44; C G Hartley, *The Truth About Women* (London, 1914), p355
15 *Scottish Diaries and Memoirs*, edited J G Fyfe (Stirling, 1942), p332
16 Vanda F Neff, *Victorian Working Women* (London, 1966), p208
17 R De Bruce Trotter, *Galloway Gossip or the Southern Abbanich 80 Years Ago* (Dumfries, 1901), p103; E J Guthrie, *Old Scottish Customs* (Glasgow, 1885), p109
18 Marie Stopes, *Marriage in My Time* (London, 1935), p202
19 O'Malley, op cit, p328
20 David Gilmour, *Paisley Weavers of Other Days* (Paisley, 1876), p126
21 Hawkie (William Cameron) told John K Hunter of his very unusual experience with working-class women in Glasgow in the 1830s: 'The wives, puir creatures, were for once fairly out-talked'. John K Hunter, *Life Studies of Character* (London, 1870), p144
22 Thomas Johnston, *The History of the Working Classes in Scotland* (Glasgow, 1920), p53

23 Stone, op cit, p655
24 Barbara Ehrenreich and Deirdre English, *For Her Own Good* (London, 1979), p7
25 Population of Great Britain. Occupation Abstract. *Parliamentary Papers*, Vol XXVII, 1844, passim
26 James E Handley, *The Irish in Scotland* (Glasgow, 1964), p328 and p277; *Scottish Population History*, edited Michael Flinn (Cambridge, 1977), p365
27 James Dawson Burn, *The Autobiography of a Beggar Boy*, edited with an introduction by David Vincent (London, 1978), p41
28 Abram Combe, *Metaphorical Sketches of the Old and the New Systems* (Edinburgh, 1823), p165
29 J F C Harrison, *Robert Owen and the Owenites in Britain and America* (London, 1969), p83
30 *Tait's Edinburgh Magazine*, January 1849
31 Elizabeth I Spence, *Sketches of the Present Manners of Scotland* (London, 1811), pp98-100
32 'Paisley and Glasgow 52 Years Ago', *The Chartist Circular*, 25 April 1840
33 Robert Chambers, *The Picture of Scotland* (Edinburgh, 1847), Vol 2, p9
34 Robert Dale Owen, *Treading My Own Way* (London, 1874), p88
35 Eden and Cedar Paul, 'A French Comrade's View of the British Labour Movement', *The Worker*, 1 November 1919
36 'After Empire', *New Edinburgh Review*, No 37, 1977
37 David Craig, *Scottish Literature and the Scottish People, 1680-1830* (London, 1961), p36
38 Sheila Rowbotham, *Hidden from History* (London, 1977), p32
39 *Collected Writings of Dugald Graham*, edited by George MacGregor (London, 1883), Vol 2, p232
40 Henry G Graham,*The Social Life of Scotland in the Eighteenth Century* (London, 1906), p189
41 Johnston, op cit, p86
42 E P Thompson, 'Patrician Society and Plebeian Culture', *Journal of Social History*, Vol 7, No 4, 1974; E P Thompson, *The Making of the English Working Class* (New York, 1966), p403; Patrick Joyce, *Work, Society and Politics. The Culture of the Factory in Later Victorian England* (Brighton, 1980), pp292-301
43 'Factory Bill — Beneficial to England, But Not to Scotland, Without the Introduction of Poor Laws', *The Radical Reformers' Gazette*, 26 January 1833
44 Thompson, 'Patrician Society', op cit, p393
45 Frederick Engels, *The Origin of the Family, Private Property and the State* (Peking, 1978), p156 and p160
46 John Fraser, *The Humourous Chap-Books of Scotland* (New York, 1873), Vol 2, p94
47 Patrick Walker, *Biographia Presbyteriana* (Edinburgh, 1827), Vol 1, p131
48 Robert Chambers, *Traditions of Edinburgh* (Edinburgh, 1868), p23; I Lettice,*Letters on a Tour through various parts of Scotland* (London, 1794), p86
49 Gail Malmgreen, *Neither Bread nor Roses* (Brighton, 1978), p23; Peter F Anson, *Fishing Boats and Fisher Folk on the East Coast of Scotland* (London, 1930), p74
50 Martha Vicinus, *The Industrial Muse* (London, 1975), pp5-45
51 *Statistical Account of Scotland* (Edinburgh, 1790-1794), Vol XVI, p18; *Personal Recollections of Mary Somerville* (London, 1873), edited Martha Somerville, p14; Robert Chambers, *Picture of Scotland*, Vol 2, op cit, pp107 and 162
52 Graham, *Collected Writings*, Vol 2, op cit, p55
53 Children's Employment Commission, *Parliamentary Papers*, Vol XVI, 1842, p475; A Millar, *Coatbridge. Its Rise and Progress* (Glasgow, 1864), p181
54 William Thom, *Rhymes and Recollections of a Hand-Loom Weaver*, edited W Skinner

(Paisley, 1880), p6; *Statistical Account of Scotland* (Edinburgh, 1790-1794), Vol VII, p329

55 Millar, *Coatbridge*, op cit, p177; Anonymous, *Chapters in the Life of a Dundee Factory Boy* (Dundee, 1850), p21; George Legman, *The Horn Book* (Dundee, 1850), p361

56 Hunter, *Life Studies*, op cit, p277

57 *Glasgow Free Press*, 24 May 1834

58 John Ashton, *Gossip* (London, 1903), p58

59 Letter in the National Library of Scotland, MS 4027

60 Hawkie, *The Autobiography of a Gangrel*, edited John Strathesk (Glasgow, 1885), p14

61 David Vincent, *Bread, Knowledge and Freedom. A Study of Nineteenth-Century Working-Class Autobiography* (London, 1981), p42

62 *Northern Star*, 10 January 1846 and 25 March 1848; Vincent, *Bread, Knowledge and Freedom*, op cit, pp66 and 146; Thomas Johnston, *Old Kirkintilloch* (Kirkintilloch, 1927), p132

63 Engels, *The Origin of the Family*, op cit, p55

64 *Edinburgh Review*, Vol 36, 1821, p251

65 Millicent G Fawcett, *Women's Suffrage* (London, 1912), p7

66 William C Lehmann, *John Millar of Glasgow, 1735-1801* (Cambridge, 1960), p224

67 Michael Ignatieff, 'Marxism and Classical Political Economy', *People's History and Marxist Theory* (London, 1981), edited Ralph Samuel

68 Harrison, *The Owenites,* op cit, pp85-86

69 Lehmann, *John Millar*, op cit, p137

70 Ibid, p77

71 Davis D McElroy, *A Century of Scottish Clubs, 1700-1800*, PhD thesis, Edinburgh, 1979, pp148-155

72 Ian Simpson Ross, *Lord Kaimes and the Scotland of His Day* (Oxford, 1972), p339

73 John Ramsay, *Scotland and the Scotsmen of the Eighteenth Century* (Edinburgh, 1888), Vol 1, p204

74 Gladys Bryson, *Man and Society. The Scottish Inquiry of the Eighteenth Century* (New York, 1968), p189

75 Ibid, p7

76 John Langdon-Davies, *A Short History of Women* (London, 1928), pp223-225

77 Nan Wilson, 'Legal Attitudes to Slavery in Eighteenth-Century Britain: English Myth: Scottish Social Realism and Their Wider Comparative Context', *Race*, Vol XI, No 4, 1970

78 Elizabeth Haldane, *The Scotland of Our Fathers* (London, 1933), p66; *Edinburgh Review*, No 57, 1833, p1

79 William R Waterman, *Frances Wright* (New York, 1924), passim

80 A R Schoyen, *The Chartist Challenge* (London, 1962), p204

81 Earl Barnes, *Women in Modern Society* (London, 1912), pp174-175

82 W R Greg, *Why Are Women Redundant?* (London, 1869), p4

83 G W Johnson, *The Evolution of Woman* (London, 1926), p243; Alice Zimmern, *Women's Suffrage in Many Lands* (London, 1909), p9

84 Jurgen Kuczynski claims that the first recorded women's strike occurred in America in 1824. He obviously was not aware of the Scottish women's strike in the previous century. See his *The Rise of the Working Class* (London, 1967), p120

85 Alfred, *The History of the Factory Movement from the Year 1802 to the Enactment of the Ten Hour Act in 1847* (London, 1857), p19; G J Holyoake, *Self-Help a Hundred Years Ago* (London, 1882), pp129-131; R W Cooke Taylor, *The Modern Factory System* (London, 1891), p203; *Aberdeen Journal*, 2 January 1792

86 Winifred Holtby, *Women and a Changing Civilisation* (London, 1934), p75

87 *Report of the Aberdeen Female Operatives' Union* (Aberdeen, 1834), pp3-4
88 Rowbotham, *Hidden from History*, op cit, p32
89 Jack Wade, *History of the Middle and Working Classes* (London, 1835), p570
90 'Popular education was so utterly unkown to England that the ignorance of the lower orders was considered as a positive recommendation'. Henry Cockburn, *Life of Lord Cockburn* (Edinburgh, 1852), Vol 1, p296
91 Walter Rodney, *A History of the Guyanese Working People, 1881-1905* (London, 1981), p151
92 John Foster, 'Scotland's Three Unlikely Stories', *Morning Star*, 13 April 1969
93 *Glasgow Journal*, 24 March 1768
94 I B O'Malley, *Women in Subjection*, op cit, p318
95 Hamish Henderson, 'Some Thoughts on Highland History', *Cencrastus*, No 3, 1980
96 *Glasgow Chronicle*, 27 August 1828; Handley, *The Irish in Scotland*, op cit, p24
97 Ken Logue, *Popular Disturbances in Scotland, 1780-1815* (Edinburgh, 1979), pp198-202
98 Adam Dawson, *Rambling Recollections of Past Times* (Falkirk, 1868), p10; Dorothy Thompson, 'Women and Nineteenth-Century Radical Politics', *The Rights and Wrongs of Women* (Harmondsworth, 1976), p116; Patricia Branca, *Women in Europe since 1750* (London, 1978), p70; Alexander Stewart, *Reminiscences of Dunfermline* (Edinburgh, 1886), p208
99 Logue, op cit, p203; H O Correspondence, RH 2/4/81, Scottish Records Office, Edinburgh; *Glasgow Herald and Chronicle*, 9 October 1797
100 O'Malley, op cit, pp311-313
101 Samuel Bamford, *Passages in the Life of a Radical* (London, 1893), p338
102 *Gorgon*, 22 August 1818
103 *Annual Register for 1819* (London, 1820), p348
104 Fawcett, op cit, p8
105 *Hansard*, 29 November 1819, Vol XLI, p391
106 Ivy Pinchbeck, *Women Workers*, op cit, p323
107 Edward Royle and James Walvin, *English Radicals and Reformers, 1760-1848* (London, 1982), p186
108 *The Herald to Trades' Advocate*, 16 October 1830 and the *Chartist Circular*, 14 March 1840
109 Hunter, *Life Studies,* op cit, p113; David Gilmour, *Reminiscences of the "Pen" Folk* (Paisley, 1878), p14; *Glasgow Free Press*, 16 April 1834; Elspeth King, *The Scottish Women's Suffrage Movement* (Glasgow, 1978), p9
110 *Glasgow Evening Post and Renfrewshire Reformer*, 15 March 1834; Thompson, *Women and Nineteenth-Century Radical Politics*, op cit, p123; *Glasgow Constitutional*, 20 November 1839
111 Ashton, *Gossip*, op cit, p131; Strachey, *The Cause*, op cit, p30
112 Ashton, *Gossip*, op cit, p194; quoted in Fawcett, op cit, p17

3 Women and the Class Struggle in Mid-Victorian Britain

1 Ethel Snowden, *The Feminist Movement* (London, ND, probably 1914), p132; Elizabeth Haldane, *The Scotland of Our Fathers: A Study of Scottish Life in the Nineteenth Century* (London, 1933), pp59-60

2 Elizabeth Stanton and Matilda Gage, *History of Woman Suffrage* (New York, 1970), Vol 3 p852

3 Eunice G Murray, *Scottish Women in Bygone Days* (Glasgow, 1930), p172

4 *The Woman's Book*, edited Florence B Jack (London, 1911), p697

5 John Ashton, *Gossip* (London, 1903), p298

6 Karl Marx, *Capital* (London, 1949), Vol 1, p391

7 Bessie Rayner Parkes, *Essays on Women's Work* (London, 1966), p23

8 Ibid, pp23-24

9 John Milne,*The Industrial and Social Position of Women in the Middle and Lower Ranks* (London, 1857), p233

10 Anonymous, *A Woman's Thoughts on Women's Rights* (Edinburgh, 1876), p12

11 Hamish Henderson, 'Some Thoughts on Highland History', *Cencrastus*, No 3, 1980, p16

12 Barbara Drake, *Women in Trade Unions* (London, 1921), p22

13 Ibid, p24; B L Hutchins, *Women in Modern Industry* (London, 1915), p121

14 A D Hope, *A Midsummer Eve's Dream* (Edinburgh, 1971), pp215-218

15 Sheila Lewenhak, *Women and Trade Unions* (London, 1977), p115

16 William Power, *Literature and Oatmeal* (London, 1935), p127

17 Lewis Grassic Gibbon and Hugh MacDiarmid, *Scottish Scene* (London, 1934), p324

18 Joseph L Melling, 'The Scottish Working Class and the Problems of Clydeside from the 1870s to the 1920s', Conference of Socialist Economists at the University of Stirling, May 1978

19 'Calico Printing and Turkey-Red Dyeing', *North British Daily Mail*, 18 January 1868

20 T C Smout, 'Aspects of Sexual Behaviour in Nineteenth-Century Scotland', *Social Class in Scotland*, edited A A MacLaren (Edinburgh, 1978), pp73-75

21 Lewenhak, op cit, p86

22 *The Times*, 20 November 1871

23 *North British Daily Mail*, 4 July 1873

24 Ibid, 2 November 1871

25 *Aberdeen Journal*, 25 October 1871

26 *Dunfermline Journal*, 9 November 1872

27 *North British Daily Mail*, 22 August 1873

28 Robert Gillespie, *Round About Falkirk* (Glasgow, 1878), p248

29 *Edinburgh Evening Courant*, 24 August 1868; *Kilmarnock Advertiser*, 24 June 1879

30 Quoted in Eric Richards, 'Women in the British Economy since about 1700: An Introduction', *History*, Vol LIX, 1974, p342

31 *Dunfermline Journal*, 10 April 1973

32 *North British Daily Mail*, 4 February 1875

33 Ibid, 18 February 1875

34 Vanda F Neff, *Victorian Working Women* (London, 1966), p36

35 *Dunfermline Journal*, 2 October 1875

36 Augustus Muir, *Nairns of Kirkcaldy* (Cambridge, 1956), p64

37 *Minutes of the Edinburgh Trades Council*, 27 April 1875

38 *Dunfermline Journal*, 22 September 1875

39 E P Thompson, *The Making of the English Working Class* (Harmondsworth, 1968), p401

40 Henry Hamilton, *The Industrial Revolution in Scotland* (London, 1966), p11

41 Henry Buckle, *History of English Civilisation* (London, 1914), Vol 3, p103

42 *Women as Barmaids* (London, 1905), pp1-3

43 Hope, op cit, p166

44 R De Bruce Trotter, *Galloway Gossip* (Perth, 1901), p442

45 "That's some of your English notions", said Maggie MacNab, "working women ha' nae time for dawtin (affectionate) bairns or men either". Margaret M Brewster, *Sunbeams in the Cottage or What Women May Do* (Edinburgh, 1864), p35

46 Janet Hassan, 'Clichés or Côncepts in a Scottish Setting', WEA Conference, Edinburgh, 10-11 November 1978

47 Hope, op cit, p192

48 Smout, op cit, p69

49 Henry G Graham, *Social Life in Scotland in the Eighteenth Century* (Edinburgh, 1937), Vol 2, p46

50 'Hiring Fairs and their Scandals', *Stirling Journal*, 11 May 1872

51 E J Hobsbawm, *Revolutionaries* (London, 1973), pp218-219

52 *Our Freedom and Its Results*, edited Ray Strachey (London, 1936), p183

53 *The Scotsman*, 24 February 1854

54 Alfred Leffingwell, *Illegitimacy* (London, 1892), p64; *A Scottish Working Man* (Robert Wilson), *Prostitution Suppressible* (Glasgow, 1871), p92

55 James D Burn, *The Working Classes in the United States during the War* (London, 1965), p77

56 Ibid, p79

57 AD 2/12, Scottish Records Office, Edinburgh

58 Margaret Sanger, *An Autobiography* (London, 1939), p124; Gertrude M Williams, *The Passionate Pilgrim* (London, ND), p91; Ethel M Elderton, *Report on the English Birthrate* (London, 1914), Vol 1, p234

59 A A MacLaren, 'Presbyterianism and the Working Class in a mid-Nineteenth Century City', *Scottish Historical Review*, No 142, 1968, p139

60 *Kirkintilloch Free Church Session Minutes*, 2 April 1868 and 16 December 1869, Scottish Records Office

61 *Gallatown Free Church Session Minutes*, 1 August 1876

62 Kenneth M Boyd, *Scottish Church Attitudes to Sex, Marriage and the Family, 1850-1914* (Edinburgh, 1980), p129

63 Ibid, 307

64 *Proceedings of the Free Church of Scotland*, 1873, p50

65 David Kerr Cameron, *The Ballad and the Plough* (London, 1978), p119

66 George Legman, *The Hornbook* (London, 1970), passim

67 Cameron, op cit, p131

68 Alexander Thompson, *The Licentiousness of Scotland* (London, 1861), p5

69 *Stirling Journal*, 2 June 1876

70 Michael Hechter, *Internal Colonialism* (London, 1975), p33

71 Boyd, op cit, p33

72 Andrew Wallace, 'Pauperism and the Poor Law', *Proceedings of the Glasgow Philosophical Society*, Vol X, No 1, 1877-1878, p181

73 Thomas Ferguson, *Scottish Social Welfare* (Edinburgh, 1958), p260

74 'Immorality in Scotland', *The Glasgow Sentinel*, 23 April 1870

75 Ibid, 4 June 1870

76 'The Clergy and Immorality', ibid, 1 June 1872

77 E J Hobsbawm, *The Age of Capital* (London, 1975), p256

78 See Chapter 2

79 Boyd, op cit, p1

80 Ibid, p325

81 H G Gutman, Introduction to *Working Lives*, edited by Marc S Miller (New York, 1980), pxvii

82 Willa Muir, *Mrs. Grundy in Scotland* (London, 1927), p45

83 'Outrages on Women', *North British Review*, May, 1856

84 *Annual Register*, 1851, p196
85 Ibid, 1872, p196
86 Hope, op cit, p164
87 George Borrow, *The Romany Rye* (London, 1876), p461
88 Frances Power Cobbe, 'Wife Torture in England', *Contemporary Review*, April 1878
89 *Annual Register*, 1853, p76; Arthur R Cleveland, *Women under the English Law* (London, 1896), p262
90 W M Cooper, *A History of the Rod* (London, 1864), p397
91 Quoted in Edward Abbot Parry, *The Law and the Woman* (London, 1916), p46
92 Cobbe, op cit, p63
93 By Herself, *The Life of Frances Power Cobbe* (London, 1894), Vol 2, p223
94 Frances Power Cobbe, *The Duties of Women* (Boston, 1881), p17; Annie Besant, *Marriage* (London, 1882), p14
95 A Beatrice Wallis Chapman, *The Status of Women under English Law* (London, 1909), p62; *Life of Frances Power Cobbe*, op cit, pp224-225
96 'The Lash for Wife-Beaters', *Dunfermline Journal*, 13 February 1875
97 Reports to the Secretary of State on the Law relating to Brutal Assaults, *Parliamentary Papers*, Vol LXI, 1875, p127
98 AD 56/18, Scottish Records Office
99 *Minutes of the Edinburgh Trades Council*, 13 and 27 April 1875
100 D D McElroy, *Scotland's Age of Improvement: A Survey of Eighteenth-Century Literary Clubs and Societies* (Washington State University Press, Pullman, 1969), passim
101 *Edinburgh Reformer,* 29 August 1868; Constance Rover, *Women's Suffrage and Party Politics in Britain, 1866-1914* (London, 1967), p56
102 Charles Anthony, *The Social and Political Dependence of Women* (London, 1867), p1
103 James Stuart, *Reminiscences* (London, 1912), p228
104 *Minutes of the Edinburgh Trades Council*, 10 May 1870
105 Mary A Hamilton, *Mary MacArthur* (London, 1922), pp18-22
106 Erna Reiss, *Rights and Duties of Englishwomen* (Manchester, 1934), p241
107 *Report of the British Trades Union Congress*, 1877, p17

4 Scottish and English Women and Protest, 1880-1914

1 'We are writing to you regarding the issue of differential rates of violence against wives in Scotland versus England and Wales. . . . The historical statistics are too fragmentary and incomplete and would render any attempt at direct comparison spurious. The contemporary scene is also fraught with problems. The only explicit attempt to assess the rate of official reporting of assaults on wives is our own work (in 1974) on Scottish Police records. This research reveals that wife assaults constitute about 25% of all reported crimes of violence. There is no comparable data for England and Wales.' Letter from Russell P Dobash and R Emerson Dobash to the author, 6 June 1984. Although Dobash and Dobash have not researched extensively into the historical differences between Scotland and England, we should not ignore their comments on the statistical evidence.
2 Eugene A Hecker, *A Short History of Women's Rights* (New York, 1910), passim; Ethel Snowden, *The Feminist Movement* (London, ND, probably 1914), passim
3 W E Carson, *The Marriage Revolt* (London, 1915), p292
4 Alfred Plowden, *Autobiography of a Police Magistrate* (London, ND, probably 1904), p276

5 *Recollections of the Public Work and Home Life of Louisa Stevenson,* Printed for private circulation (Edinburgh ND), p10; James Coutts, *A History of the University of Glasgow* (Glasgow, 1909), p458; A Logan Turner, *History of the University of Edinburgh* (Edinburgh, 1933), p42; S J Curtis, *History of English Education since 1800* (London, 1960), p348

6 Peter Sterns, 'Working-Class Women in Britain, 1890-1914', in *Suffer and Be Still*, edited Martha Vicinus (Bloomington, 1970), pp113 and 115

7 Matilda J Gage, *Women, Church and State* (New York, 1893), p440; *Forward*, 21 August and 11 September 1909

8

	England and Wales		Scotland	
Agriculture			Agriculture	
Male	Female		Male	Female
971,708	90,128		148,426	32,423
Mining			Mining	
Male	Female		Male	Female
1,010,834	3,570		161,812	2,537

These figures from the 1911 census underline the significant differences in the two countries. The percentage of female workers in the total labour force in England and Wales engaged in agriculture and coal mining was 8.49% and 0.35%. In Scotland the corresponding percentage was 17.93% and 1.54%

Population of England and Wales, *Parliamentary Papers*, Vol LXXIX, 1913; Population of Scotland, *Parliamentary Papers*, Vol LXXX, 1913

9 Gage, op cit, p441

10 O Jocelyn Dunlop, *The Farm Labourer* (London, 1913), p193

11 Barbara Drake, *Women in Trade Unions* (London, 1921), p21; Winifred Holtby, *Women in a Changing Civilisation* (London, 1934), p79

12 *Women's Trade Union Review*, July 1912

13 *Forward*, 1 October 1910

14 Drake, op cit, p50

15 Sylvia Anthony, *Women's Place in Industry and Home* (London, 1932), p263

16 Cecil Chapman, *Marriage and Divorce* (London, 1911), p97

17 Keir Hardie, *The Citizenship of Women* (London, 1905), p7

18 Sheila Lewenhak, 'The Lesser Trade Union Organisation of Women than of Men', *Bulletin of the Society for the Study of Labour History*, No 26, 1973

19 Agnes Mure MacKenzie, *Scotland in Modern Times* (Edinburgh, 1947), p252

20 See below

21 H F Normanton, *Magna Carta and Women* (London, 1915), p10

22 Marie C Stopes, *Marriage in My Time* (London, 1935), p202

23 Eugene A Hecker, *A Short History of Women's Rights* (New York, 1910), p180

24 Margaret Bain, 'Scottish Women in Politics', *Chapman*, No 3-4, 1980, p5

25 Mrs Archibald Colquhoun, *The Vocation of Woman* (London, 1913), pp27-28

26 Leon Trotsky, *On Literature and Art*, edited by Paul N Siegal (New York, 1970), p89

27 Hecker, op cit, p127

28 A M B Meakin, *Women in Transition* (London, 1907), pp145-146

29 Hecker, op cit, p127

30 Alfred C Plowden, *Grain or Chaff. The Autobiography of a Police Magistrate* (London, ND, probably 1904), p278

31 Annie Besant, *Marriage* (London, 1822), p14

32 Marion Holmes, *The A.B.C. of Votes for Women* (London, ND, probably 1910), p7

33 Ethel Snowden, *The Feminist Movement* (London, 1914), p228 and H G Wells, *Socialism and the Family* (London, 1907), p29

34 Elizabeth S Chesser, *Women's Charter of Rights and Liberties* (London, 1909), p17

35 J Johnson, *Wastage of Child Labour* (London, 1909), p29

36 Lady Mclaren, *The Women's Charter of Rights and Liberties* (London, 1909), p17

37 *Pall Mall Gazette*, 20 October 1882; *South Wales Daily News*, 2 May 1882; John Ashton, *The Dawn of the Nineteenth Century in England* (London, 1886), p67; Robert Briffault, *The Mothers* (London, 1927), Vol 2, p223

38 T Sharper Wilson, *The Origins of Popular Superstitions and Customs* (London, 1910), p108

39 Mrs H M Stanwick, *The Future of the Woman's Movement* (London, 1913), p79

40 Frances Power Cobbe, *The Duties of Women* (Boston, 1881), p17

41 A Beatrice Wallis Chapman, *The Status of Women under the English Law* (London, 1909), p71

42 Hecker, op cit, pp132-35

43 'A good number of Englishmen seem to think that they have a perfect right to thrash or kick their wives as the Americans had to "lick his nigger". Yes, and some of these fellows are completely astonished when a magistrate ventures to hold a different opinion.' Thomas Holmes, *Pictures and Problems from London Police Courts* (London, 1900), p73

44 James D Young, *The Rousing of the Scottish Working Class* (London, 1979), p172

45 H L Smith and V Nash, *The Story of the Dockers' Strike* (London,1889), p82

46 Jack London, *The People of the Abyss* (London, 1963), p134

47 Lady McLaren, op cit, p17

48 *Working Women and Divorce. An Account of the Evidence Given on Behalf of the Women's Co-operative Guild before the Royal Commission on Divorce* (London, 1911), p39

49 *Justice*, 9 July 1914

50 Chesser, op cit, p77

51 Report on the Judicial Statistics of Scotland for the Year 1900, Accounts and Papers, *Parliamentary Papers*, Vol CXVII, p36 and Vol C, 1914, p125

52 Anne Showstack Sassoon, *Gramsci's Politics* (London, 1980), p191

53 Thomas Johnston, *The History of the Working Classes in Scotland* (Glasgow, 1922), pp155-56

54 William Mitchell, *Rescue the Children* (London, 1882), p41

55 D Lennox, *Working Class Life in Dundee, 1878-1905*, unpublished manuscript (1905), St Andrews University library, MS DA 890, p54

56 Sheila Rowbotham and Jeffrey Weeks, *Socialism and the New Life* (London, 1977), pp63-99

57 A J P Taylor, *English History, 1914-1945* (Oxford, 1965), p163

58 Margaret Bondfield, *A Life's Work* (London, 1948), p42

59 Ethel M Elderton, *Report on the English Birthrate* (London, 1914), Vol 1, p181 and passim; James D Young, 'The Problems and Progress of the Social History of the British Working Class, 1880-1914', *Labor History*, Vol 18, No 2, 1977, pp257-266

60 Kellogg Durland, *Among the Fife Miners* (London, 1904), pp116-118

61 'They are the only people among whom the women are truly equal, participating in plays, meetings and all their affairs, an example for all others.' Elizabeth Gurley Flynn, *I Speak My Own Piece* (New York, 1955), p200

62 Ethel M Elderton, *Report on the English Birthrate* (London, 1914), p121

63 Interview with the veteran socialist, Bob Selkirk, Cowdenbeath, 11 July 1972

64 Alexander Paterson, *Across the Bridges* (London, 1911), p210 and *Studies of Boy Life*,

edited E J Urwick (London, 1904), pp82-83
65 Stanley Reynolds, *The Lower Deck* (London, 1912), p29
66 Young, *The Rousing*, op cit, pp134-185
67 James H Muir, *Glasgow in 1901* (Glasgow, 1901), p190
68 Mari Jo Buhle, *Feminism and Socialism in the United States, 1820-1920*, PhD thesis, University of Wisconsin, Madison, 1974, p128
69 Harry McShane, *No Mean Fighter* (London, 1978), p34
70 Samson Bryher, *An Account of the Labour and Socialist Movement in Bristol* (Bristol, 1929), p33
71 *I.L.P. News*, August 1903
72 Andrew Rosen, *Rise Up, Women* (London, 1974), p50
73 Interview with Bob Selkirk, 19 May 1972
74 William Ferguson, *Scotland: 1689 to the Present* (Edinburgh, 1968), p350
75 Stephen Maxwell, 'Women in Scotland', Q, 27 May 1977
76 Lady Frances Balfour, *Ne Oliviscaris. Dinnae Forget* (London, 1930), Vol 2, p140
77 *The Case for Women's Suffrage*, edited Brougham Villiers (London, 1907), pp33-34
78 Ferguson, op cit, p351
79 Bain, op cit, p5
80 *Justice*, 4 January 1896
81 Sandy Macfarlane, 'The Position of Women among the Early Christians', *Justice*, 17 August 1895
82 Arthur Keep, 'The Proletarian of the Home', *Justice*, 9 January 1897
83 Archibald McLaren to R F Muirhead, 24 June 1888. McLaren-Muirhead Archives, Baillie's Library, Glasgow
84 Diary of Andreas Scheu, International Institute of Social Hitory, Amsterdam
85 Bob Duncan, *James Leatham* (Aberdeen, 1978), p30
86 Ibid, p68
87 For details of the Suffragettes' incendiarism in Glasgow, see *The Suffragette*, 12 June 1913
88 *Justice*, 30 July 1914
89 Daniel De Leon, *The Ballot and the Class Struggle* (New York, 1971), p73
90 *Justice*, 25 October 1913
91 Antonia Raeburn, *The Militant Suffragettes* (London, 1973), p125
92 MacKenzie, op cit, p259
93 Richard Bell, *Trade Unionism* (London, 1907), p82
94 Sheila Lewenhak, *Women and Trade Unions* (London, 1977), p102
95 Snowden, op cit, p192
96 *Minutes of the Glasgow Trades Council*, 13 November 1912
97 Minutes of the East London Federation of Suffragettes, 27 January 1914, International Institute of Social History, Amsterdam
98 *Forward*, 13 January 1914
99 Arthur Gleason and Paul U Kellog, *British Labour History and the War* (New York, 1919), p141 and Mary A Hamilton, *Mary MacArthur* (London, 1925), p57
100 Ibid, p88
101 R S Neale, *Class and Ideology in the Nineteenth Century* (London, 1972), p151
102 Lewenhak, *Women and Trade Unions*, pp114-115
103 Emilia F S Dilke, 'The Seamy Side of Trade Unionism for Women', *New Review*, May 1890, p418
104 *The Woman Worker*, 26 June 1908
105 *Report of the British T.U.C.*, 1910, p210
106 A A Bulley and M Whitley, *Women's Work* (London, 1894), pp99-100

107 Socialist League Archives, F274, International Institute of Social History, Amsterdam

108 Geoffrey Drage, *The Labour Problem* (London, 1896), p99; A M Bulley and M Whitley, *Women's Work* (London, 1894), p84

109 A M Anderson, *Women in the Factory* (London, 1922), p119

110 Margaret H Irwin, *Women's Industries in Scotland* (Glasgow, 1896), p17

111 Robert H Sherard, *The Child Slaves of Britain* (London, 1905), p187

112 'Falkirk's Immorality', *Falkirk Mail*, 20 and 27 December 1913

113 George L Bolen, *Getting A Living*, (New York, 1903), p478

114 Young, *The Rousing*, op cit, pp168-69

115 Drake, op cit, p24

116 Gertrude Tuckwell, *et al*, *Women in Industry from Seven Points of View* (London, 1908), p79; Hamilton, *Mary MacArthur*, op cit, p148

117 Ibid, p96

118 W H Marwick, *A Short History of Labour in Scotland* (Edinburgh, 1967), pp54-56; Lewenhak, *Women and Trade Unions*, op cit, pp80-81

119 Thomas Don to Sidney Webb, 14 November 1892, Webb Collection, The Library of the London School of Politics and Economics

120 Joseph Claydon, *Trade Unions* (London, ND, probably 1914), p85

121 Charles Watney and James A Little, *Industrial Warfare* (London, 1912), p262

122 Margaret H Irwin, *Home Work Amongst Women* (Glasgow, ND), p17

123 Socialist League Archives, Miscellaneous File

124 Drake, op cit, p42

125 Royal Commission on Labour, Fifth and Final Report, 1894, *Parliamentary Papers*, Vol XXXV, p539

126 Drake, op cit, p29

127 Watney and Little, op cit, p122

128 *Falkirk Herald*, 18 January 1896

129 Emilia F S Dilke, 'Trade Unionism for Women', *New Review*, January 1890, p49

130 Nan Milton, *John Maclean* (London, 1973), p50

131 Daniel M'Iver, *An Old-time Fishing Town* (Greenock, 1906), p226

132 Archie Crawford, 'Capitalism in Shetland', *International Socialist Review*, October 1914

133 M'Iver, op cit, pp226-227

134 Anderson, op cit, p32

135 Michael Sneed, 'The Real "Norma Rae" says union brought J. P. Stevens to its knees', *Chicago Tribune*, 26 October 1980

136 *The Woman Worker*, 28 August 1908

137 Young, *The Rousing*, op cit, pp180

138 See Ernest Mandel's brilliant introduction to Leon Trotsky, *The Struggle Against Fascism* (Harmondsworth, 1975), ppxiv-xv

139 Antonio Labriola, *Essays on the Materialist Conception of History* (Chicago, 1908), pp14-17

140 Hamish Henderson, 'Some Thoughts on Highland History, *Cencrastus*, No 5, 1980, pp14-17

141 Crawford, op cit, p1102

142 James D MacDougall, 'The Scottish Fisherman', *Nineteenth Century and After*, September 1927, p702

143 Ray Strachey, *The Cause. A Short History of the Women's Movement in Great Britain* (London, 1928), p290

144 Hamilton, *Mary MacArthur*, op cit, p102

145 *The Kirkcaldy Times*, 25 September and 25 and 29 December 1912
146 Ibid, 28 August 1912 and 12 February 1913
147 Ibid, 2 November 1912 and 19 February 1913
148 Marwick, op cit, p81
149 *Fife Free Press*, 9 April 1898
150 Ibid, 11 June 1898
151 G Von Shulze-Gaevernitz, *Social Peace* (London, 1893), p277; B O Hutchins, *Women in Modern Industry* (London, 1915), p115; *The Socialist*, April 1906
152 Mary Brooksbank, *No Sae Lang Syne. A Tale of This City* (Dundee, ND, probably 1973), p20
153 *The Case for Women's Suffrage*, edited Brougham Villiers (London, 1907), p61; Flora Thompson, *Lark Rise to Candleford* (Oxford, 1939), p204; O J Dunlop, *The Farm Labourer* (London, 1913), passim
154 Sheila Lewenhak, 'Women in the Leadership of the Scottish Trades Union Congress, 1897-1970', *Journal of the Scottish Labour History Society*, No 7, 1973, p3

5 British Women,
Class Struggle and 'Emancipation', 1914-1927

1 Millicent G Fawcett, *The Women's Victory and After* (London, 1920), p106
2 B L Hutchins, *Women in Modern History* (London, 1915), p69
3 Mary A Hamilton, *Margaret Bondfield* (London, 1924), p115
4 Vera Brittain, *Women's Work in Modern England* (London, 1928), p12
5 Hamilton, op cit, p116
6 Hubert L Smith, *The New Survey of London Life and Labour* (London, 1930), Vol 1, p379
7 Conversation with Bob Selkirk, veteran Fife socialist, 4 June 1973
8 J J Astor and A L Bowley, *Third Winter of Unemployment* (London, 1922), p174
9 Arabella Kennealy, *Feminism and Sex-Extinction* (London, 1920), p284
10 *Pargraves Dictionary of Political Economy*, edited Henry Higgs (London, 1926), Vol 2, p855
11 G W Johnston, *The Evolution of Woman* (London, 1926), p193
12 E M White, *Woman in World History* (London, 1924), p384
13 Catherine Webb, *The Woman with the Basket* (Manchester, 1927), p24
14 John Montgomery, *The Twenties* (London, 1957), p57
15 Leslie Baily, *Scrapbook for the Twenties* (London, 1925), p28
16 *Our Freedom and Its Results* (London, 1936), edited Ray Strachey, p131
17 A L Bowley and H M Hogg, *Has Poverty Diminished?* (London, 1925), p152
18 R M Fox, *The Triumphant Machine* (London, 1928), p32
19 Annual Report of the Chief Inspector of Factories and Workshops, *Parliamentary Papers*, Vol VII, 1922, p91
20 T F Henderson and F Watt, *Scotland of Today* (London, 1907), p32; Gilbert McAllister, *James Maxton* (London, 1935), p93
21 Ibid, p16
22 Bob Selkirk, *The Life of a Worker* (Dundee, 1967), p13
23 Ibid, p12
24 In 1907 and 1909 the Social Democratic Federation published two important and well-researched pamphlets by Dora Montefiore. They were *Some Words to Socialist*

Women and *The Position of Women in the Socialist Movement*.

25 Conversations with the late George Lindsay in 1955. A headmaster in Falkirk in the late 1950s, George Lindsay frequently had tea with John Maclean in the early 1920s.

26 John Collier and Iain Laing, *Just the Other Day* (London, 1932), p201

27 John Montgomery, *The Twenties* (London, 1957), p164

28 Marie C Stopes, *Married Love* (London, 1918), p90

29 Margaret Sanger, *An Autobiography* (London, 1939), p267

30 William Bolitho, *The Cancer of Empire* (London, 1924), p28

31 Smith, *New Survey*, op cit, p33

32 Charlotte Haldane, *Motherhood and Its Enemies* (London, 1927), p96

33 Henry S Salt, 'I was in Prison', *Daily Echo*, 21 March 1892

34 Maud I Crofts, *Women under the English Law* (London, 1925), p39; Helena Normanton, *Everyday Law for Women* (London, 1932), p386; Minnie Pallister, *Socialism for Women* (London, 1929), p23

35 Arthur Marwick, *The Deluge* (London, 1965), p107

36 Bennett, *A Picture of the Twenties*, op cit, p79

37 *Daily Herald*, 19 April 1924

38 John Peel, 'Birth Control and the British Working Class Movement', *Bulletin of the Society for the Study of Labour History*, No 7, 1963, p20

39 Eveline Hunter, *Scottish Woman's Place* (Edinburgh, 1978), p5

40 David Kennedy, *Birth Control in America* (New Haven, 1970), pp21-22

41 Conversation with Harry McShane, 4 October 1968

42 Guy Aldred, *No Traitor's Gait*, Vol III, No 1, 1963

43 Conversation with Bob Selkirk, 4 April 1972

44 *Workers' Dreadnought*, 10 March 1923

45 Sinclair, op cit, p14

46 H Fyfe, *Revolt of the Women* (London, 1933), p101

47 Conversation with Peter Kelly, veteran miner, Kirkintilloch, 4 June 1967; and conversation with James Dick, veteran miner and jack-of-all-trades, 20 October 1981

48 Sheila Rowbotham, *Hidden from History* (London, 1974), p142

49 Eleanor F Rathbone, *The Disinherited Family* (London, 1924), p88

50 Margaret L Eyles, *The Woman in the Little House* (London, 1922), p141

51 Charlotte Luetkens, *Women and a New Society* (London, 1946), p20, and Millicent Fawcett, *Women Victory, op cit, p107*

52 Civil and Judicial Statistics for England and Wales, *Parliamentary Papers*, Vol XXX, 1929-1930

53 Smith, *New Survey*, op cit, p397

54 Mess, *Facts*, op cit, p91

55 *The Proceedings of the Conference on Christian Politics, Economics and Citizenship* (London, 1924), pp140-41

56 Arnold Bennett, *Our Women* (London, 1923), p162

57 Henry T Waddy, *The Police Court and Its Work* (London, 1925), p104

58 Alfred Fellows, *The Case Against English Divorce Law* (London, 1932), p118

59 Hermann Mannheim, *Social Aspects of Crime in England between the Wars* (London, 1940), p177

60 James Leatham, 'Glasgow in the Limelight', *The Gateway*, mid-way 1923, p5

61 See Chapter four

62 E Llewelyn Lewis, *The Children of the Unskilled* (London, 1924), pp54-59

63 Stuart Macintyre, *Little Moscows* (London, 1980), pp140-142

64 Judicial Statistics for Scotland for 1920, *Parliamentary Papers*, Vol XX, 1921, p115

65 Eunice G Murray, *A Gallery of Scottish Women* (London, 1935), p30
66 A Scottish Hotel Servant, 'Keeping Up Appearances' in *Memories of the Unemployed*, edited H L Beales and H S Lambert (London, 1934), pp255-263
67 Marie Stopes, *Mother England* (London, 1929), p174
68 Conversation with Bob Selkirk, 4 June 1972
69 Macintyre, p142
70 Sheila Rowbotham, Lynne Segal and Hilary Wainwright, *Beyond the Fragments* (London, 1979), p121
71 Macintyre, op cit, p155
72 James D Young, 'Totalitarianism, Democracy and the British Labour Movement before 1917', *Survey*, Vol 90, No 1, p42
73 Sandra Holton, *Feminism and Democracy. The Women's Suffrage Movement in Britain, with particular reference to the National Union of Women's Suffrage Societies, 1807-1918*, PhD thesis, University of Stirling, 1980, p383
74 Martin Pugh, *Electoral Reform in War and Peace, 1906-1918* (London, 1978), pp358-9
75 Conversation with Harry McShane, 4 October 1981
76 James D MacDougall, 'The Position of Women after the War', *The Vanguard*, November 1915
77 John J Clarke, *The Housing Problem* (London, 1920), p142
78 *Forward*, 24 January 1920
79 Helen Fraser, *Women and War Work* (New York, 1918), p132
80 Helen R Vernon, *The Socialist Labour Party and the Working Class Movement on the Clyde, 1903-1921*, MPhil thesis, University of Leeds, 1968, p126 and p143
81 Sheila Rowbotham, *Women, Resistance and Revolution* (Harmondsworth, 1972), p130
82 *Minutes of the East London Federation of Suffragettes*, 17 January 1916, International Institute of Social History, Amsterdam.
83 *Minutes of the Workers Suffrage Federation*, 16 May 1919
84 Constance Williams, *How Women Can Help in Political Work* (London, 1920), p25
85 Eyles, *Little House*, op cit, p19
86 *Glasgow Herald*, 6 March 1917
87 Holton, op cit, p383
88 Nan Milton, *John Maclean* (London, 1973), passim
89 *We Shall Be All*, edited Laurie Flynn (Glasgow, 1978), pp18-33
90 I owe this information to Bob Duncan, the author of *James Leatham*, who is now researching into the history of the labour movement in Lanarkshire.
91 James D Young, 'Towards a History of the Labour Movement in Stirlingshire', *Forth Naturalist and Historian*, Vol 4, 1979, p132
92 Bolitho, op cit, p16
93 Walter Kendall, *The Revolutionary Movement in Britain, 1900-1921* (London, 1969), p107
94 Helen Vernon, op cit, passim
95 Ibid, p185
96 Commission of Enquiry into Industrial Unrest. Report of the Commissioners for Scotland, *Parliamentary Papers*, Vol VX, 1917-1918, p8
97 *The Times*, 6 May 1918
98 *Glasgow Herald*, 2 May 1918
99 *Forward*, 11 May 1918
100 E J Hobsbawm, *Revolutionaries* (London, 1973), p18
101 *Glasgow Herald*, 20 November 1918
102 Ibid, 2 May 1919, 3 May 1920 and 3 May 1921
103 Ibid, 3 May 1920

104 Ibid, 2 May 1923

105 Bennett, *A Picture*, op cit, p31

106 C F G Masterman, *The New Liberalism* (London, 1920), p189

107 Harriet S Blatch and Alma Lutz, *Challenging Years* (New York, 1940), p255

108 Leonora Eyles, *Women's Problems of Today* (London, 1926), pp10 and 40

109 Ibid, p56

110 Roger Dataller, *From a Pitman's Notebook* (London, 1925), p29

111 Interview with Bob Selkirk, 14 June 1972; *Militant Miners*, edited Ian MacDougall (Edinburgh, 1981), p101

112 Mary Brooksbank, *No Sae Lang Syne. A Tale of This City* (Dundee, ND, probably 1973), p24

113 For biographical details of Mary Docherty, see Macintyre, pp128-9

114 Interview with Mary Docherty, 4 June 1972

115 Fox, op cit, p19

116 N L, 'Shirt Maker', Pollock, op cit, p243

117 F W Ticker, *Women in English Economic History* (London, 1923), p222

118 Eyles, *Little House*, op cit, p14

119 Brooksbank, op cit, p24

120 Bowley and Hogg, *Poverty*, op cit, p23

121 Baily, op cit, p152

122 Marion Philips, *Women and the Miners* (London, 1927), p78

123 Gladys Boone, *The Women's Trade Union League in Great Britain and the United States of America* (New York, 1942), p40

124 Irene O Andrews, *Economic Effects of the War Upon Women and Children in Great Britain* (New York, 1921), p218

125 *Glasgow Herald*, 8 September 1926

126 A Communist Party pamphlet, *Women in the Class Struggle* (London, ND, probably 1926), p4

127 A Gleason, *What the Workers Want* (London, 1920), p227

128 MacDougall, *Militant Miners*, op cit, passim

129 Robert Rayner, *The Story of Trade Unionism* (London, 1929), p257

130 Fox, op cit, p85

131 Collier and Lang, op cit, p200

6 Images of Women

1 Cairns Craig, 'Peripheries', *Cencrastus*, No 9, 1982, p8

2 Ian Campbell, *Kailyard* (Edinburgh, 1981), p89

3 Gail Braybon, *Women Workers in the First World War* (London, 1981), pp220-223

4 Willa Muir, 'Women in Scotland', *Left Review*, October 1936, p58

5 Sally O'Sullivan, *Sunday Standard*, 17 March 1982

6 Eunice G Murray, *A Gallery of Scottish Women* (London, 1935), p28

7 The unpublished manuscript is in the Marx Library, London. It is clear that Helen Crawfurd's iconoclastic opinions on women and the national question persuaded the Communist Party publishers not to publish it, though it is a fascinating and sensitive book.

8 Stephen Maxwell, 'Women in Scotland', Q, 27 May 1977

9 Eunice G Murray, *Scottish Women in Bygone Days* (London, 1930), p239

10 Margaret Cole, *Women of Today* (London, 1938), p153

11 A Beatrice Wallis Chapman, *The Status of Women under the English Law* (London, 1909), pp63 and 66

12 David Vincent, *Bread, Knowledge and Freedom* (London, 1891), p21

13 Sheila Lewenhak, *Women and Trade Unions* (London, 1977), p111

14 Mary A Hamilton, *Mary MacArthur* (London, 1925), pp6 and 27

15 Cole, *Women of Today*, op cit, p100

16 R S Neale, *Class and Ideology in the Nineteenth Century* (London, 1972), p144

17 'Thus, the fashionable relegation of the law to the rank of a super-structural derivative phenomenon obscures the degree of autonomy it creates for itself'. Eugene D Genovese, *Roll, Jordan, Roll* (New York, 1976), p25
'The point is only that a mature historical materialism can accept that there are differences between peoples that are not themselves economic ones'. David Rubin, 'Marxism and the Jewish Question', *Socialist Register*, edited John Saville and Ralph Miliband (London, 1983), p220

18 Rosalind Mitchison, *A History of Scotland* (London, 1982), p406

19 Quoted by Dora Montefiore, *The Position of Women in the Socialist Movement* (London, ND, probably 1911), p3

20 August Bebel, *Women under Socialism* (New York, 1904), pp222 and 229

21 Eveline Hunter, *Scottish Woman's Place* (Edinburgh, 1979), p3

22 Murray, *Scottish Women in Bygone Days*, op cit, p218

23 Ashley Montage, *Touching* (New York, 1978), pp283-285

24 Henry Buckle, *History of Civilisation in England* (London, 1904), Vol 3, pp275 and 253

25 James Hogg, *The Three Perils of Woman* (London, 1923), Vol 2, p233

26 'Scottish National Character', *Blackwood's Edinburgh Magazine*, June 1860, pp719-725; James Logan, *The Scottish Gael* (London, 1831), p360

27 James M Barrie, *Margaret Ogilvy* (London, 1896), pp21-22; Anthony Ross, 'Ressurection', *Whither Scotland*, edited Duncan Glen (London, 1971), p123; Harry M Johnson, *Sociology* (London, 1961), pp108 and505; Neil Gunn, *Highland River* (London, 1960), p77

28 Annie Besant, *An Autobiography* (London, 1893), p134

29 Neale, op cit, p147

30 Bebel, op cit, p111

31 Besant, op cit, p229

32 E P Thompson, 'Homage to Tom Maquire' *Essays in Labour History*, edited Asa Briggs and John Saville (London, 1969), p315

33 Lawrence Thompson, *The Enthusiasts* (London, 1971), p93

34 James H Muir, *Glasgow in 1901* (Glasgow, 1901), p189

35 Robert Haddow, 'The Miners of Scotland', *Nineteenth Century and After*, September 1888, p368

36 Peter N Sterns, 'Working Class Women in Britain, 1890-1914', *Suffer and Be Still*, edited Martha Vicinus (Bloomington, 1972), p113

37 Joyce Macmillan, 'Writing in the Women's Movement', *Cencrastus*, No 5, 1981

38 R J Morris, 'Skilled Workers and the Politics of the "Red Clyde"', *Scottish Labour History Society Journal*, No 18, 1983, p9

39 Barrie, op cit, pp21-22

40 Elizabeth Fox-Genovese, 'Placing Women in History', *New Left Review*, No 133, 1982, p31

41 See Chapter 5

42 'The Syndicalist is a "race suicider". He knows that children are a detriment to him in his daily struggles, and that by rearing them he is at once tying a millstone

around his neck and furnishing a new supply of slaves to capitalism. He, therefore, refuses to commit this double error and carries on an extensive campaign to limit births among workers'. Earl Ford and William Z Foster, *Syndicalism* (Chicago, 1909), p7. Bob Selkirk gave me a sight of this important pamphlet when I interviewed him on 4 April 1972.

43 Margaret Bondfield, *A Life's Work* (London, 1948), p40; Robert Roberts, *The Classic Slum* (Harmondsworth, 1973), p128; Caroline Nelson, 'The Control of Child-Rearing', *International Socialist Review*, March 1914

44 John Peel, 'Birth Control and the British Working-Class Movement', *Bulletin of the Society for the Study of Labour History,* No 7, 1963

45 See 'Domestic Servants Revolt in Aberdeen', *Forward*, 18 May 1912, etc

46 Ibid, 16 May 1908

47 'Report on equal pay demand of Scottish Socialist Teachers' Association', *The Vote*, 16 November 1912. I owe this reference to Elspeth King.

48 Jeremy Seabrook, *What Went Wrong* (London, 1978), p23; Neale, op cit, p159

49 E Sylvia Pankhurst, *The Home Front* (London, 1932); Helen Crawford, 'The Rent Strike', *Workers' Dreadnought*, 17 April 1920

50 James D MacDougall, 'The Position of Women after the War', *The Vanguard*, November 1915; John Maclean, 'Independent Working-Class Education', *Workers' Dreadnought*, 3 November 1917

51 Mary Brooksbank, *No Sae Lang Syne: A Tale of This City* (Dundee, ND, probably 1973), p36

52 Ibid, p16

53 Fenner Brockway, *Hungry England* (London, 1930), p192

54 Douglas and Quaine Bain, 'Women in Scotland: Scotch Reels and Political Perspectives', *Cencrastus*, No 11, 1983

55 Montefiore, op cit, p8

56 Sheila Rowbotham and Jeffrey Weeks, *Socialism and the New Life* (London, 1977), p119

57 Harry McShane, *No Mean Fighter* (London, 1978), p34

58 Sheila Rowbotham, 'The Women's Movement and Organising for Socialism', in *Beyond the Fragments*, edited Sheila Rowbotham, Lynne Segal and Hilary Wainwright (London, 1979), p121

59 Tony Cliff, *The Class Struggle and Women's Liberation* (London, 1984), passim; Montefiore, op cit, p12

Afterword

1 Beatrix Campbell, *Wigan Pier Revisited* (London, 1984), pp101-102

2 Tony Cliff, *Class Struggle and Women's Liberation* (London, 1984), p229

3 Elizabeth Fox-Genovese, 'Placing Women's History in History', *New Left Review*, No 153, 1982

4 Frederick Engels, *The Origin of the Family, Private Property and the State* (Peking, 1978), p75

5 Wilhelm Liebnecht, 'Reminiscences of Marx', *Karl Marx Through the Eyes of Their Contemporaries* (Moscow, 1972), pp69-70

6 Peter Worsley, *Marx and Marxism* (Chichester, 1982), p51

7 Dora B Montefiore, *The Position of Women in the Socialist Movement* (London, ND,

probably 1913), p6

  8 Ibid, p8
  9 'Linda Gordon', *Visions of History*, edited Henry Abelove (New York, 1984), p92
 10 Cliff, op cit, p12
 11 Charlotte Luetkens, *Women and a New Society* (London, 1946), p20
 12 E M White, *Woman in World History* (London, 1924), p284
 13 Millicent G Fawcett, *Women and Soldiers* (London, 1918), p104; *Our Freedom and Its Results*, edited Ray Strachey (London, 1936), p245
 15 Peter Worsley, *The Three Worlds* (London, 1984), pp337–338
 16 Sally Alexander, Anna Davin and Eve Hostettler, 'Labouring Women', *History Workshop*, No 8, 1979, p181
 17 Ruth Richardson, 'In the Posture of a Whore? a reply to Eric Hobsbawm', *History Workshop*, No 14, 1982, p137
 18 Sarah Benton, 'A conference of one's own', *New Statesman*, 23 March 1984
 19 Sarah Benton, 'Take the money and Run', *New Statesman*, 4 December 1981
 20 Alice Henry, *The Trade Union Woman* (New York, 1915), p121; Ron Edwards 'Underneath, they're all redundant', *New Stateman*, 19 February 1982
 21 Roger Dataller, *From a Pitman's Notebook* (London, 1925), p29; J G Sinclair, *Easingden* (Oxford, 1926), p14
 22 Peter Worsley, 'Britain — Unknown Country', *The New Reasoner*, summer 1958, p53; Campbell, op cit, pp111 and 106
 23 Chris Burkham, 'Last Stand at the Alamo', *New Statesman*, 27 April 1984
 24 Jane Inham, 'Women and the pit strike', *Militant*, 10 August 1984
 25 Vanessa Loraine, 'Women fight for future', *Militant*, 5 October 1984
 26 Ray S Baker, *The New Industrial Unrest* (New York, 1920), p55
 27 'Miners face Tory hard line', *The Observer*, 12 August 1984
 28 'Numerous women have told me that they now watch and read the news with an interest they never had before. They see the coverage of industrial disputes is distorted, and as so different from the reality of those involved. . . . Many had no real reason to discuss "politics" before. Numerous women who had no previous experience of speaking in public have now addressed meetings to explain why women are supporting the strike'. Val Woodward, 'Not Just Tea And Sandwiches', October 1984
 29 'Hard day's strike', *Morning Star*, 3 November 1984
 30 'Miners' wives have come into their own. Debbie Alan, from the Yorkshire Women's Support Group, ironically acknowledges Mrs Thatcher's contribution to their new-found self-confidence and political activism — "She has released energies in women that will never be suppressed again", she said'. Steve Vines, 'Coal Strike', *The Observer*, 18 November 1984
 31 Beatrix Campbell, 'The other miners' strike', *New Statesman*, 27 July 1984

A Select Bibliography on Scottish Women

Books

Anderson, James, *The Ladies of the Covenant* (Edinburgh, 1850)
Anderson, James, *The Ladies of the Reformation* (Glasgow, 1854)
Autobiography of Elizabeth Stories, a Native of Glasgow (Glasgow, 1859)
Balfour, Frances, *Dr Elsie Inglis* (Edinburgh, 1918)
Balfour, Frances, *Ne Obliviscarie (Dinnae Forget) — The Memoir of Lady Frances Balfour* (London, 1930)
Boyd, Kenneth, *Scottish Church Attitude to Sex, Marriage and the Family, 1850-1914* (Edinburgh, 1980)
Brewster, Margaret M, *Sunbeams in the Cottage or What Women May Do* (Edinburgh, 1864)
Brooksbank, Mary, *No Sae Lang Syne. A Tale of This City* (Dundee, ND, probably, 1973)
Cameron, David Kerr, *The Ballad and the Plough* (London, 1979)
Chambers, Robert, *The Domestic Annals of Scotland* (Edinburgh, 1858)
Chambers, Robert, *The Picture of Scotland* (Edinburgh, 1828)
Fraser, John, *The Humourous Chap-books of Scotland* (New York, 1873)
Fraser, Patrick, *Treatise of the Law of Scotland as applicable to the Personal and Domestic Relations* (Edinburgh, 1846)
Graham, Henry, *The Social Life of Scotland in the Eighteenth Century* (London, 1906)
Haldane, Elizabeth, *The Scotland of Our Fathers* (London, 1928)
Hunter, Eveline, *Scottish Woman's Place* (Edinburgh, 1978)
Irwin, Margaret, *Women's Industries in Scotland* (Glasgow, 1896)
Keary, M R, *Great Scotswomen* (London, 1933)
King, Elspeth, *The Scottish Women's Suffrage Movement* (Glasgow, 1978)
Knox, John, *The First Blast of the Trumpet against the Monstrous Regiment of Women*, in *The Works of John Knox*, edited David Laing (Edinburgh, 1855)
Larner, Christina, *Enemies of God. The Witch-Hunt in Scotland* (London, 1981)
Legman, George, *The Horn Book* (London, 1978)
Marshall, Rosalind, *Virgins and Viragos. A History of Women in Scotland from 1080 to 1980* (London, 1983)
Marwick, W H, *A Short History of Labour in Scotland* (Edinburgh, 1967)
Murray, Eunice G, *A Gallery of Scottish Women* (London, 1935)
Murray, Eunice G, *Scottish Women in Bygone Days* (Glasgow, 1930)
Muir, Willa, *Mrs Grundy in Scotland* (London, 1936)
Paterson, Elizabeth, *Mary Somerville, 1780-1872* (Oxford, 1979)
Personal Recollections from the Early Life to the Old Age of Mary Somerville, edited Martha Somerville (Edinburgh, 1973)
Reid, Mrs H, *A Plea for Women* (Edinburgh, 1843)
Smith, Joan and McShane, *Harry, No Mean Fighter* (London, 1978)
Spence, Elizabeth, *Sketches of the Present Manners of Scotland* (London, 1811)
Todd, Margaret, *The Life of Sophia Jex-Blake* (London, 1918)
Thompson, Alexander, *The Licentiousness of Scotland* (London, 1861)
Walker, Patrick, *Biographia Presbyteriana* (Edinburgh, 1827)
Wilson, Robert, *Prostitution Suppressible* (Glasgow, 1871)
Young, James D, *The Rousing of the Scottish Working Class* (London, 1979)

Articles

Bain, Douglas and Quaine, 'Women in Scotland', *Cencrastus*, No 11, 1983
Bain, Margaret, 'Scottish Women in Politics', *Chapman*, No 28, 1980
Dilke, Lady E F S, 'The Seamy Side of Trade Unionism for Women', *New Review*, May 1890
Dilke, Lady E F S, 'Trade Unionism for Women' *New Review*, January 1890
Henderson, Hamish, 'Some Thoughts on Highland History', *Cencrastus*, No 3, 1980
Lewenhak, Sheila, 'Women in the Leadership of the Scottish Trades Union Congress', *Journal of the Scottish Labour History Society*, No 7, 1973
MacDougall, James, 'The Position of Women after the War', *The Vanguard*, November 1915
Maxwell, Stephen, 'Women in Scotland', *Q*, 27 May 1977
Muir, Willa, 'Women in Scotland', *Left Review*, October 1936
Young, James D, 'Social Class and the National Question: the Dialectics of Scottish History', unpublished paper, 1978
Young, James D, 'Radicalism and Scottish Women, 1770-1850', *Radical Scotland*, April/May 1983
Young, James D. 'Wife-Beating in Britain: A Socio-Historical Analysis, 1850-1914', American Sociological Association, New York, August 1976
Young, James D, 'The Condition of Scotland Question', *Bulletin of the Society for the Study of Labour History*, No 36, 1978
Young, James D, 'The Problems and Progress of the Social History of the British Working Classes', *Labor History*, Vol 18, No 2, 1977

General Books with useful information on Scottish Women

Drake, Barbara, *Women in Trade Unions* (London, 1921)
Harrison, J F C, *Robert Owen and the Owenites in Britain and America* (London, 1969)
Langdon-Davies, John, *A Short History of Women* (London, 1938)
Lewenhak, Sheila, *Women and Trade Unions* (London, 1977)
Macintyre, Stuart, *Little Moscows* (London, 1980)
Hamilton, Mary, *Mary MacArthur* (London, 1925)
Schoyen, A R, *The Chartist Challenge* (London, 1962)
Snowden, Ethel, *The Feminist Movement* (London, 1914)

Index